Janet and James M. Hawley

Adelaide, South Australia

October, 1970

KENNETH JACK

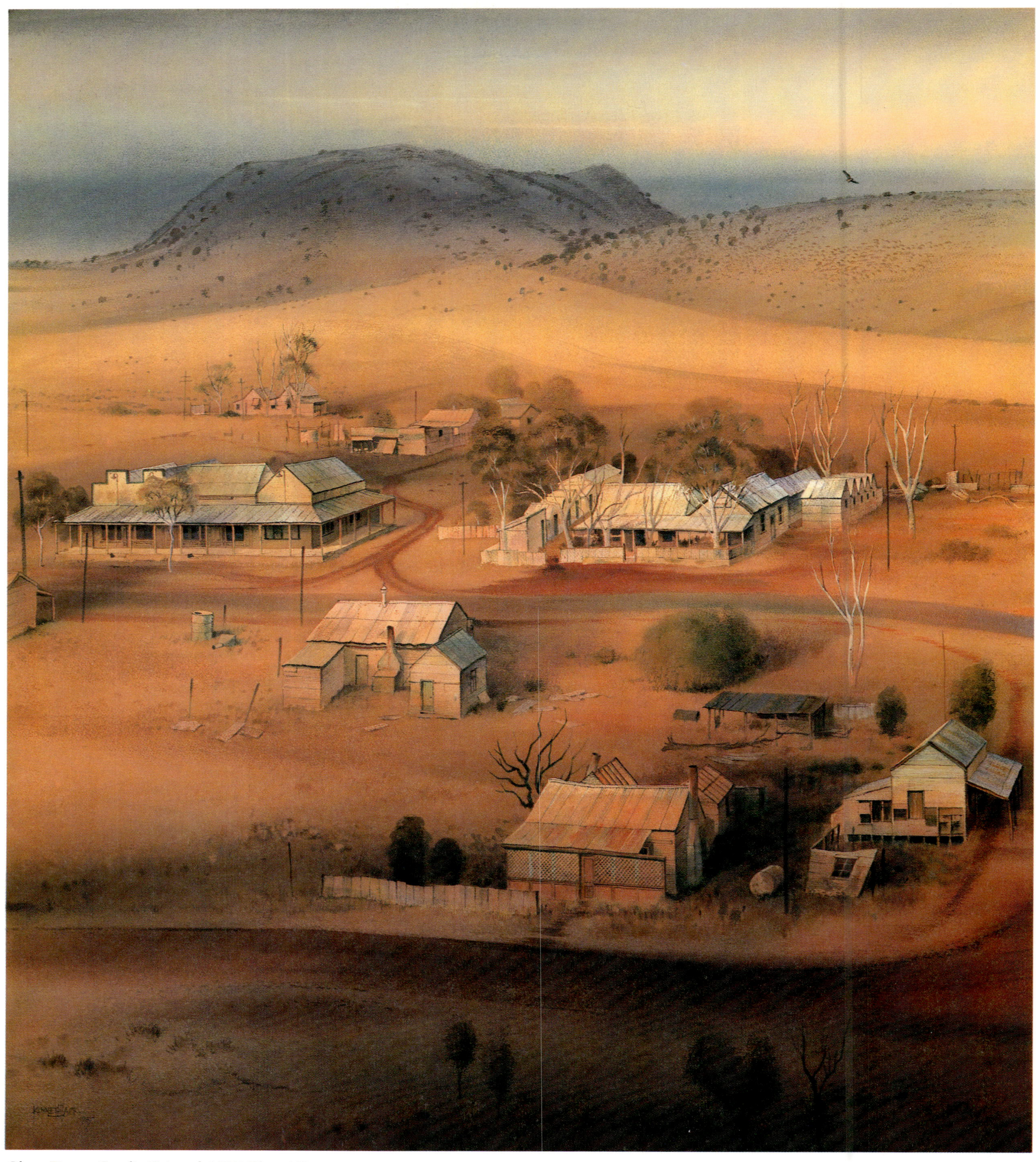

Ghost Town, Gwalia Triptych 1987 (Plate 19)
Left Panel: *Mt. Leonora, General Store, Rooming House*
Watercolour, 113 × 101 cm

KENNETH JACK

LOU KLEPAC

BAY BOOKS
Sydney and London

The artist and the author wish to dedicate this book to the memory of John Brackenreg (1905–1986) who did much to promote the art and artists of Australia.

ACKNOWLEDGEMENTS

Many people assisted me in the preparation of this book. I am grateful to Anne and Stuart Purves of the Australian Galleries, Melbourne; Brian Johnstone, Brisbane; Philip and Julie Brackenreg of the Artarmon Galleries, Sydney and David Dridan — all early supporters of the artist — for help in locating works and reviews of exhibitions. Barry Pearce of the Art Gallery of New South Wales; Hendrik Kolenberg of the Tasmanian Museum and Art Gallery; Anne Gray of the Australian War Memorial; the National Library, Canberra and the La Trobe Library, Melbourne all helped with various enquiries.

I would also like to express my thanks to all the private collectors whose works are reproduced in this book. The staff at Bay Books have been a pleasure to work with and I am grateful to Harry Bettison, Annette Robinson and Sheridan Carter. I am particularly grateful to Bruce Semler who edited the text and Susan Kinealy who designed the book. I would also like to thank David Jack for providing photographs of his father and of the drawings, and Samuel Critchley who photographed most of the works reproduced in the book.

Most of all I wish to thank Kenneth and Betty Jack for their unstinting help, support and hospitality.

Published by Bay Books,
61–69 Anzac Parade, Kensington,
NSW 2033

National Library of Australia
card number and ISBN 1 86256 320 9

Designed by Susan Kinealy
Typesetting by Savage Type Pty Ltd
Printed in Singapore by Toppan
Printing Co

BB88

CONTENTS

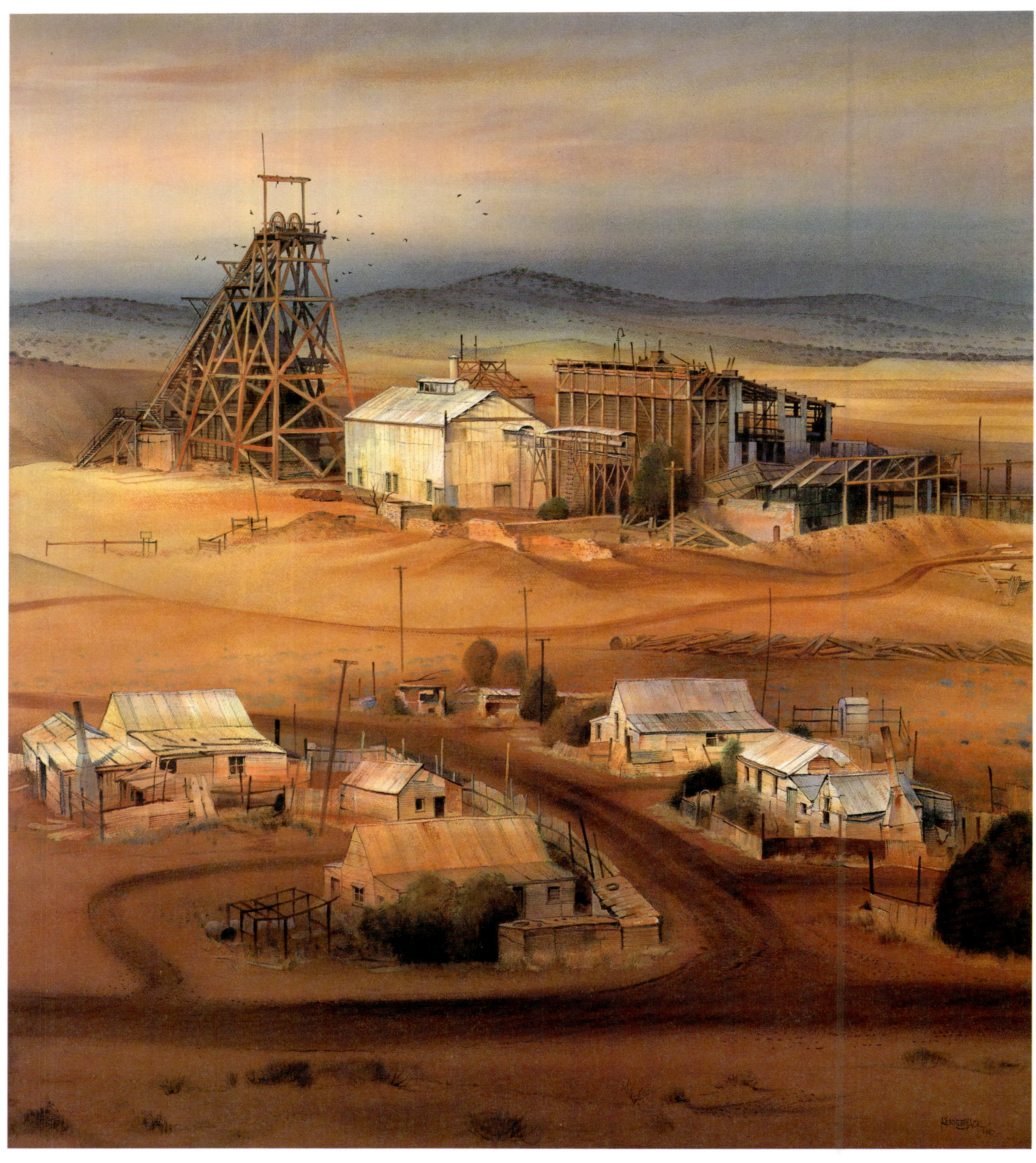

Ghost Town, Gwalia Triptych 1987 (Plate 19)
Right panel: *Sons of Gwalia Mine, Miners' Houses*
Watercolour, 113 × 101 cm

INTRODUCTION

Kenneth Jack occupies an unusual place in Australian art. He has made a successful career of drawing and painting what has attracted him most — the Australian landscape and its typical country towns. He sought them out first by bicycle, then by bus, later still by car and finally by air and four-wheel drive as his circumstances improved and his interests developed.

Jack has been almost everywhere in Australia on a mission that might be compared to the explorations of geologists and mining engineers. He has travelled as much and as far as any of them in order to know at first hand and to draw and sketch those places which for him represent the essence of Australia.

This immense gesture of love for his country has been supported by the public but not by the art establishment. Since the mid-1960s he has rejected the flat picture plane which he at first explored in paintings and prints and has found himself out of step with the rest of the art world, which meanwhile has passed through several phases and directions from abstract expressionism and colour field to hard edge and photo-realism. Even the advent of the last has not helped to redeem Jack's chosen style of painting.

Fortunately, many collectors have shared his interest in what he paints and for more than twenty years there has been a steady demand for his work. Consequently, in 1968 he was able to give up teaching to become a full-time painter. Although he was advised against it Kenneth Jack has never looked back.

He is one of the most industrious of painters and one of the happiest. He enjoys working in his studio, listening to his beloved Mozart, who more than any of his other favourite composers — Haydn, Beethoven and Schubert — satisfies his spiritual needs. He first heard Mozart's music when he was twelve, without knowing what it was, but it found a deep response in him. Music has been the consolation of what Jack calls the lonely life of the artist. If he is not travelling to find his subjects he is hard at work in the studio. If at times he feels sluggish, music comes to the rescue: he might put on a Rossini overture to stir himself up.

Although he was born in the city, he developed an interest in landscape as a child and loves the country towns in which he finds an expression of the essential down-to-earth Australian character. The Australian spirit beats in his heart and his background and his life merge in the subject matter of his art.

His unequalled mastery of Victorian architecture has developed over a lifetime. A remarkably able drawing of the Adelaide General Post Office clock made from a photograph when he was sixteen shows the direction his work would take for the next fifty years (Fig. 2).

Kenneth Jack's Australia may seem fashionable today but he began painting it long before many people appreciated its beauty and charm; there were times when not one work was sold from his exhibitions. His devotion to his subject matter fulfils a social and historical function beyond its artistic purpose, but he paints it because he must. He is well aware of the difference between painting in a style which is accessible to many people and painting to please the ignorant.

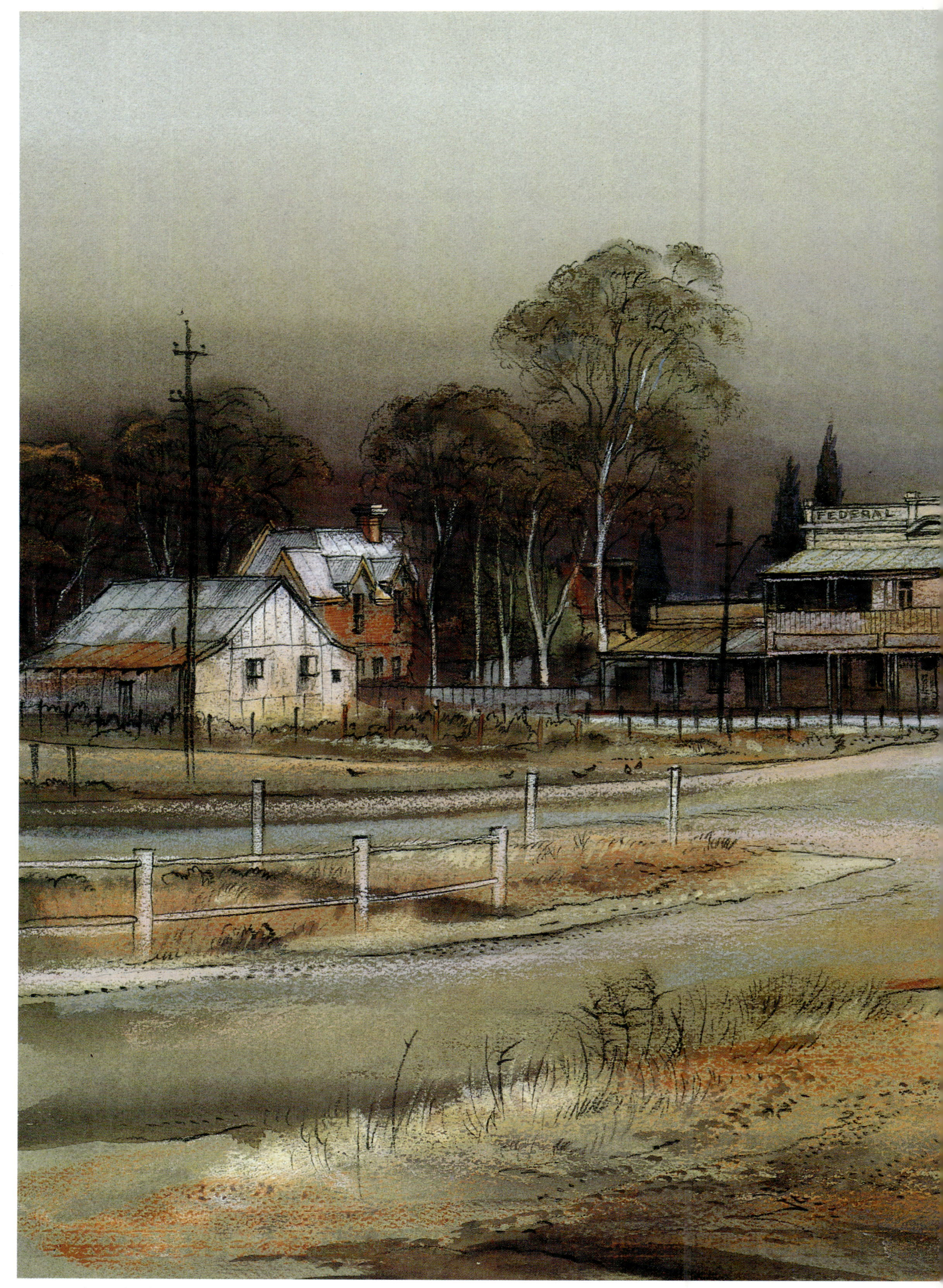

Plate 1 *The Federal Hotel, Kalgoorlie* 1985 (Western Australia) pencil, oil pastel and watercolour, 37 × 54.5 cm

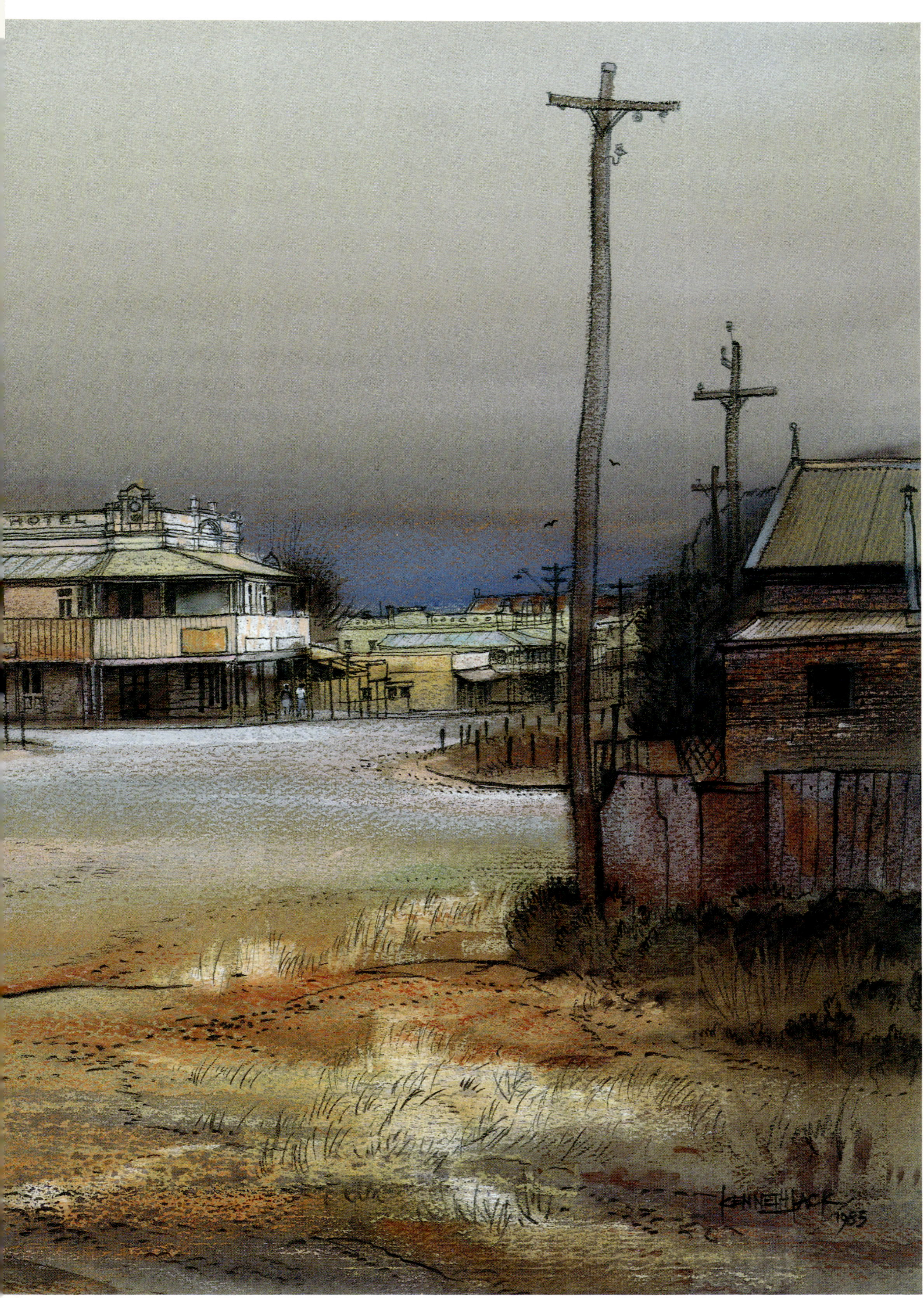

HOTEL
KENNETH JACK
1985

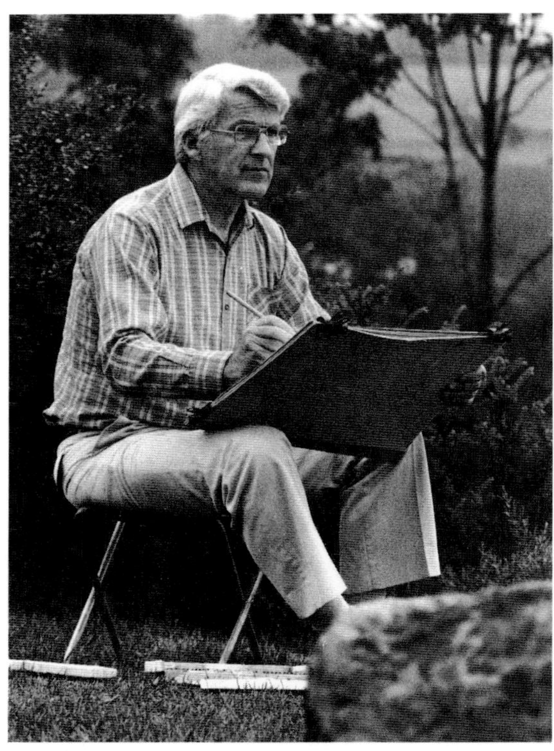

Kenneth Jack painting   *Photograph: David Jack*

He is delighted to see that his popularity is increasing, but he never lets anything out of his studio until he is totally satisfied by what he has done. His work is characteristically detailed because he feels that he must paint so that the picture can work not only from a distance but also yield its detail on closer inspection. This is how he was taught: to look long and hard at the subject so as to understand it beneath the surface.

It is possible superficially to criticise his work as mechanical but the mood and atmosphere he captures are beyond the mechanical. A master craftsman, he does not need to labour over his perspective for accurate draughtsmanship is second nature to him, but he does feel the need to allow himself to paint more intuitively. Commenting on his own work in the early 1970s he humbly pointed out that there was always something which seemed to elude him. That it still does gives him the impulse to keep on working.

At sixty-three, Jack has already achieved a body of work which would shame two fully active artists. Recently, he has challenged the traditional small scale of watercolour by painting two massive works each twelve feet long (Pls. 19 & 46). They are not only extraordinary technical feats, but an endeavour to get to grips with the spirit and timelessness of the Australian landscape in a medium which has its own magic. He has a special love for watercolour and is particularly proud of being the only full member of the Royal Watercolour Society outside Britain. The Society has a long and distinguished history and some of the greatest watercolour artists have been among its members.

Note: The extended captions in *italics* under plates are written by the artist.

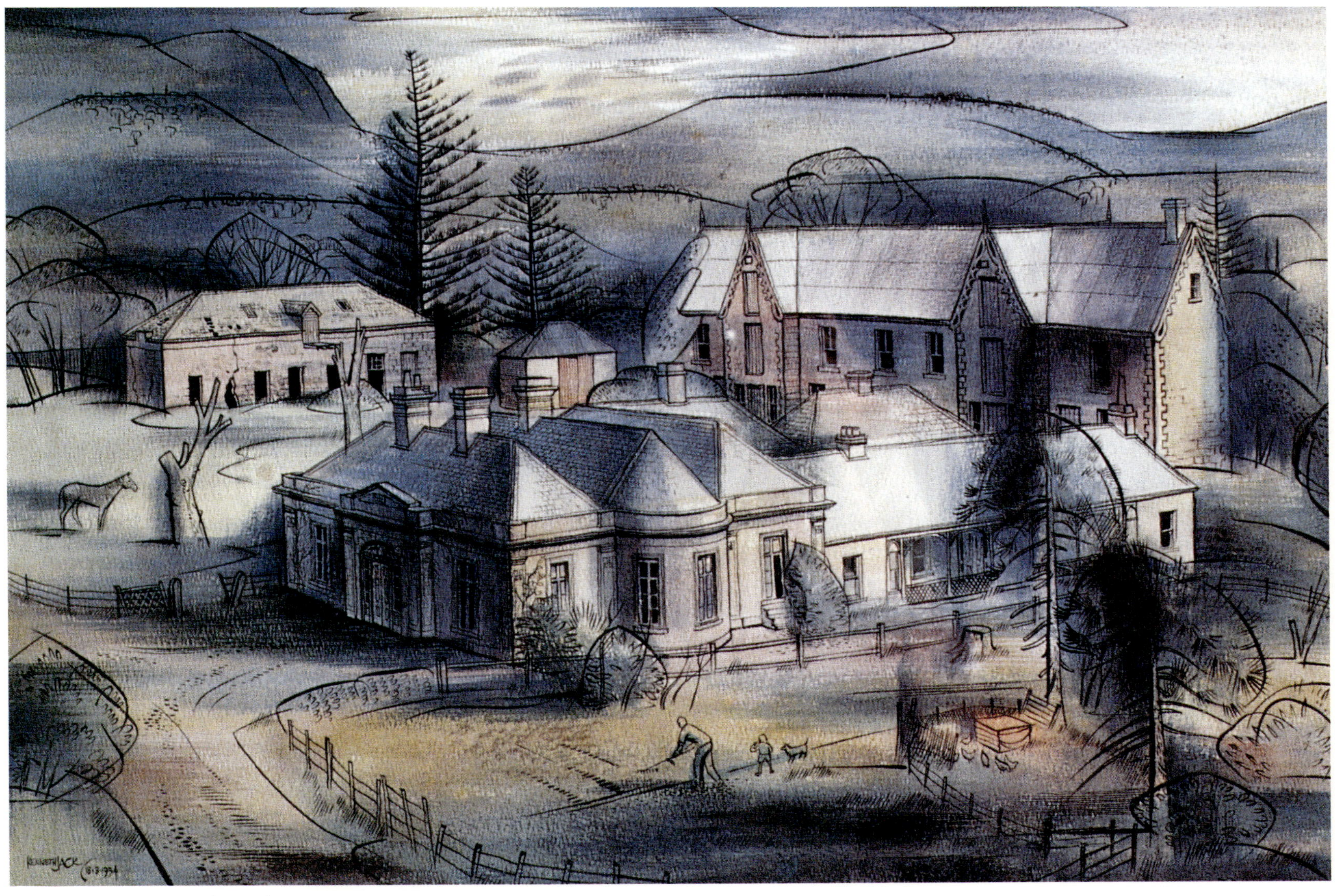

Plate 2 *Newtown Park, Hobart* 1954, watercolour, 35 × 53 cm

I first 'discovered' this wonderful subject in 1949 when making drawings for Sydney Ure Smith's publication of my drawings of Tasmania's capital city called The Charm of Hobart. *I spent a day at the old farm making drawings of the homestead, stables and barn from several different directions. The beautiful old house, built of Tasmanian freestone, was built in the 1830s. It is one of the best examples left of early colonial architecture — of note is the fine facade and doorway with fanlight.*

Five years after my first visit, using my drawings, I decided to make a watercolour of the whole complex. To do this I chose a birds-eye viewpoint since at ground level one could not see it all. From this imaginary high viewpoint I could also include the mountain setting. The precise linework and the semi-abstract symbolism I used across the open colour areas is influenced by several engravings in copper and perspex I was also making at the time.

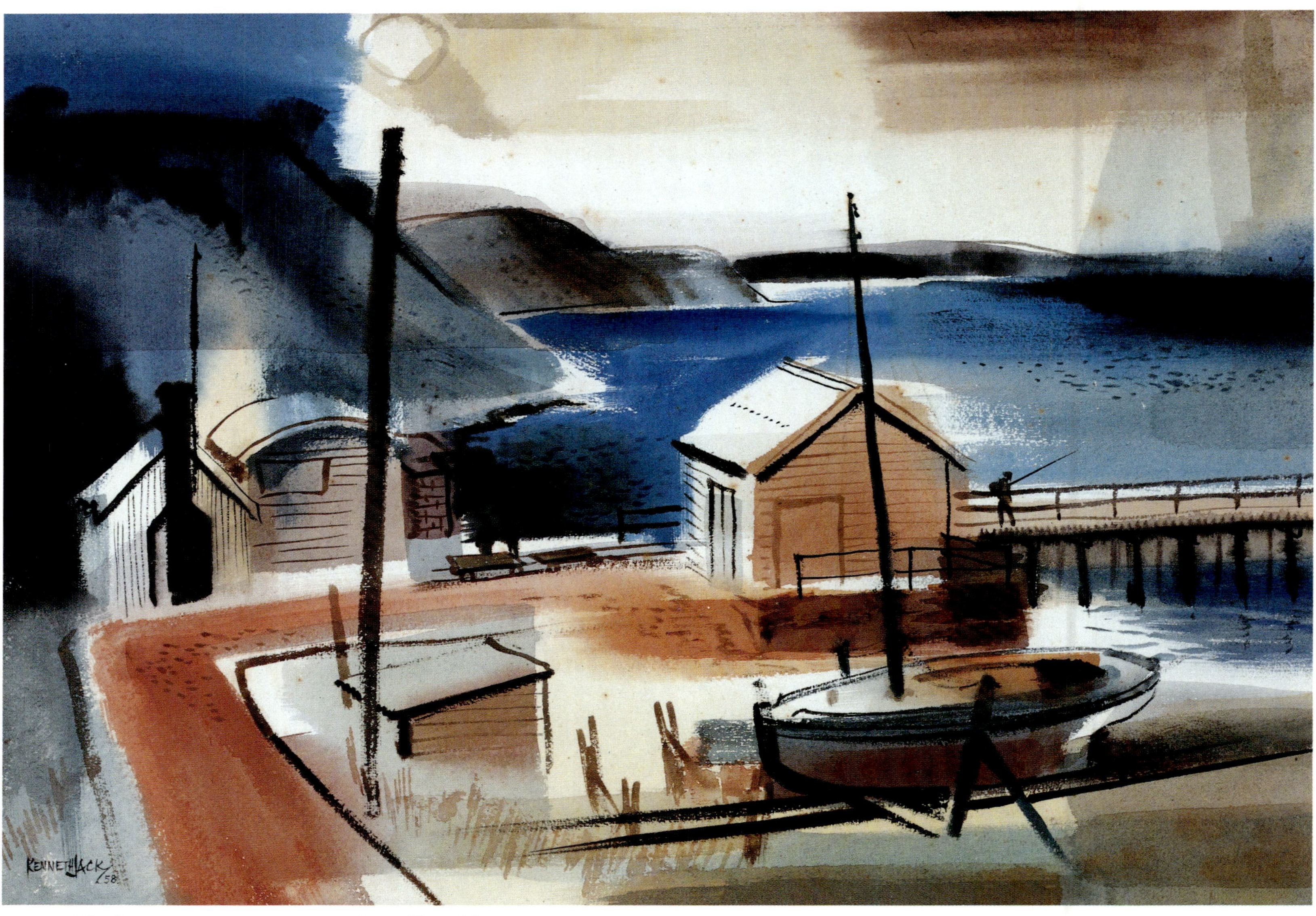

Plate 3 *Flinders* 1958 (Victoria) watercolour, 38 × 55 cm

THE STUDENT

Kenneth Jack was born at Caulfield, Melbourne, on 5 October, 1924. His father had studied architecture for three years before family circumstances forced him to take a job as a commercial artist with Victorian Railways, for which he worked for fifty years from 1922 to 1972.

The boy showed an early interest and ability in drawing and his father encouraged him and provided him with materials. He watched his father drawing and doing ticket writing and learnt quickly. From the beginning he wanted to draw accurately and searched for ways to improve his work. Among his father's books was Walter Shaw Sparrow's *Advertising and British Art,* which was an important early influence. The book deals with the period of great British posters by artists such as the Beggarstaff Brothers (James Pryde and William Nicholson), E. McKnight Kauffer, Frank Brangwyn and Fred Taylor. Jack was particularly interested in the way in which Taylor rendered buildings in his well-known posters for the London Underground and British Railways. By copying these works he learned to resolve problems of perspective and simplify an architectural subject to make a strong image without losing the character of the place.

Jack decided quite early that he wanted to become an artist and in order to support himself determined to take a job as a commercial artist. On his first day at Melbourne High School all the first-year students[1] were seated in the Great Hall to be put into their various classes. The assembled students gradually disappeared to the classes of their choice until Kenneth Jack was the only pupil still sitting in the hall. He was asked by a teacher what he wanted to be and as he answered 'commercial artist' he was sent to join a 'commercial' class. The second word, 'artist', went unheard. Later, when he decided that he wanted to become an art teacher rather than a commercial artist, he discovered that he should have studied different subjects in order to complete his Leaving Certificate and had to repeat the third year.

Partly because he had lost a year but also because of his determined and industrious character, he decided that he would speed things up. While still studying for his Leaving Certificate during the day, he attended evening classes on three nights a week and Saturday mornings at Melbourne Technical College (now RMIT) to prepare for both the Drawing Teachers Primary Certificate and the Secondary Certificate. At the end of his final year at Melbourne High School he had to sit for fourteen subjects, six for day school and eight for night school. In his Leaving Certificate he topped the State in art, while at the same time he had also completed, part time at night, the equivalent of a three-year full-time course.

The war was already on, and on 22 December 1942 he joined the Royal Australian Air Force as a survey draughtsman. He spent a year at Victoria Barracks in Melbourne, drawing maps and lettering, which he had always enjoyed. He was allowed to live at home and in his spare time he continued to attend evening art classes conducted by John Rowell at Melbourne Technical College.

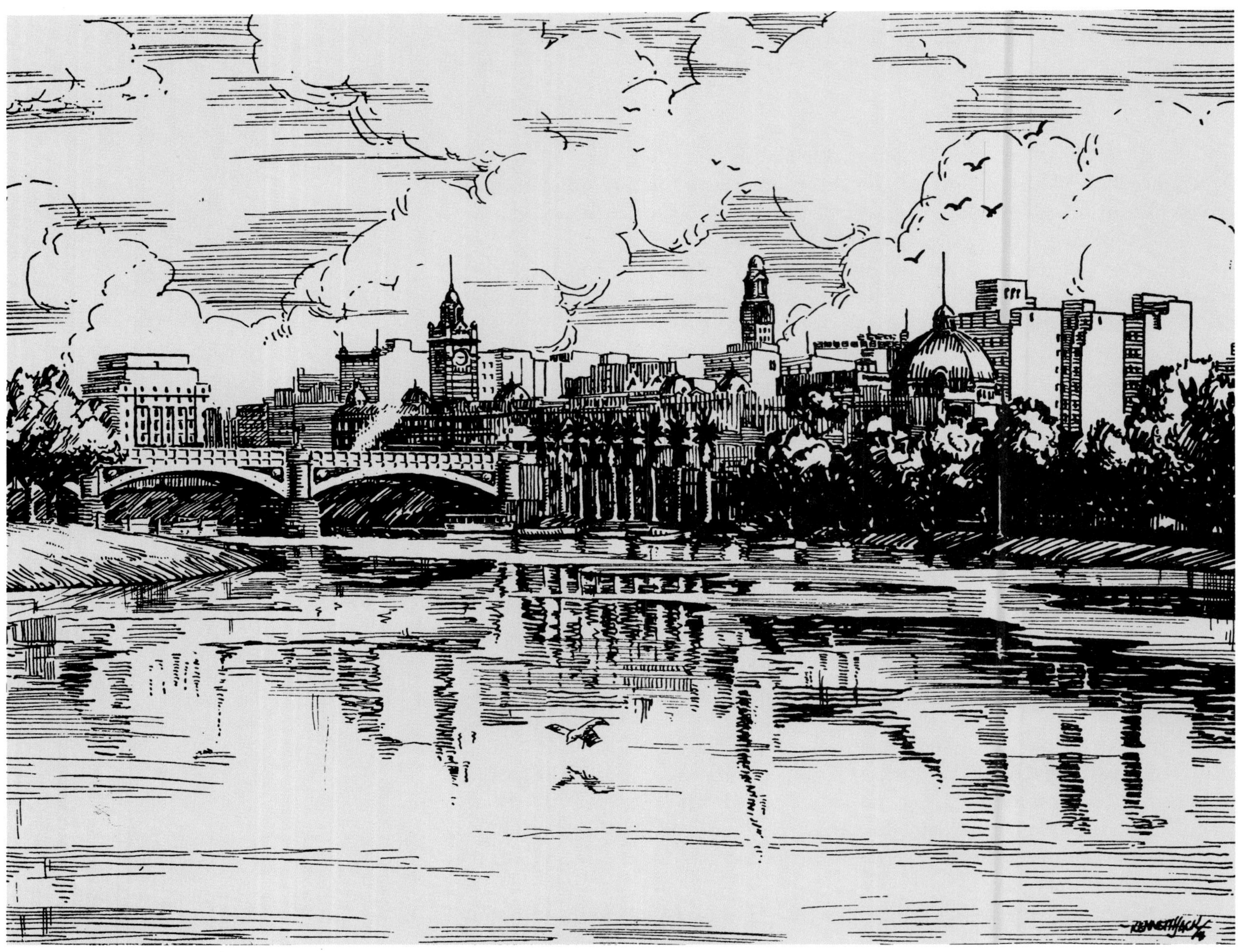

Fig. 1 *Melbourne's Skyline from the River Yarra* 1941, pen and ink, 17 × 24 cm

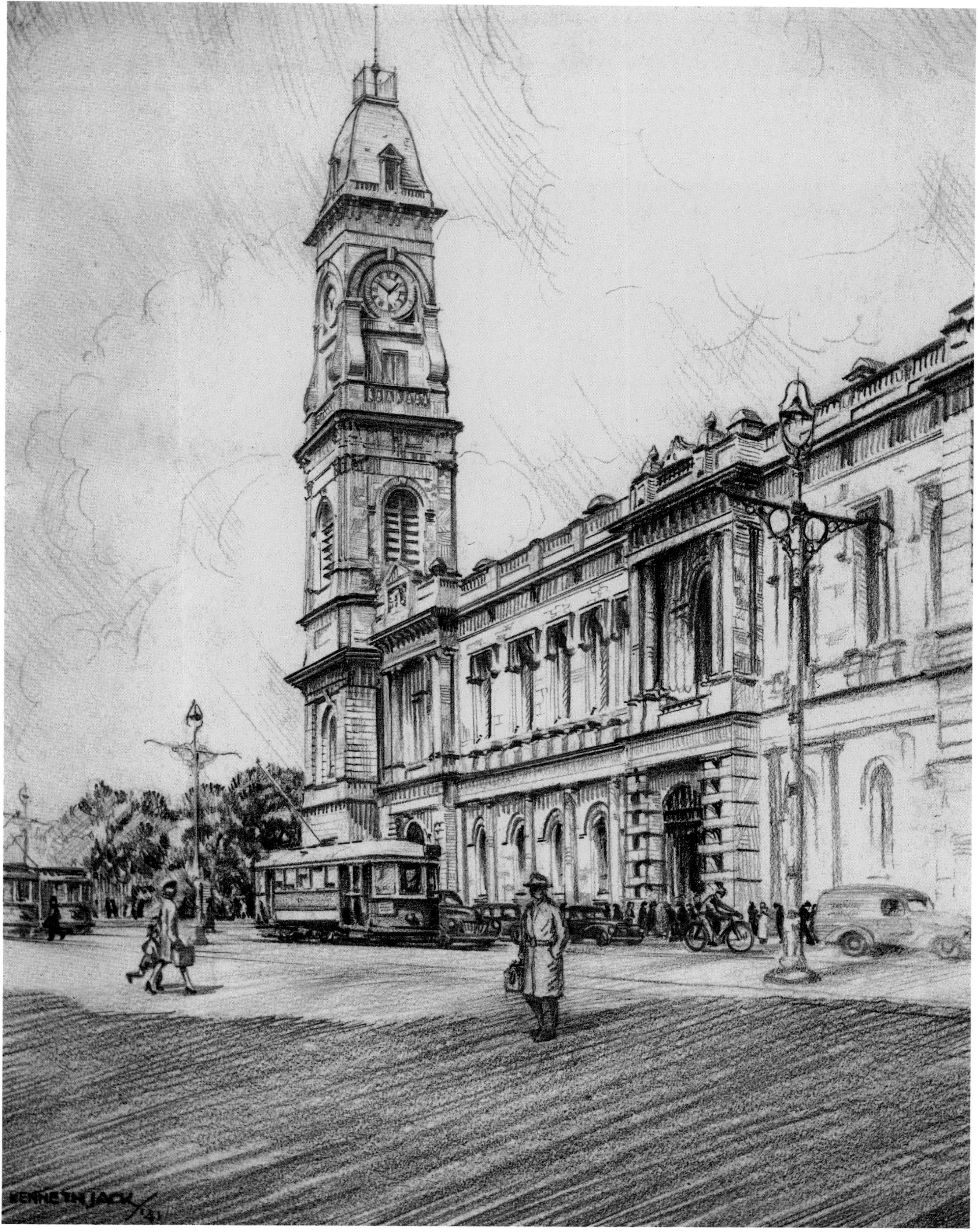

Fig. 2 *General Post Office, Adelaide* 1941, pencil, 26.5 × 21 cm

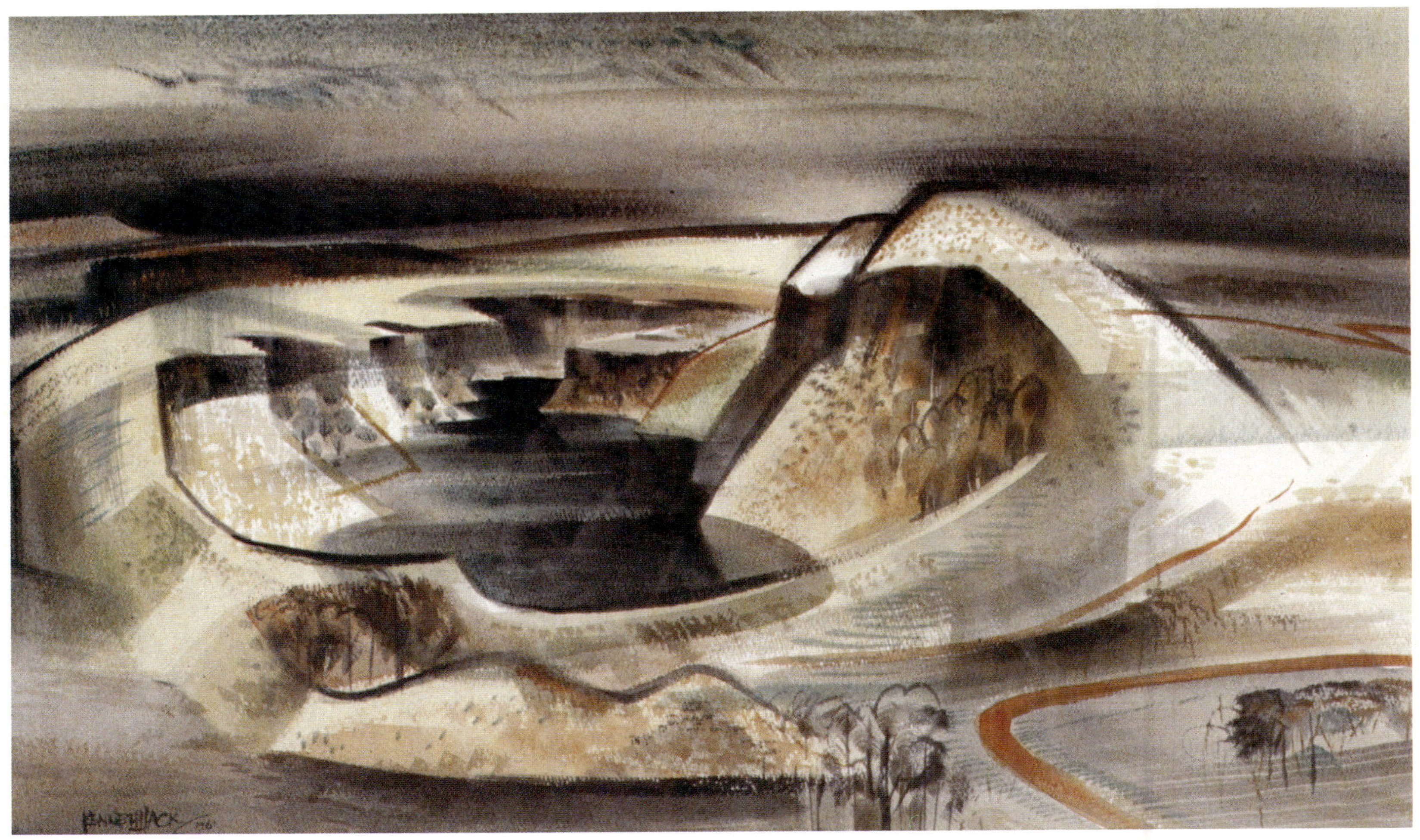

Plate 4 *Crater Lake, Western Australia* 1961, watercolour, 33 × 55 cm

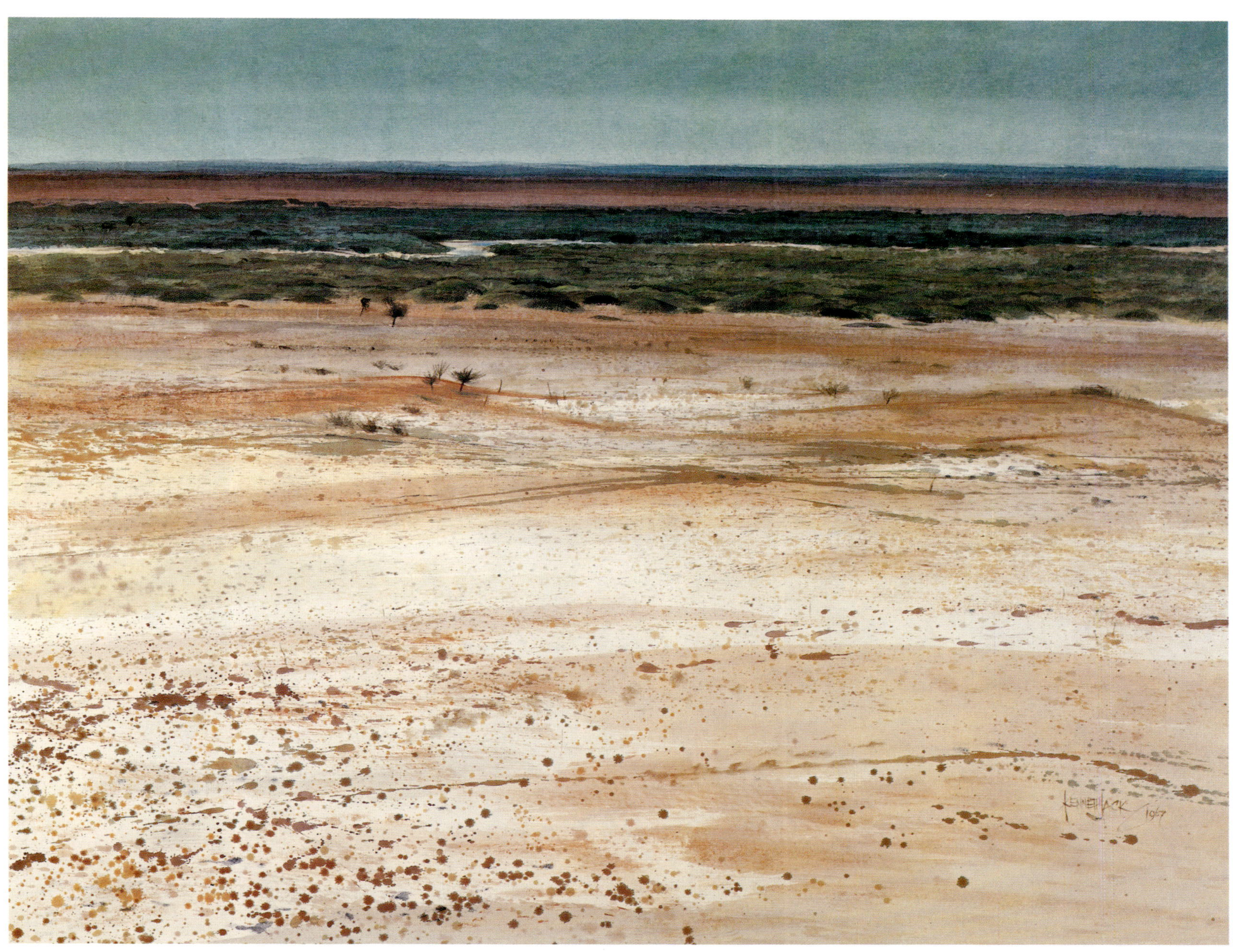

Plate 5 *The Diamantina* 1967, watercolour, 91 × 122 cm

In his late teens Jack had discovered the National Gallery of Victoria, then still in its old building in Swanston Street. One of his favourite paintings was Arthur Streeton's *The Purple Noon's Transparent Might,* in front of which he would sit for a long time. On a day's leave in 1944, when he spent a fortnight in the RAAF camp at Liverpool, New South Wales, prior to his departure for New Guinea, he took a train to Richmond on the Hawkesbury River. Walking towards the river he saw a high spot on the opposite bank some distance downstream. He made his way to it and found what he was looking for; the place where Streeton painted *The Purple Noon's Transparent Might* in 1896. From the same spot he made a small watercolour sketch in homage to Streeton and years later he visited it again to show it to his wife Betty. Today the place is inaccessible, having been built up with houses and fences, and the wonderful view is lost to the artist and the public.

It was fortunate for Jack that when he joined the RAAF it was realised that his art training would make him useful in the surveying section. While stationed

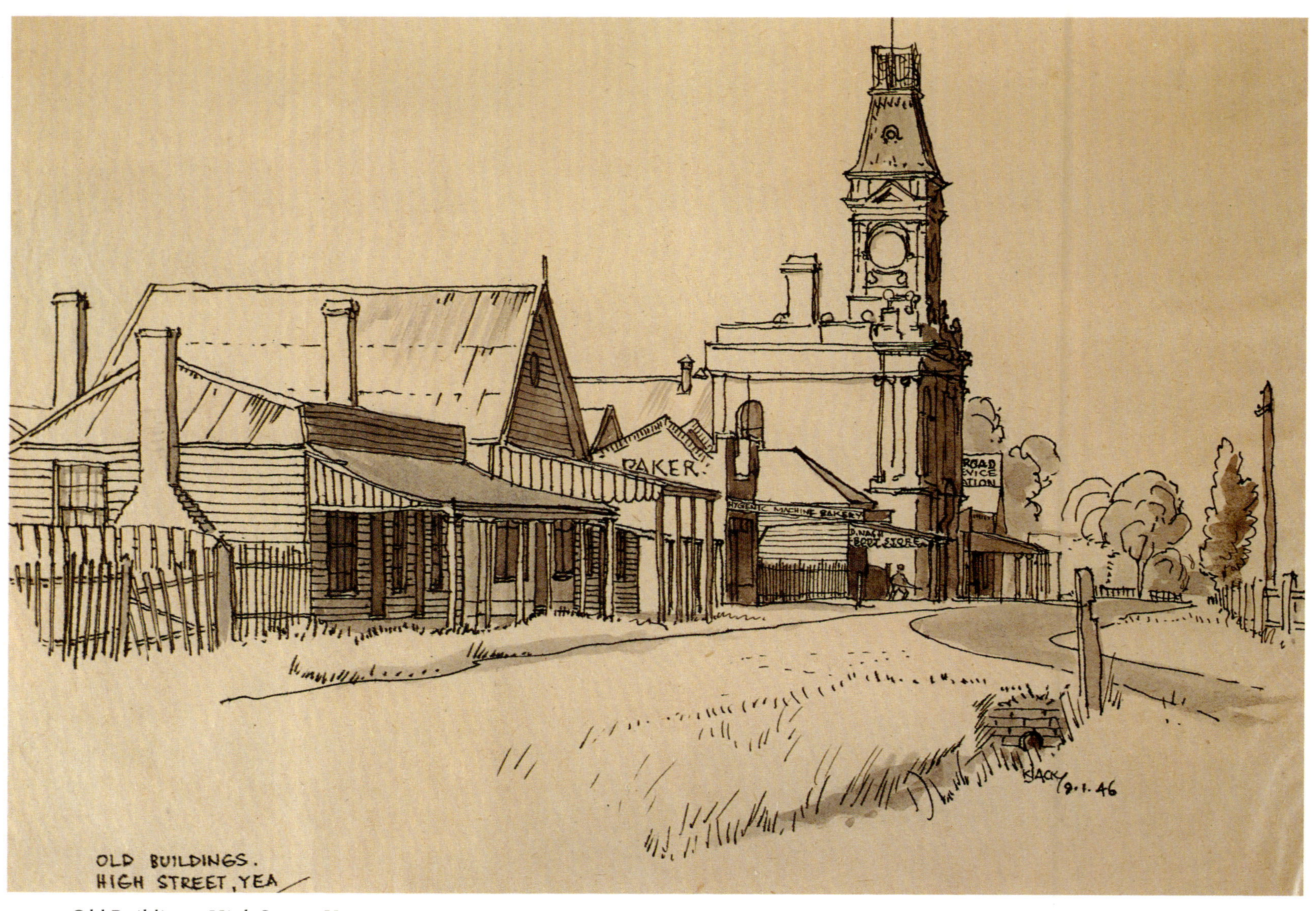

Fig. 3 *Old Buildings, High Street, Yea* 1946 (Victoria) pen, ink and wash, 18.5 × 27.5 cm

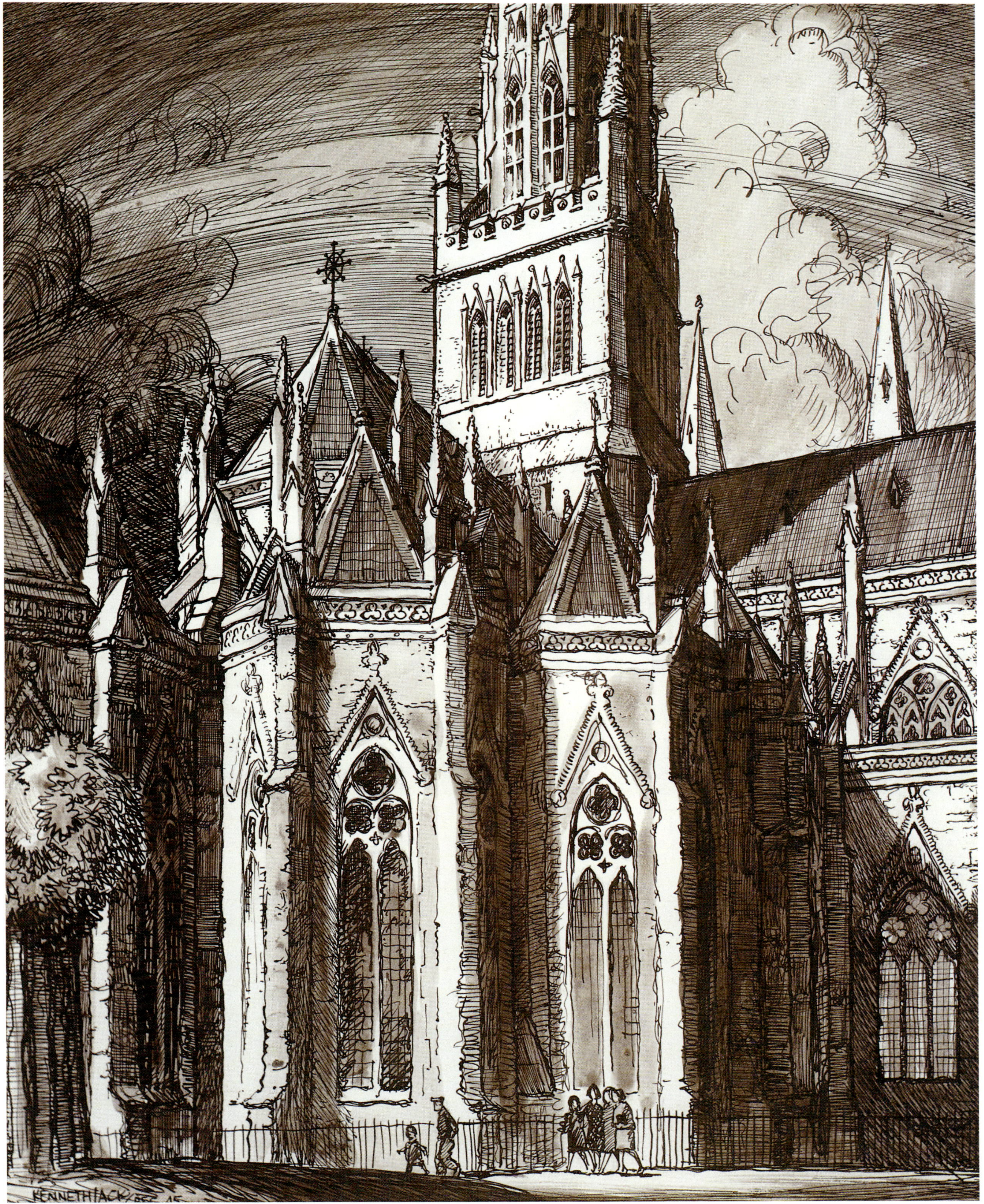

Fig. 4 *St. Patricks Cathedral, Melbourne* 1945, pen, ink and wash, 30 × 24.5 cm

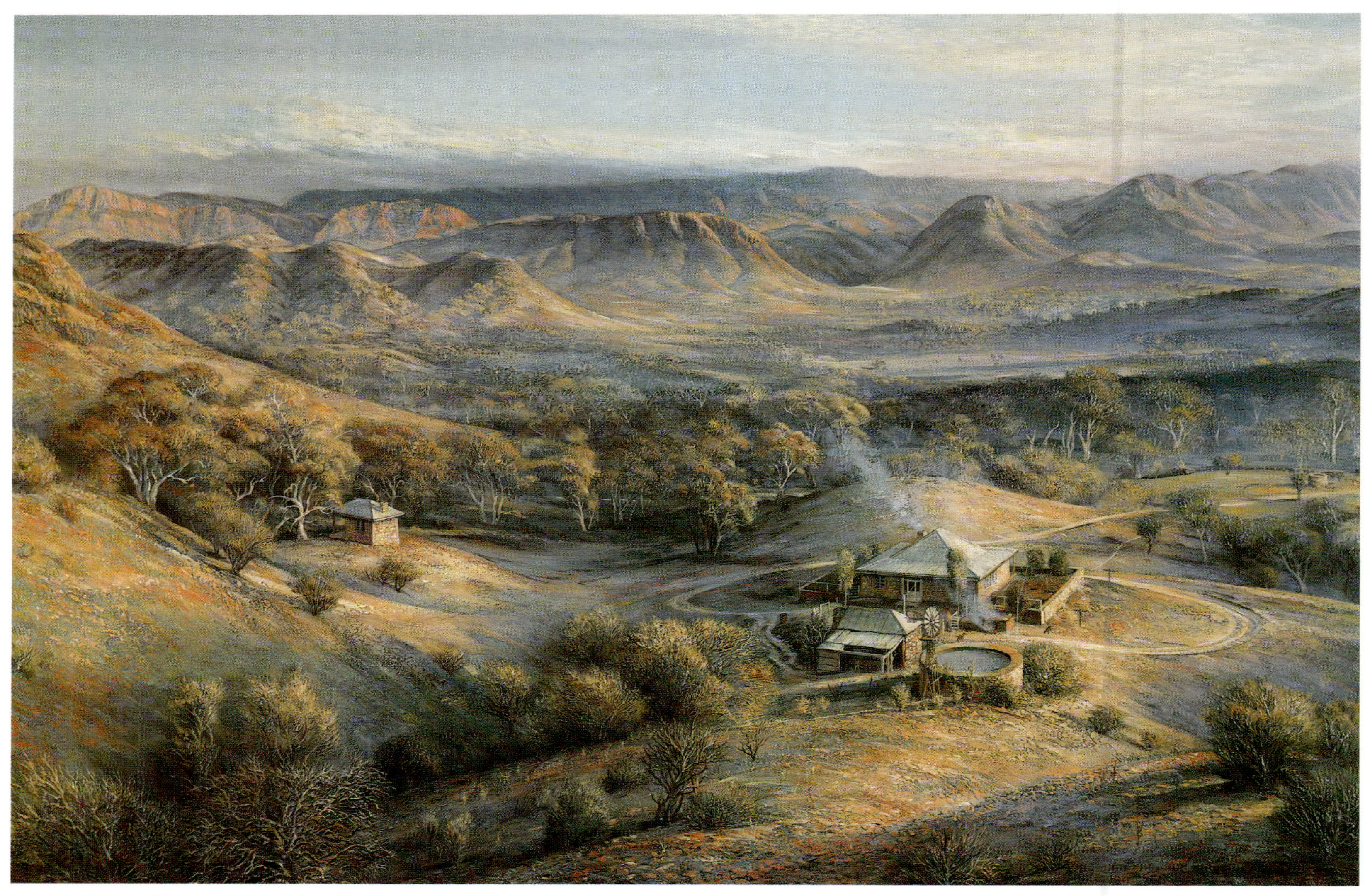

Plate 6 *Grindell's Hut, North Flinders Ranges* 1973 (South Australia) acrylic, 91 × 137 cm

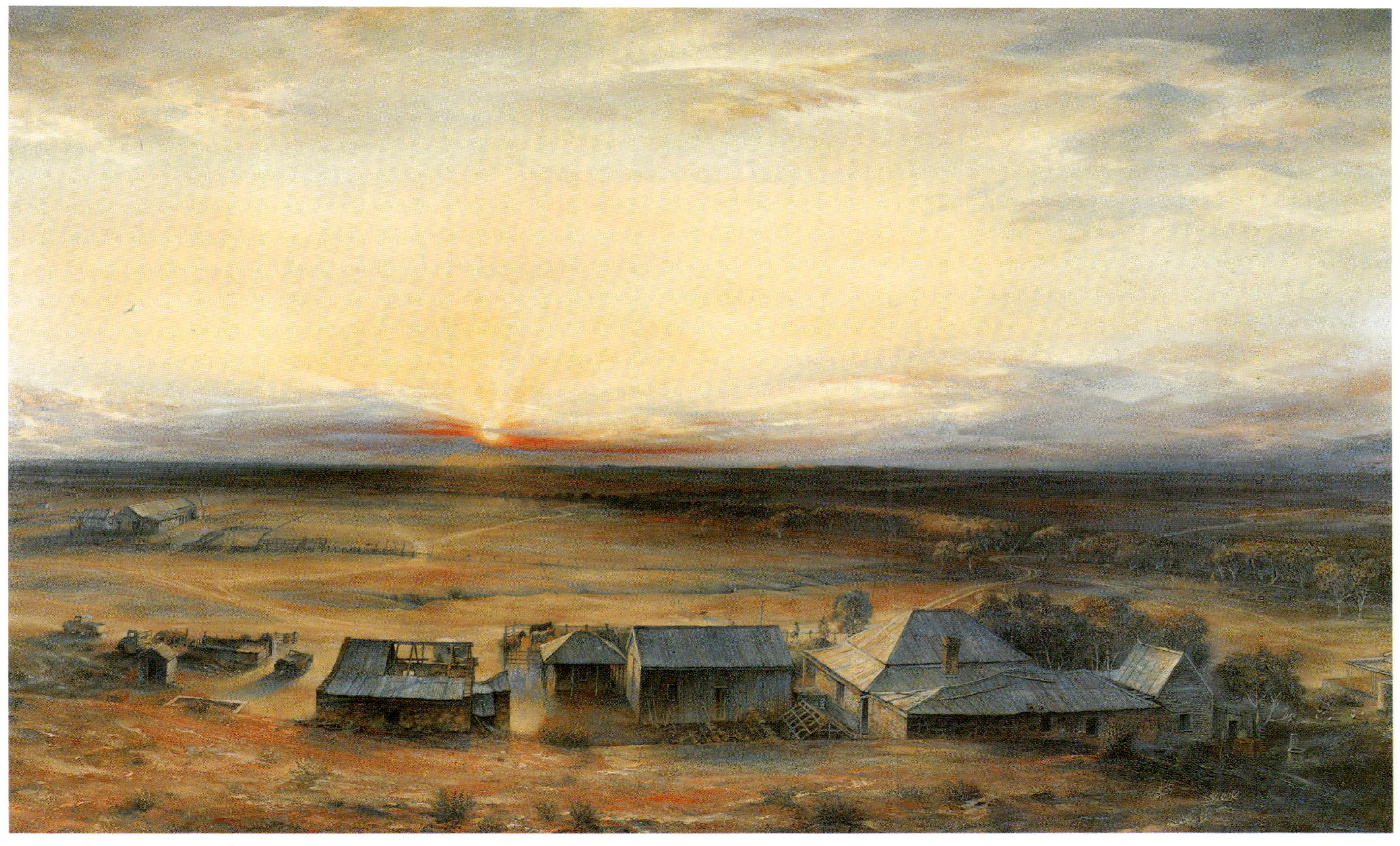

Plate 7 *Sunrise, Drought Country* 1973–74, acrylic, 167 × 274 cm

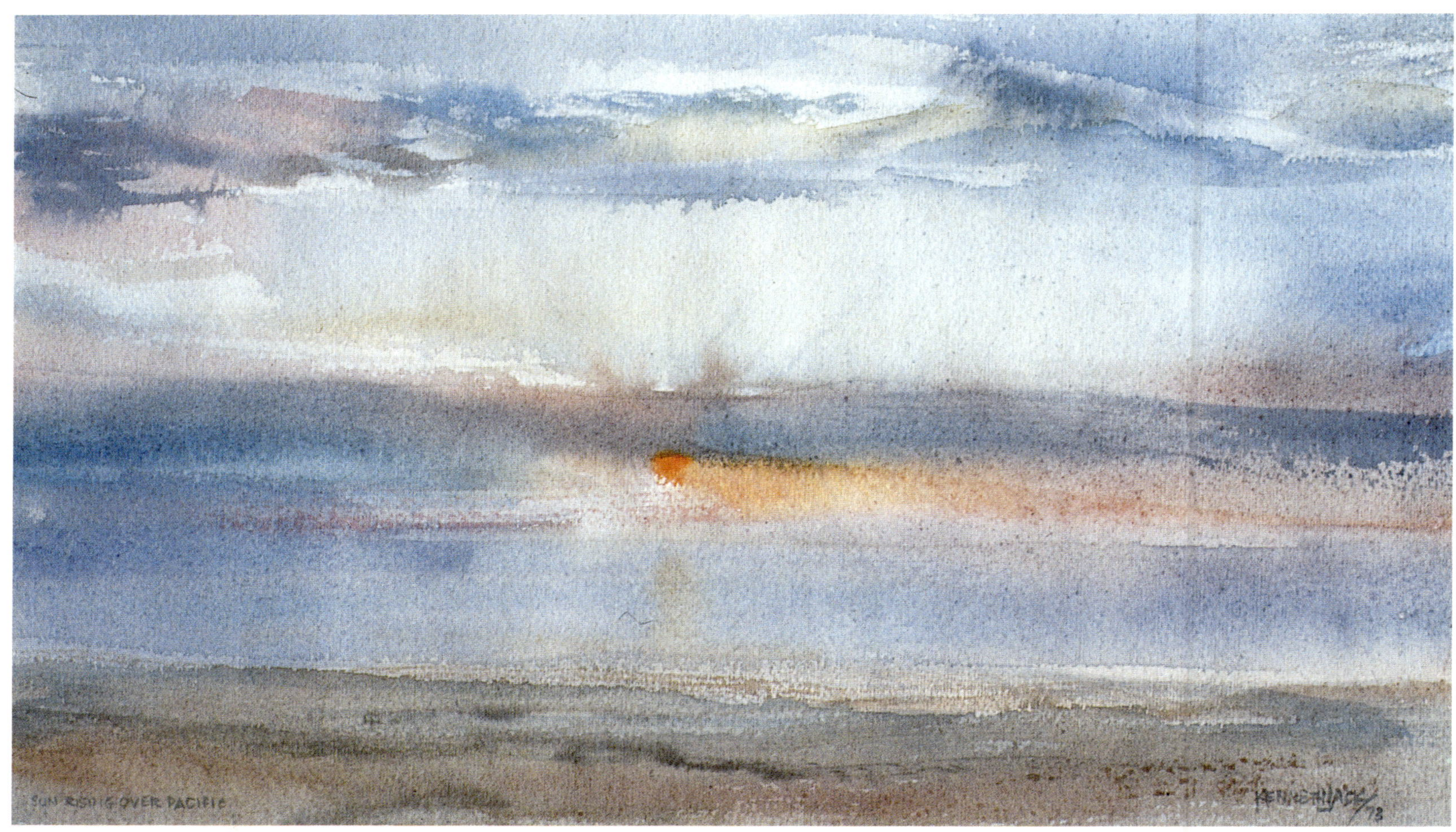

Plate 8 *Sun Rising over the Pacific* 1973, watercolour, 16 × 29 cm

My family and I were staying at Gerringong with Lloyd and Marjory Rees, which we felt was a great privilege. Their house almost overlooks the beach and looks the other way to a river and mountain landscape. The area is rich in coastal and mountain subjects for drawings and I was out every day enjoying concentrated sketching and painting.

One morning I decided to rise very early to see the sun coming up over the Pacific Ocean. The beach was empty except for a few seagulls and one friendly dog. The view south along the beach had a magical early light which I had rarely seen, so I took out my watercolours and painted quickly to capture the colours and general feeling.

By the time I had finished the sun was rising to my left, so I put the first painting aside and commenced this one. The sun was breaking through clouds on the horizon — the beautiful effects far too complicated for any artist to reproduce. Nevertheless I tried a simplified version, and when one doesn't have nature to compare it with, the painting takes on a life of its own. Painting and observing this beautiful sunrise gave me the basis for one of my largest paintings — Sunrise, Drought Country (Plate 7) painted a few months later. Then fourteen years after my original small watercolour, I used it again as a reference for a very large watercolour Sunrise — Wallaga Lake (1987).

at Victoria Barracks he met Harold Freedman, who was then in charge of RAAF publications and later became an official war artist. Freedman took an interest in Jack's work, gave him some useful criticism and published some of his drawings in publications such as *RAAF Log, RAAF Saga, Victory Roll* and the magazine *Wings*.

In 1944–45 he spent eighteen months in New Guinea, Morotai Island and Labuan, North Borneo, where he continued to draw in his spare time. His father kept him supplied with art materials, which he kept in an extra kitbag. In spite of the unpleasant tropical conditions, which caused him some skin disorders, he made more than five hundred drawings. He sold a few to American soldiers and presented the others recently to the Australian War Memorial.

While he was serving in North Borneo in 1945 with an airfield construction squadron, Jack met Donald Friend, who was attached to the same unit. Friend had been appointed a war artist late in the war and was then twenty-eight years old. As Kenneth Jack was the only other artist in the area, Friend would come and sit in his tent in the evenings and amuse him and his friends with hilarious stories which he told 'by the hour'.

> He used to write up his daily diary on blank pages, doing many drawings in pen and wash (he used spit and smudge), a technique I hadn't used. I watched him working, learning a lot just by watching his extremely brilliant left hand creating pictures very rapidly as if by magic. I had at this stage abolished the use of pencil blockouts and the use of erasers, drawing directly in pen line, usually with shading. But Donald Friend's speed and facility made me seem slow, and really amazed me. He used to talk about artists like Gauguin, Van Gogh, Dobell and Drysdale and although I was at this time twenty years old, the work of these artists was unknown to me. I can remember promising myself to find out about them on my return to civilisation.[2]

Jack kept in touch with John Rowell, who suggested he try to make some pen-and-wash drawings and explained how. In return Jack kept Rowell supplied with pipe tobacco, which was issued to him but he didn't need. He also had some oil paints and when time was available he occasionally painted outdoors on very heavy canvas from old American army tents. These were the only *plein air* oil paintings he has ever done.

When he was finally discharged Jack resumed his art studies in Melbourne through the Commonwealth Rehabilitation Training Scheme for ex-servicemen and women. He recalls that so many were studying art at the Melbourne Technical College that one could hardly move in the life class. Some students had to sit on the window sills to draw and others sat on the floor; it was hard even to see the model and very awkward for John Rowell to move around the class to see the students' work.

Jack joined the art school for the last term of 1945 and all of 1946. Impatient as always, he did two years of the Art Teachers Certificate (degree equivalent) in one and then in 1947 attended Melbourne Teachers College to obtain his Trained Teacher's Certificate (Manual Arts). He was also art editor of the college student magazine *The Trainee*. His first teaching post was at Box Hill Boys High School, where he taught for a term in 1948. He then taught at Upwey High School until the end of 1950.

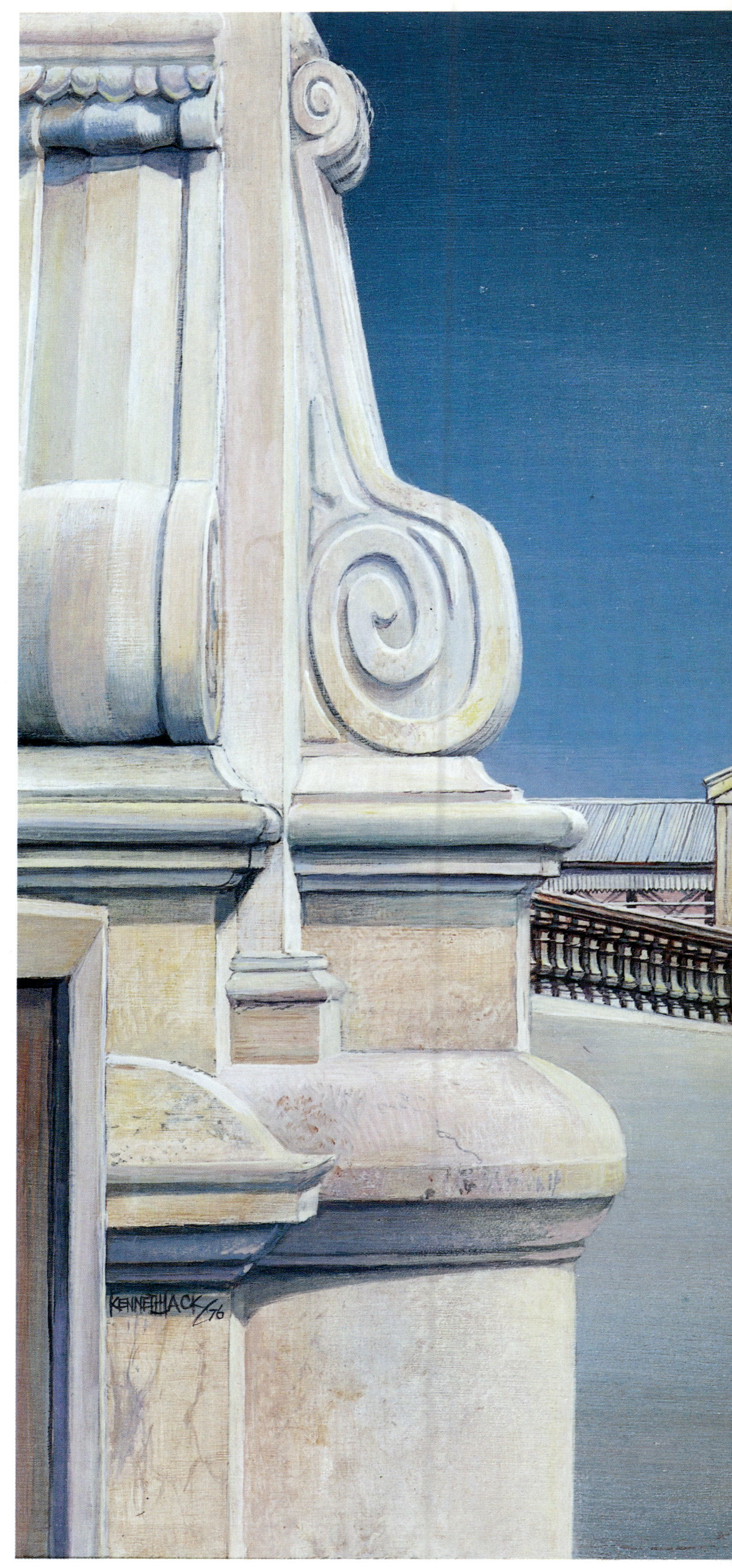

Plate 9 *Booking Office, Railway Station, Perth* 1976, acrylic, 46 × 61 cm

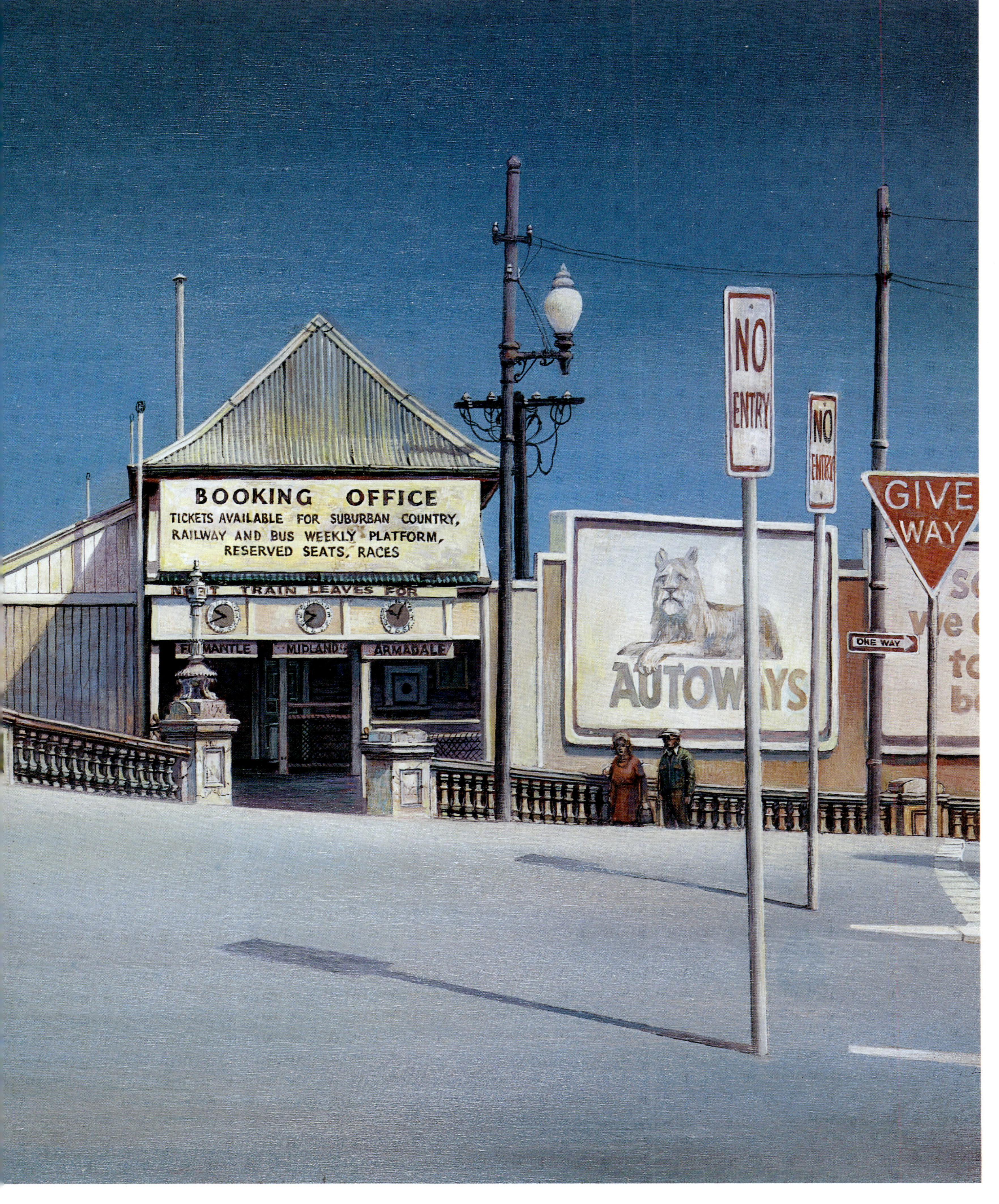
BOOKING OFFICE
TICKETS AVAILABLE FOR SUBURBAN COUNTRY,
RAILWAY AND BUS WEEKLY PLATFORM,
RESERVED SEATS, RACES
NEXT TRAIN LEAVES FOR
FREMANTLE   MIDLAND   ARMADALE
NO ENTRY
NO ENTRY
AUTOWAYS
GIVE WAY
ONE WAY

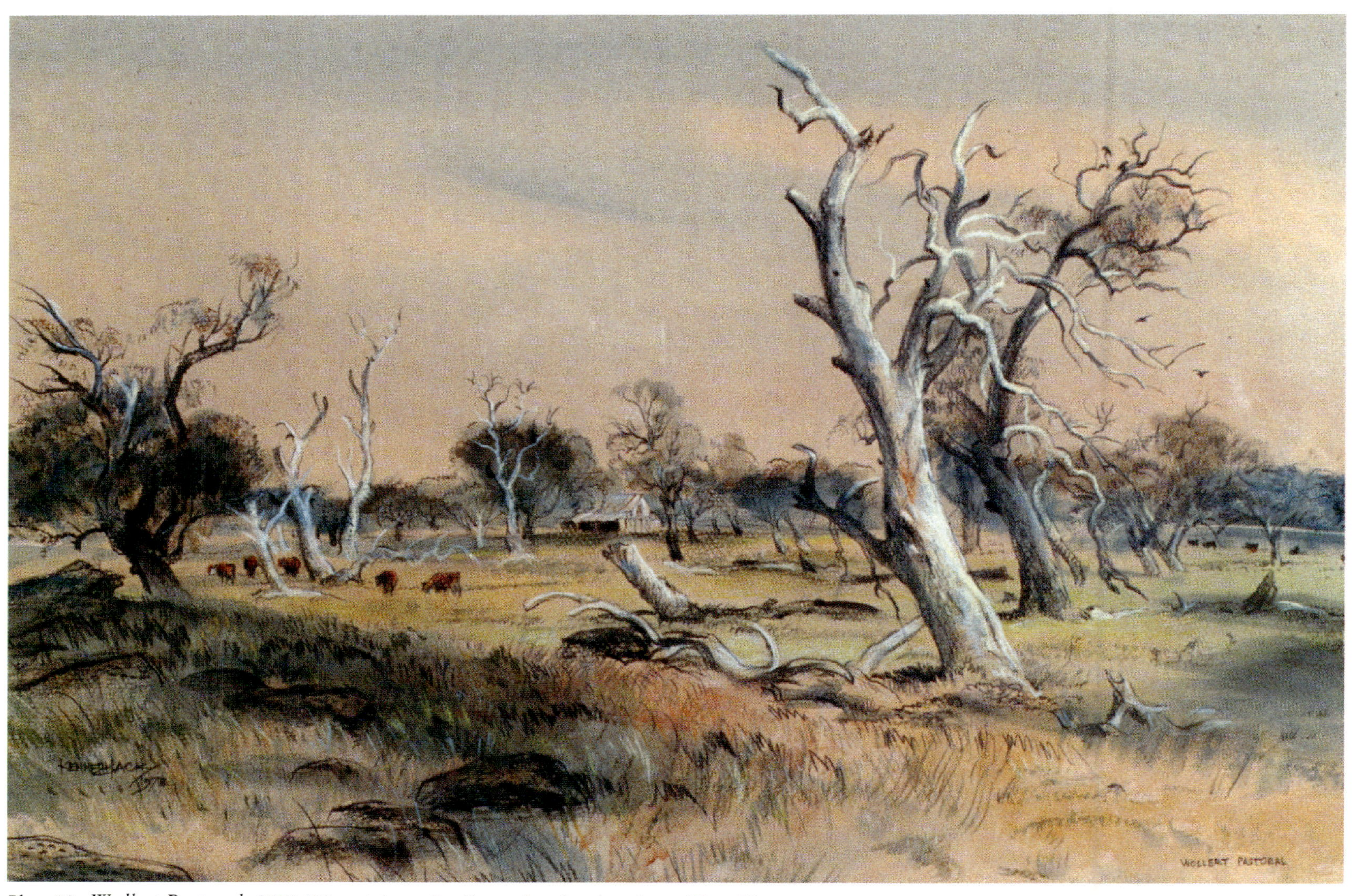

Plate 10 *Wollert Pastoral* 1973 (Victoria) pencil, oil pastel and watercolour, 37 × 53 cm

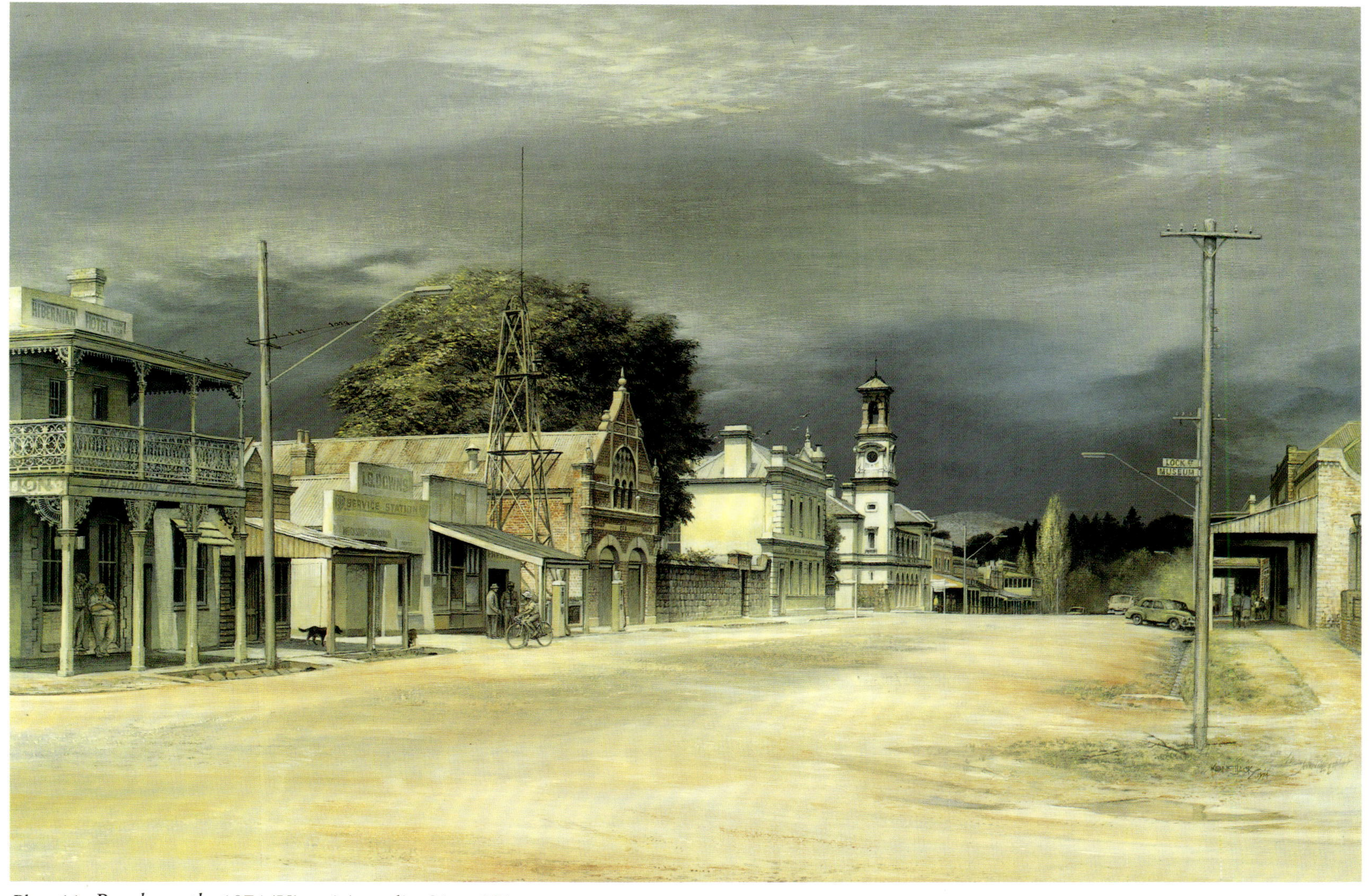

Plate 11 *Beechworth* 1974 (Victoria) acrylic, 81 × 121 cm

This old gold mining town in north-east Victoria has over thirty of its very fine buildings rated by the National Trust. It is one of the best preserved and most beautiful towns in Victoria. The painting shows a vista along a street, past a verandahed hotel, shops, the fire station, and a bank to the very elegantly-proportioned post office with its Italianate tower at the crossroads of the two principal streets. The great width of the street here is something which is very typical of Australian towns. For this painting I limited my palette to just four tubes of paint — white, black, lemon yellow and raw sienna.

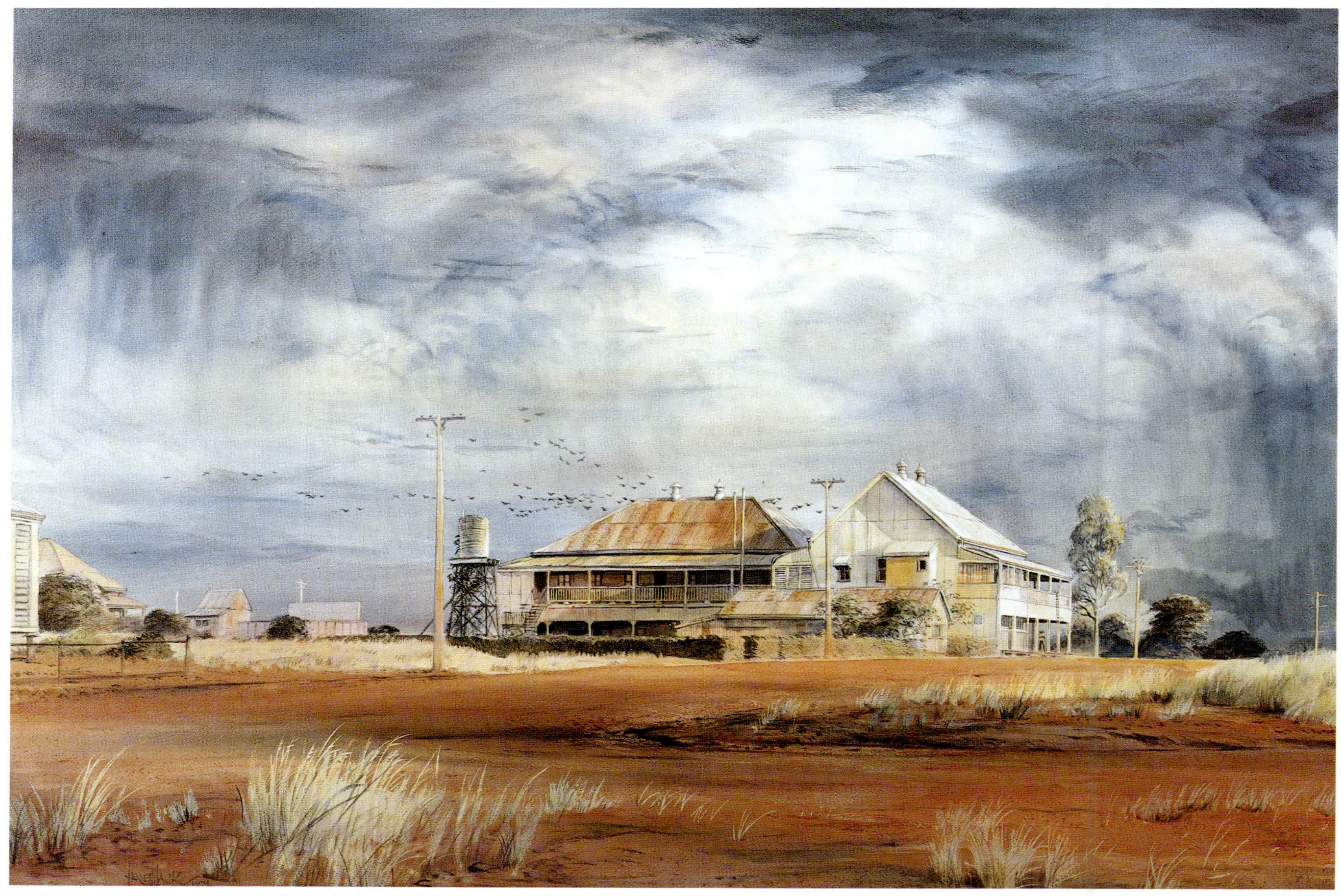

Plate 12 *Monsoon at Normanton* 1974 (Queensland) watercolour, 68 × 101 cm

*Normanton used to have a population in the gold
days of the 1890s of 3 000 people — today it has less
than 1 000. It is the main town in the Gulf Country
of North Queensland.*

*The challenge to me in painting this watercolour
was to design a huge monsoonal cumulus cloud over
the old hotel. It had to look threatening. The flight
of birds hurrying before it helps to convey some of
this atmosphere. The cloud is an imagined one, as
the sky remained cloudless the whole time I was in
Normanton.*

*The old hotel is viewed from down the hill and
three-quarter back view. To the left is an open-air
picture theatre with the screen and the projection
booth visible.*

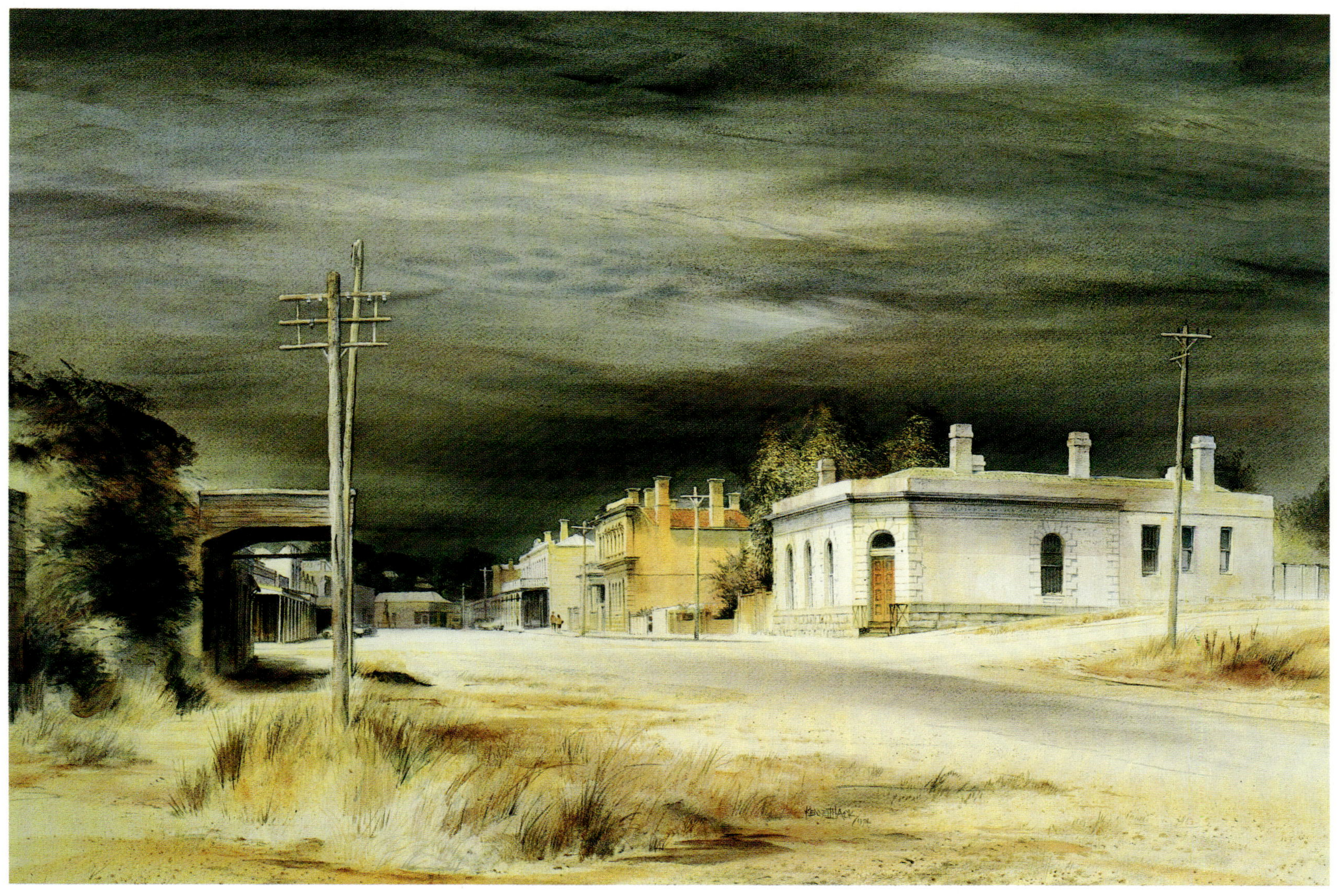

Plate 13 *Clunes* 1974 (Victoria) watercolour, 68 × 102 cm

Clunes is one of my favourite Victorian towns. It has many interesting buildings and is the town in which gold was first discovered in Victoria in 1851. It is situated along the road midway between Ballarat and Maryborough. The wide main street is typically Australian with its many shops and hotels, all with verandahs. I always feel excited when I approach this town, which I have done dozens of times over many decades, as it presents so many interesting aspects.

I remember when making a line drawing of this subject on site, a man in a car pulled up in the middle of the street to talk to a chap who happened to be crossing the street at that moment; they were obviously friends. I kept on drawing for about another hour while the two talked on. No traffic moved past or required them to move in this time — it seemed so typical of some of our country towns where life moves much more slowly than in the big cities.

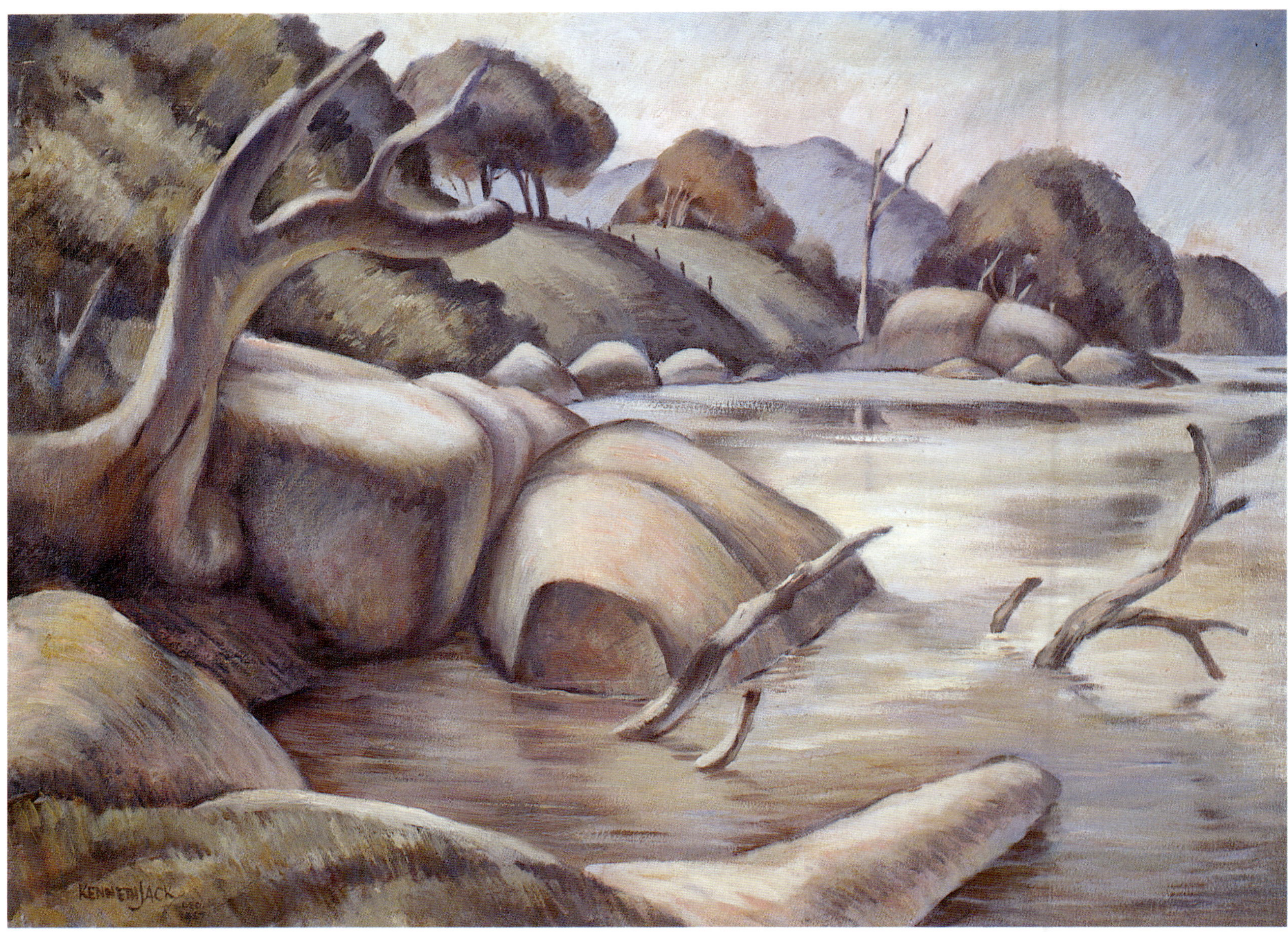

Fig. 5 *Banks of the Goulburn* 1947 (Victoria) oil, 62 × 87 cm

The Artist and Teacher

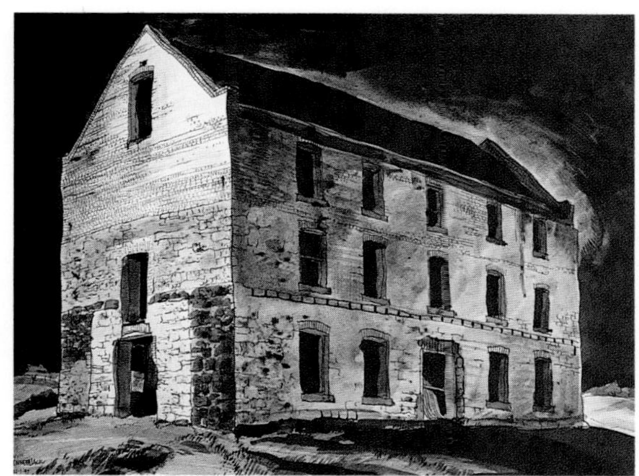

Fig. 6 *The Old Mill, Bacchus Marsh*
1947 (Victoria) pen and wash, 25 × 35 cm

Kenneth Jack's precocious talent for drawing made him more concerned with mastering technique than interested in art as revolution. He did not know of nor did he see the great *Herald* exhibition of contemporary art which came to Melbourne in 1939. Selected by Basil Burdett and sponsored by Sir Keith Murdoch, the exhibition marked the beginning of a cultural revolution which Australia went through during and just after the war. It included paintings by all the giants of twentieth-century painting including a good selection of works by Cézanne. Jack was fifteen at the time and might have profited by seeing the exhibition but his father's taste would probably have been too orthodox for him to take an interest in it. The event caused a good deal of critical controversy and caused the jolt which made the first crack in the Edwardian isolationism of Australian visual culture.

Nevertheless, while Jack was at Melbourne Teachers College in 1947 he did show allegiance to contemporary ideas when he defended the new outlook to art in a letter to the student newspaper. Replying to another correspondent who had asked why most of the paintings in the College collection were of a particular type, Jack explained that most of the works were by Impressionists. It is the 'painting the majority of the people like best, because it is what they *see* with their own eyes … Broadly speaking, the "modern" movement in Australian art is trying to put something more solid into its art than did the Impressionists. Therefore, though one's appreciation may not have extended beyond a Streeton or Heysen, we must respect these newer artists. There are things like colour harmony, form, design and unity, which must underlie a work of art if it is to stand the test of time. Whether we like it or not the work of men like William Dobell and Russell Drysdale will live because their work possesses these necessary qualities . . .'[3] He went on to say that a new 'collecting approach' should seek to acquire works by artists such as Douglas Annand, John D. Moore, Kenneth MacQueen, Dobell, Drysdale, 'Rupert Bunny (now an old man)', Douglas Dundas, Eric Wilson, Noel Counihan etc. 'All these artists can hold their own in the field with artists from overseas, but they don't receive the encouragement from the Australian public that they deserve.'

Today we may not realise that in 1947 artists such as Dobell and Drysdale were still treated with considerable contempt by some members of the art public. One need only remember the controversy in Sydney when Dobell's portrait of Joshua Smith was awarded the 1943 Archibald Prize or the furore caused in Adelaide in 1949 when Drysdale was awarded a prize for his *Woman in a Landscape*.

By the time he began teaching, Kenneth Jack was becoming quite well known as an artist. In 1945 he was awarded the Bendigo Art Gallery's Watercolour Prize and in January 1946 and July 1947 Sydney Ure Smith published some of his drawings in his important art journal *Australia, National*

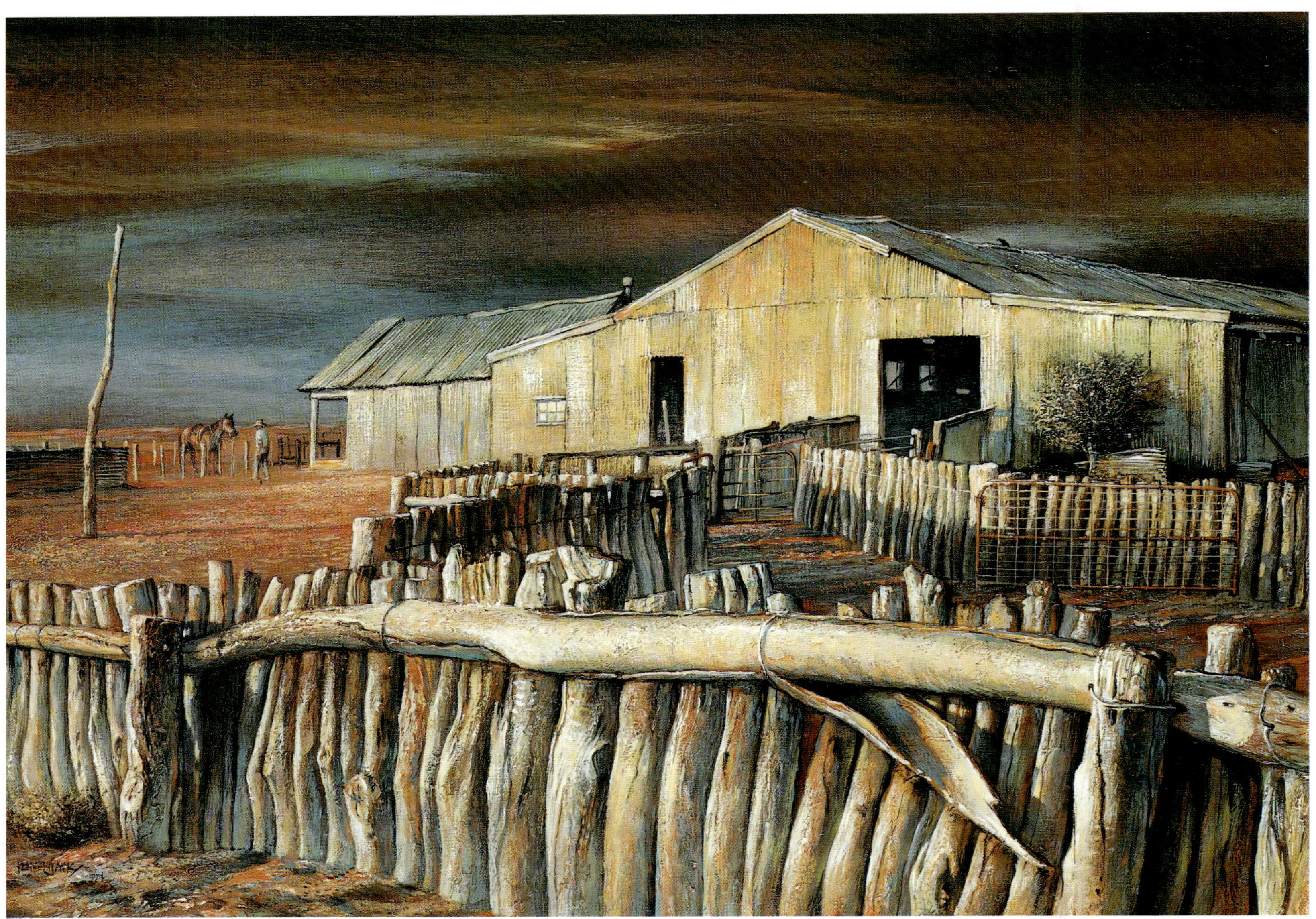

Plate 14 *Mulga Fences, Mt. Poole Shearing Shed* 1974 (New South Wales) acrylic, 40 × 56 cm

*The main reason for painting this acrylic work was
to depict the marvellous forms of the mulga fence in
front of the old galvanised iron shearing shed.
I chose a late afternoon light to emphasise the forms,
and I searched the tree-trunk posts for any
differences, for example, the bark peeling off a
nearer one, to add more interest and variety. This
shearing shed is in the desolate north-west corner of
New South Wales (near Sturt's Depot Glen) and is a
subject, together with its homestead buildings,
I have drawn and painted many times from
different angles.*

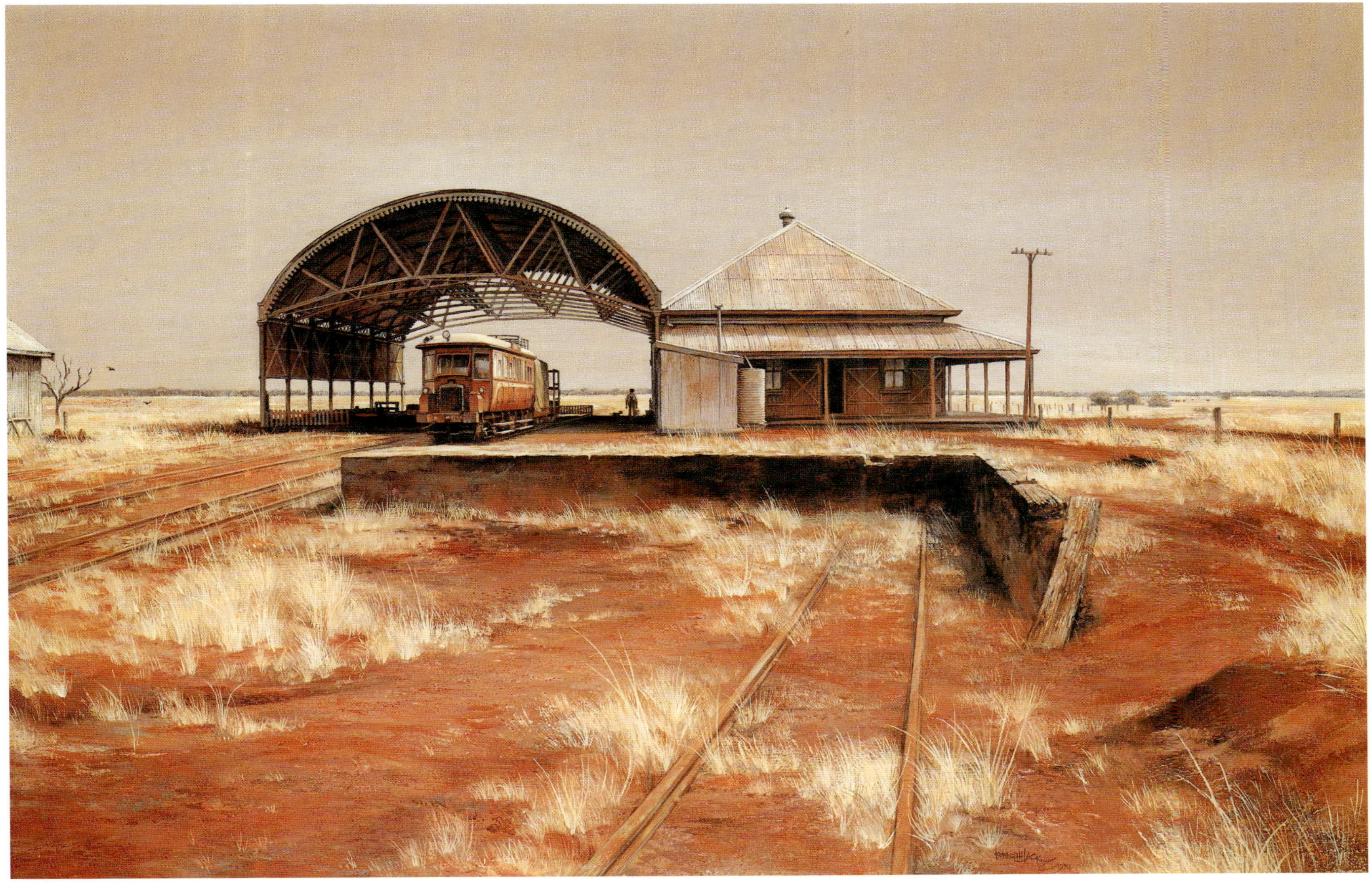

Plate 15 *Normanton Railway Station* 1974 (Queensland) acrylic, 61 × 91 cm

Situated out on the edge of the town on a flat plain covered in long, yellow grass, this very large, ornate and unusual railway station would be the most exciting subject of its type I have ever seen. It seemed so extraordinarily grandiose in conception for a small remote North Queensland town — to me it was an irresistible subject. I have made several paintings of it and a lithograph, all from different angles.

The train ('The Gulflander') is pulled by a very antiquated rail motor and travels only about 150 kilometres to the south-east to the old gold mining town of Croydon. The railway is not connected to any other rail system. Since the road between the towns sometimes becomes flooded after particularly heavy rains, the railway maintains a link, going over creeks on higher bridges.

Journal. Ure Smith had probably seen some of his drawings in *Wings* and had asked him to contribute.

Sydney Ure Smith was not only an influential figure in the Australian art world and an important publisher,[4] but was also an accomplished draughtsman and etcher. He had just published a small volume of his own drawings of Sydney and was considering following it with one devoted to Melbourne. The text was to be written by Clive Turnbull and Kenneth Jack was asked to make the drawings; he was only twenty-three when Ure Smith entrusted the project to him. The book was published in 1948 and the short biographical note on the artist, most probably written by Ure Smith, said 'It is difficult to believe that the artist who is responsible for the work in this book is only twenty-four years of age.'

As was his way when a young artist's work impressed him, Ure Smith also tried to interest his friends in Jack's drawings. He arranged an exhibition for him at Walter Taylor's Grosvenor Galleries in Sydney in November 1949, the artist's first one-man show, from which works were acquired both by the Art Gallery of New South Wales and the Mitchell Library. Douglas Dundas,[5] who was then teaching at the East Sydney Technical College, purchased the drawing *Princess Theatre, Melbourne* and remembered how excited Sydney Ure Smith was about his discovery of a draughtsman of quality in Melbourne.

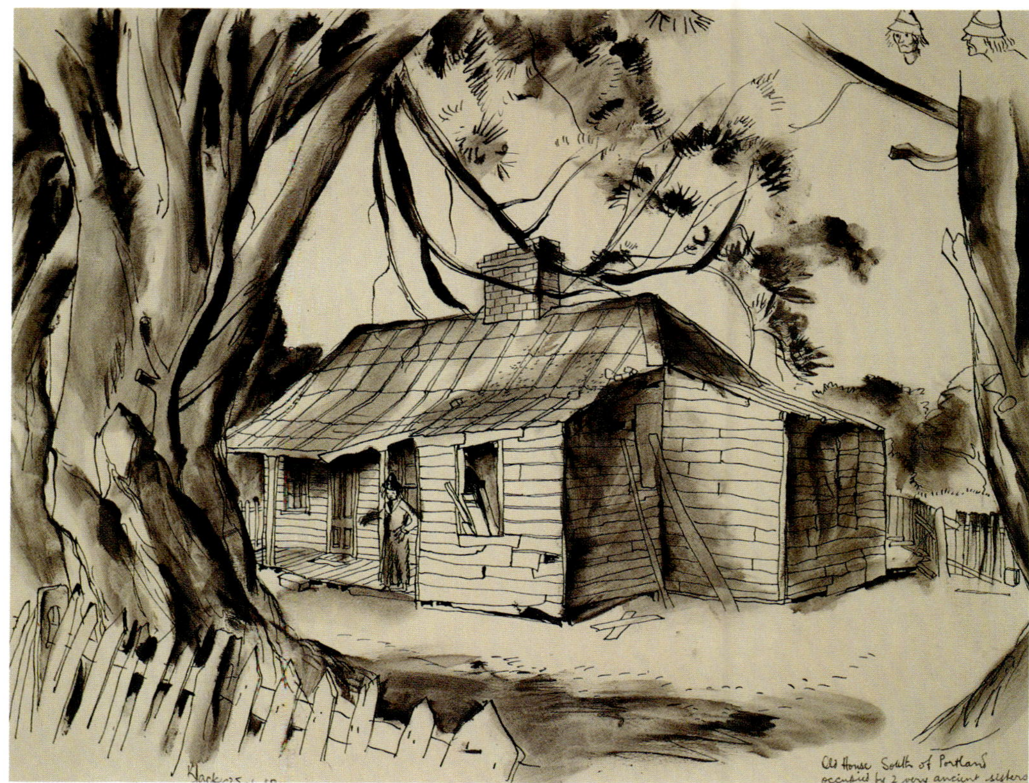

Fig. 7 *Old House, South of Portland* 1948 (Victoria) pen, ink and smudge, 26.5 × 36 cm

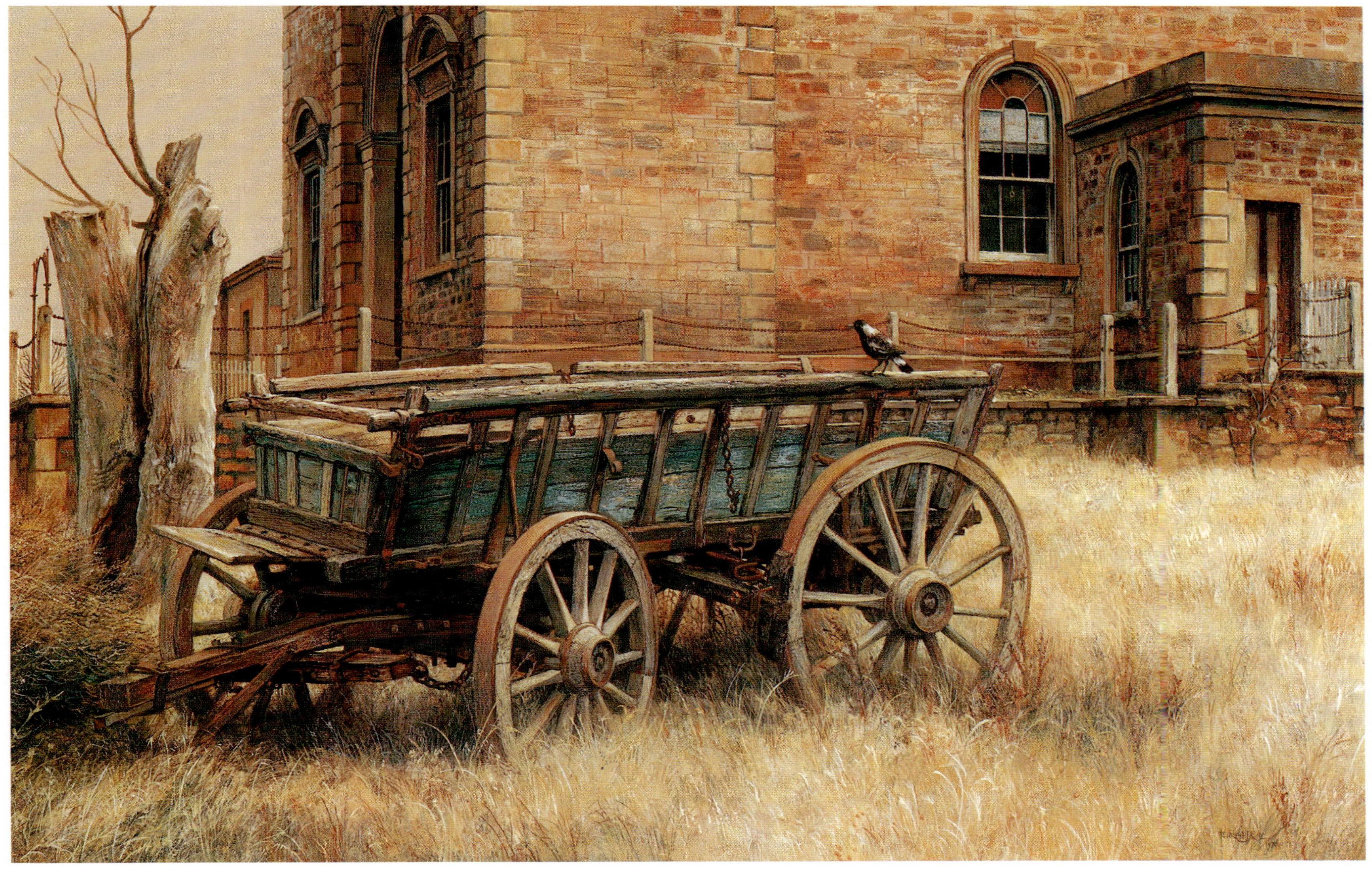

Plate 16 *Wagon at Kapunda* 1974 (South Australia) acrylic, 53 × 84 cm

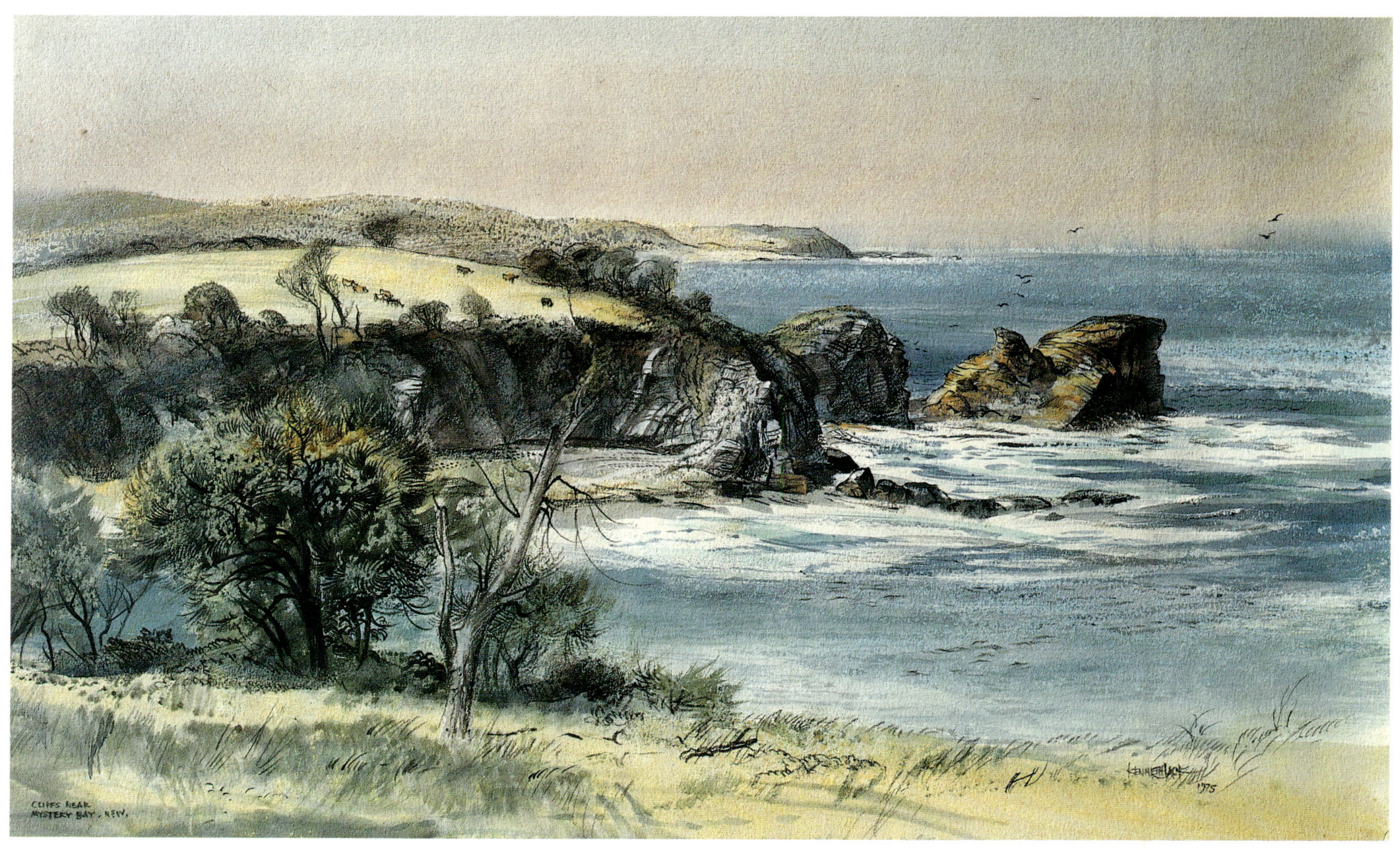

Plate 17 *Cliffs near Mystery Bay* 1975 (New South Wales) pencil, oil pastel and watercolour, 31 × 50 cm

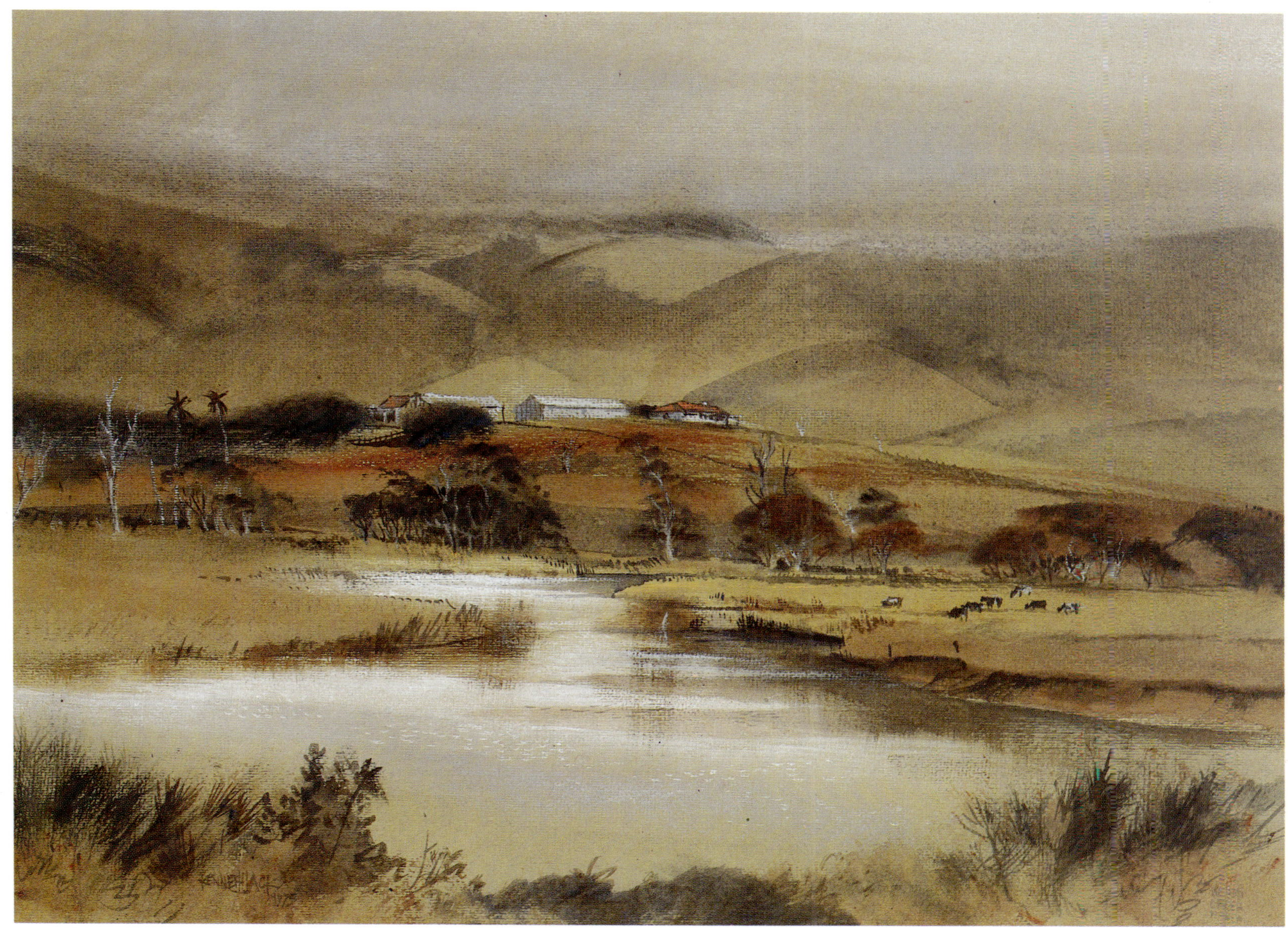

Plate 18 *Werrie Creek* 1975 (New South Wales) watercolour with pastel, 34 × 47 cm

Carrying on his business from his sick bed late in 1948, Ure Smith wrote to Kenneth Jack to say that he was planning a volume on Hobart using reproductions of colonial prints, but wanted to include several original drawings of historic buildings by Jack. As he had already arranged to go to Hobart on a sketching trip during the school holidays in January 1949, Jack said he would be happy to make the drawings and agreed to meet Ure Smith's editor Gwen Morton Spencer, who would be in Hobart to prepare the book.

He flew to Hobart with an architect friend whose interest in sketching was rather similar to his own. The holiday lasted twelve days and in that time Jack completed eighty-eight drawings, working from morning until dark, colouring some of them after the evening meal at the hotel. He had no transport apart from public trams and buses and a lot of time was spent searching out subjects. At the end of the sketching holiday he was exhausted.

> But I must point out that exploring and drawing at a concentrated rate was really quite exciting, and it is a thing that I do periodically, right up to the present day. I enjoy seeing new places and cannot resist the intense urge to draw what moves me strongly . . .[6] The exacting nature of drawing directly in ink line, without preliminary pencil guidelines . . . of drawing proportions correctly, of using perspective reasonably correctly, without ruler or set square, but by eye, to judge angles, not taking expressionistic liberties with the subject, making subtle emphases, and design allowances for form in space and the relationships between buildings and their surroundings . . . such things tire one mentally.[7]
>
> One of the advantages I have had since I was a teenage artist, is to be able to visualise the drawing on the blank paper; this enables me to place the subject, so that I rarely run out of space on the sides and also means I don't need the eraser. I've found that the degree of uncertainty in drawing directly on the blank paper in a pen line creates a certain nervous quality in line, which is absent if a drawing has a prior pencil block out.[8]

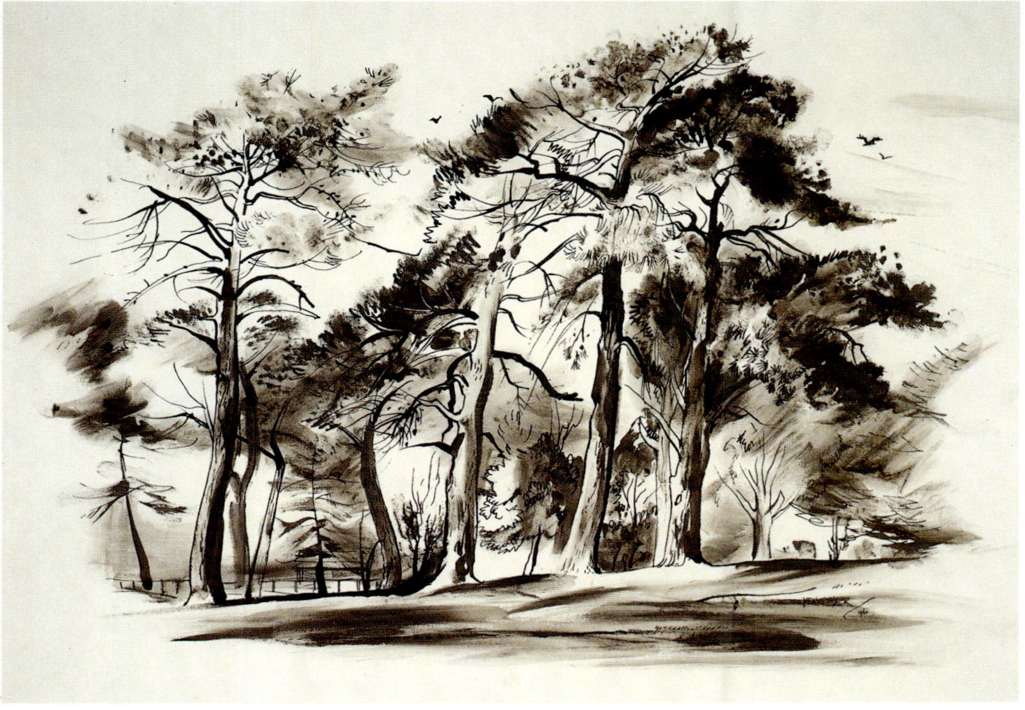

Fig. 8 *Pines, Caulfield Park* 1960 (Victoria) pen, ink and smudge, 32 × 48 cm

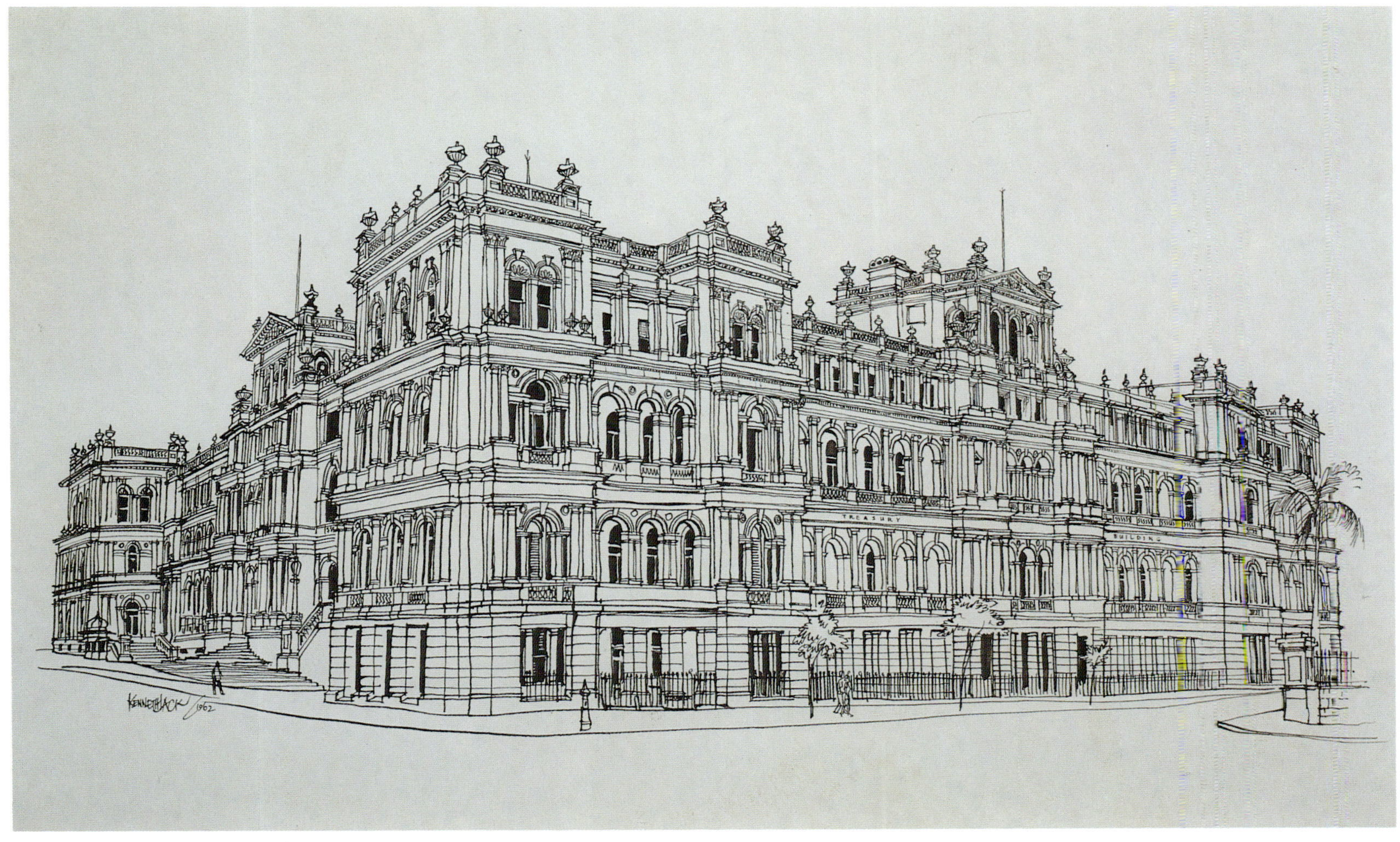

Fig. 9 *Treasury Buildings, Brisbane* 1962, pen line, 30.5 × 50.8 cm

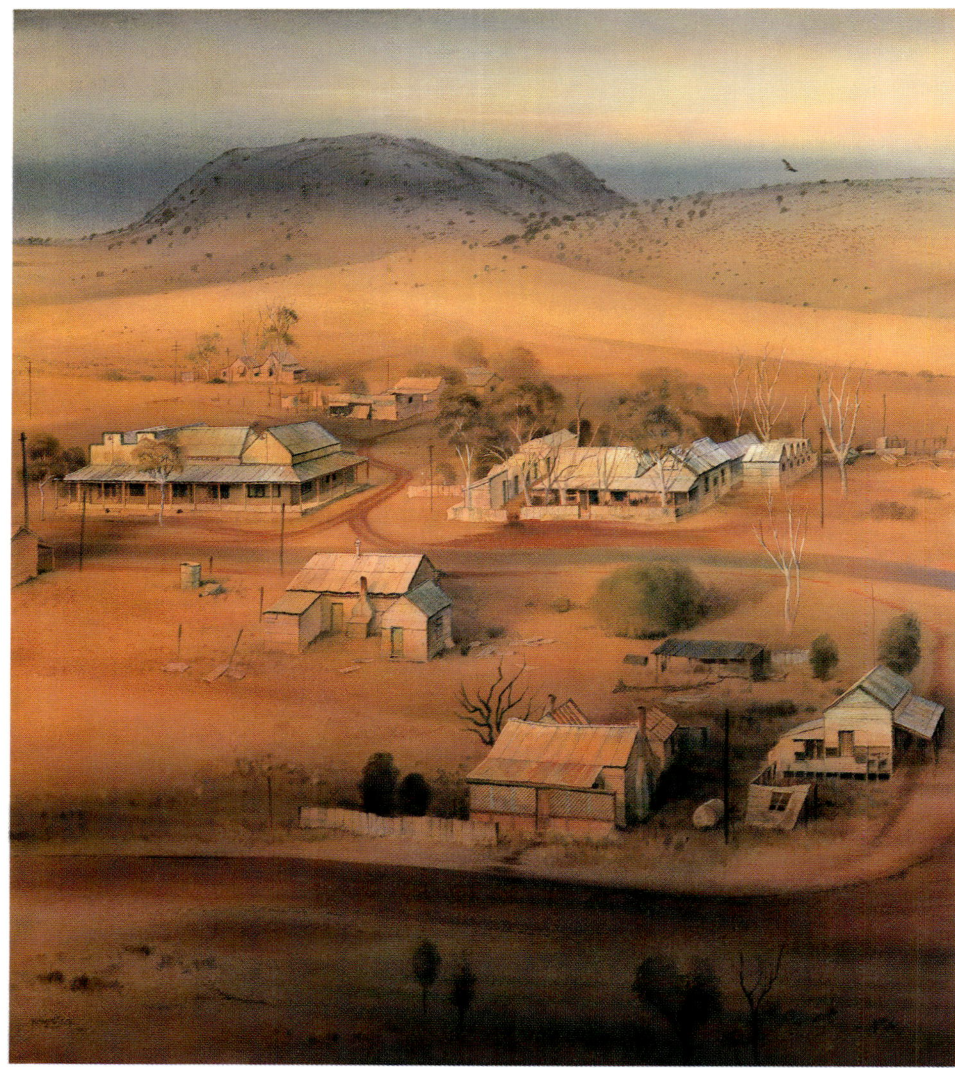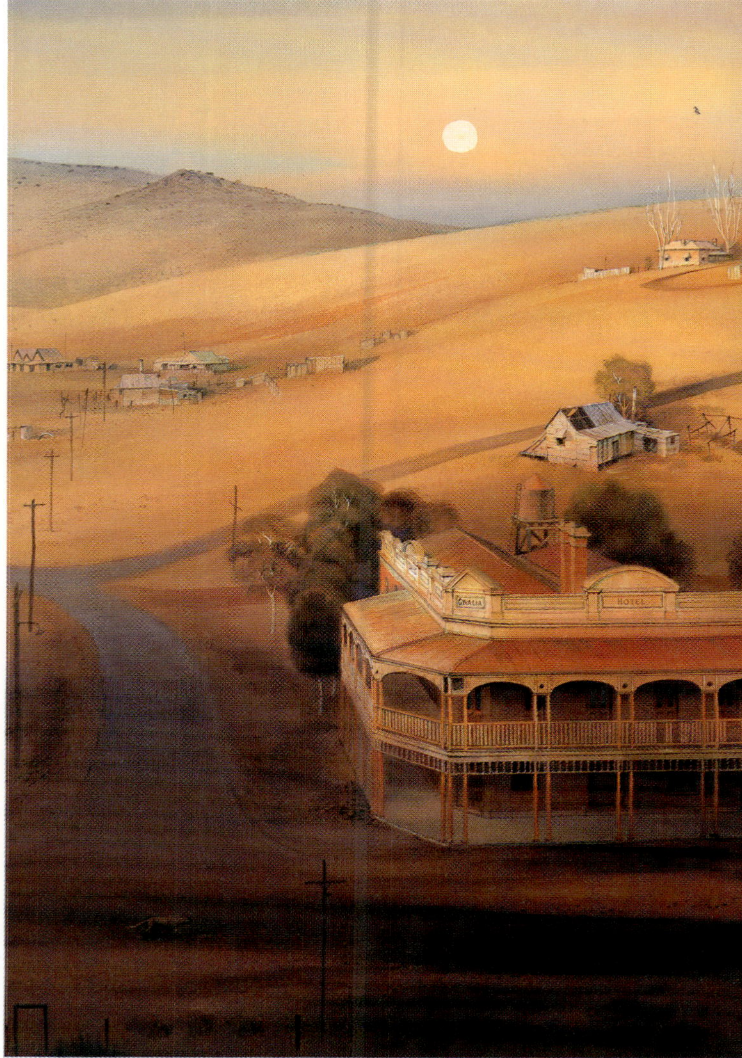

Plate 19 *Ghost Town, Gwalia Triptych* 1987 (Western Australia) 113 x 364 cm

Left panel: *Mt. Leonora, General Store, Rooming House* watercolour, 113 x 101 cm
Centre panel: *Hotel and Mine Manager's Hill* watercolour, 113 x 162 cm
Right panel: *Sons of Gwalia Mine, Miners' Houses* watercolour, 113 x 101 cm

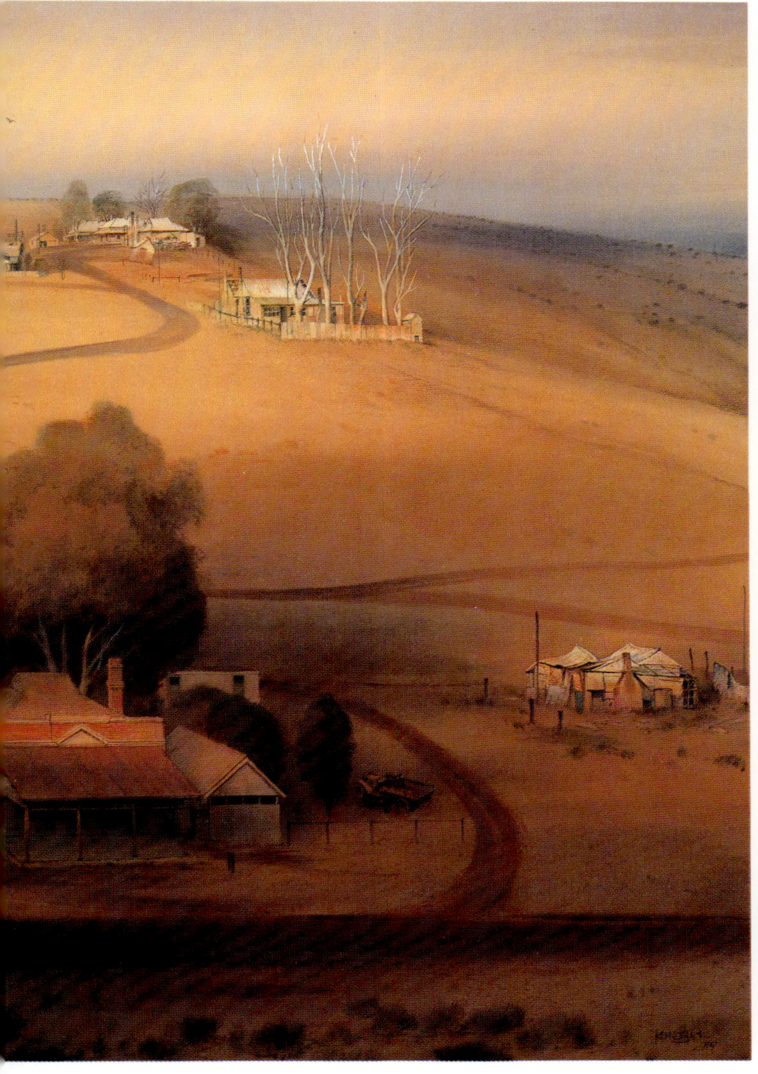 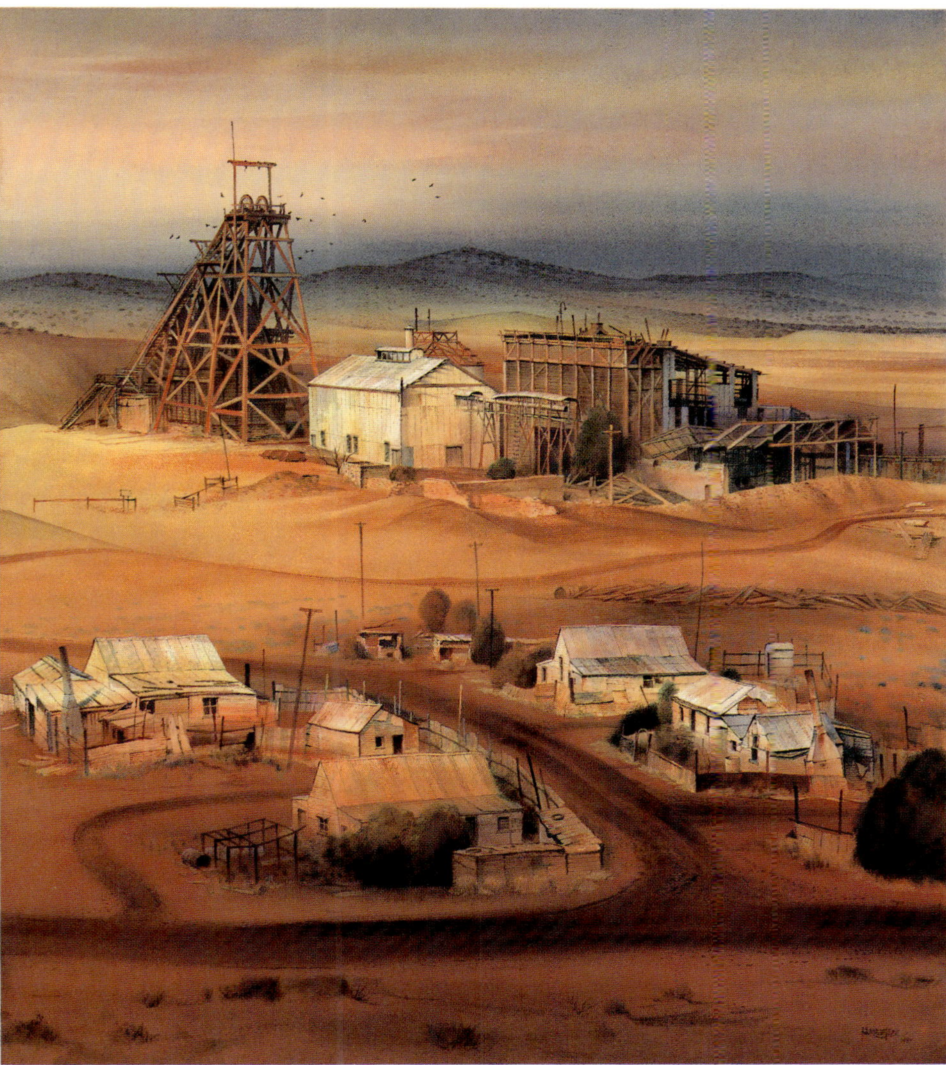

In a triptych each section should make a complete composition in itself, and yet the overall design must bind all three sections successfully into one large composition. Choosing a subject for a triptych is not just a matter of dividing a subject, any subject, into three. I had drawn and painted many different aspects of Gwalia over the years and wanted to paint a more overall view.

Gwalia, an old mining town, is mostly built of timber frame buildings with roofs and walls covered in galvanised iron. Most of the buildings are tumbling down and one gets an eerie feeling when the wind causes the sheets of iron to flap and the crows overhead screech. The feeling of a once busy town, now almost deserted, is overwhelming.

To achieve the view I wanted, I had to imagine myself in an elevated position, as in a balloon or from a birds-eye view, out over the clay pan and saltbush flats. To do this I used many of the five hundred or so photographs I'd taken over the years. For the lighting and colouring in the painting I chose moonrise at sunset to suggest the association of dying day, dying town.

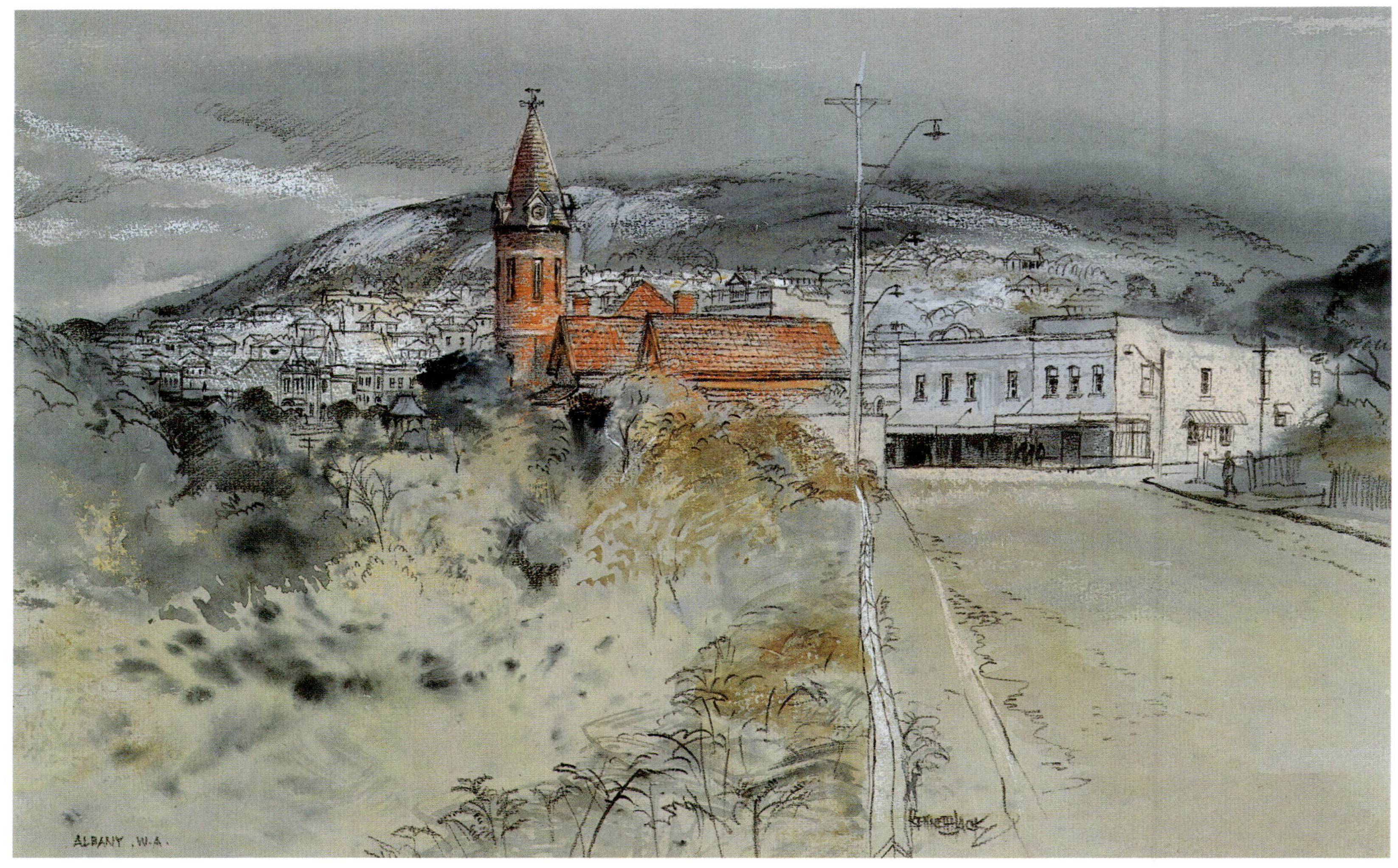

Plate 20 *Albany* 1976 (Western Australia) pencil, oil pastel and watercolour, 25 × 40 cm

In February 1949, Jack sent the entire set of Hobart drawings off to Ure Smith, who liked them so much that he scrapped the original idea of the book and devoted it entirely to these original works, using fifty-two of them. This is how *The Charm of Hobart* came into being. The negotiations were conducted from Sydney Ure Smith's hospital bed in St Lukes, where he died late in 1949 just when the book was in production.

Jack passed his final examinations for his Art Teacher's Diploma in 1950, the year he married Betty Dyer. His thesis, 'On the Drawing of Architecture', had taken him two years to prepare; obtaining the Diploma was a long, complicated affair and only seven diplomas were awarded before the course was restructured. The thesis impressed the Art Inspector of Technical Schools and Jack was appointed his assistant (1952–55); at the same time he became a part-time lecturer at Caulfield Institute of Technology. It was a period of intense activity. Besides the responsibilities of two jobs and looking after a young family there was much to learn, discover, assimilate and draw, draw, draw.

On his return from war service Jack again met Harold Freedman, who was one of his teachers at Melbourne Technical College. In 1952 Freedman invited a group of experienced artists to attend evening sessions at the College and use the printmaking facilities.[9] Besides Jack, Mary Macqueen, Harry Rosengrave, Tate Adams, Barbara Brash, Kenneth Hood, Ian Armstrong and occasionally Fred Williams and several others took part. It was the beginning of a revival of printmaking, which had been in the doldrums ever since it had 'crashed' during the Depression.

He also threw himself into printmaking about this time, experimenting in all aspects of the medium. In the biographical notes he sent to the Art Gallery of New South Wales in 1951 he listed the printmaking media he employed as etching, drypoint, engraving, mezzotint, aquatint, lithography and lino cutting and said of himself:

> I lean towards a finished picture having romantic tendencies with classical design, but designed subtly. I insist on good draughtsmanship, ability to draw with the minimum of line to suggest form. Artists should be able to see the abstract shapes beneath their subjects. I believe in an artist drawing as often as possible and deplore those artists who mostly talk art and create occasionally.

His favourite artist at this time was Rembrandt but he also became interested in the work of Turner, Cotman and Cézanne and he was attracted by the work of several English artists whose work he discovered in the series of art volumes published by Penguin during the war. John Piper, Graham Sutherland, Edward Bawden, Henry Moore, Paul Nash, Ben Nicholson and Victor Pasmore were among them. His special favourite was Piper, who was a fine draughtsman, particularly of architecture, with a strong romantic tendency (shared with several colleagues who had rediscovered the work of Samuel Palmer) and a highly dramatic and decorative sense which appealed to a generation which felt a need to incorporate contemporary elements into its work. Both Piper and Sutherland, through the Penguin volumes, had been important influences on Drysdale and Friend during the war.

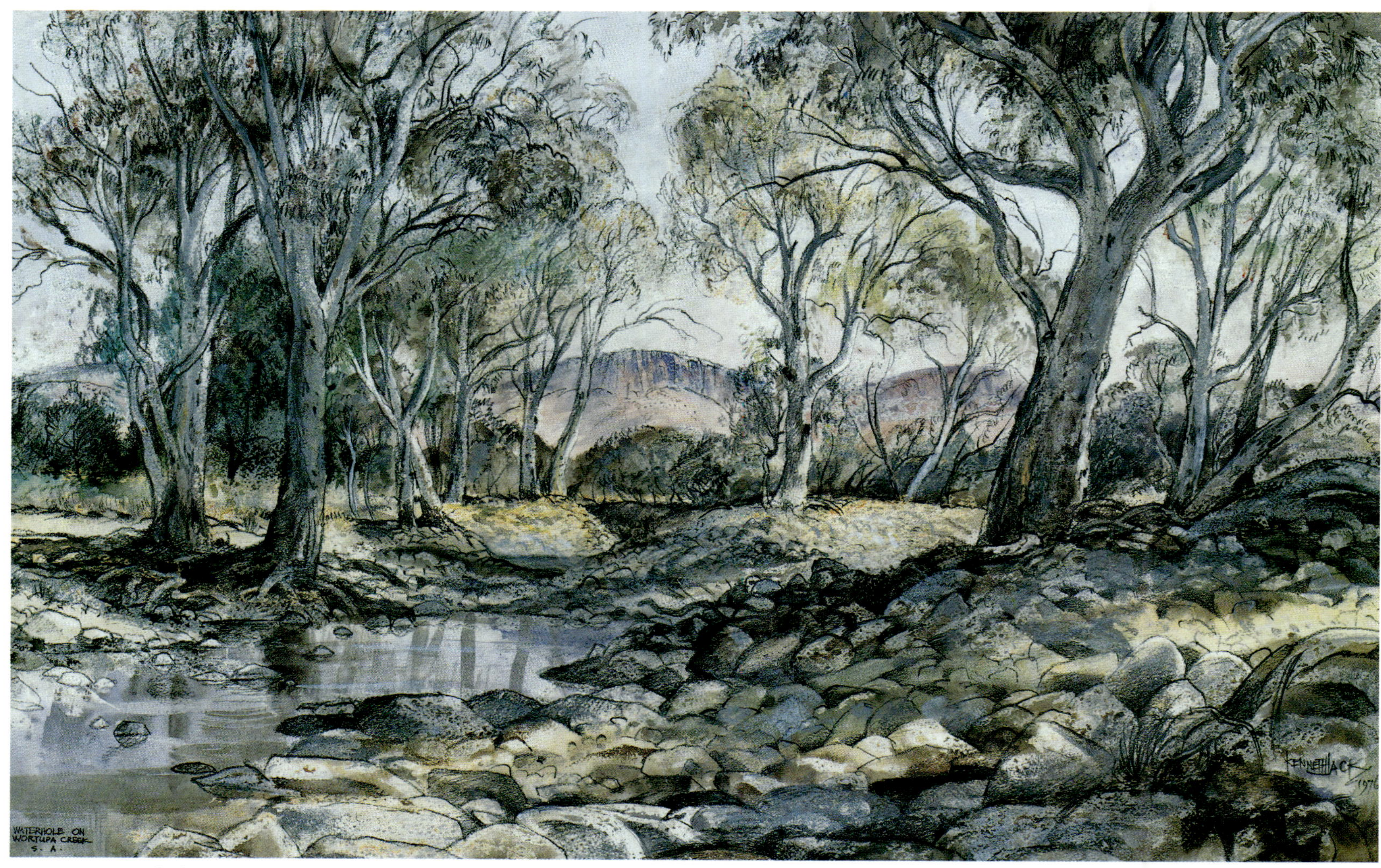

Plate 21   *Waterhole on Wortupa Creek* 1976 (South Australia) pencil, oil pastel and watercolour, 34 × 55 cm

*This drawing was made outdoors on site and is in a
very wild section of the North Flinders Ranges close
to Grindell's Hut. Jock Grindell hid from police in
this remote area after murdering his son-in-law,
George Snell, in 1918 after an argument. In the
distance of the painting are the Gammon Ranges, an
area so hard to penetrate that very few people have
ever been into it. The foreground of rocks marks
where the rough track from Balcanoona Homestead
crosses Wortupa Creek on the way to Grindell's.
Before attempting the crossing we had to stop the
heavily loaded Landcruiser to remove rocks and fill
hollows. We crossed very carefully in low gear, the
rocks moving under our weight and the vehicle
tipping at all angles.*

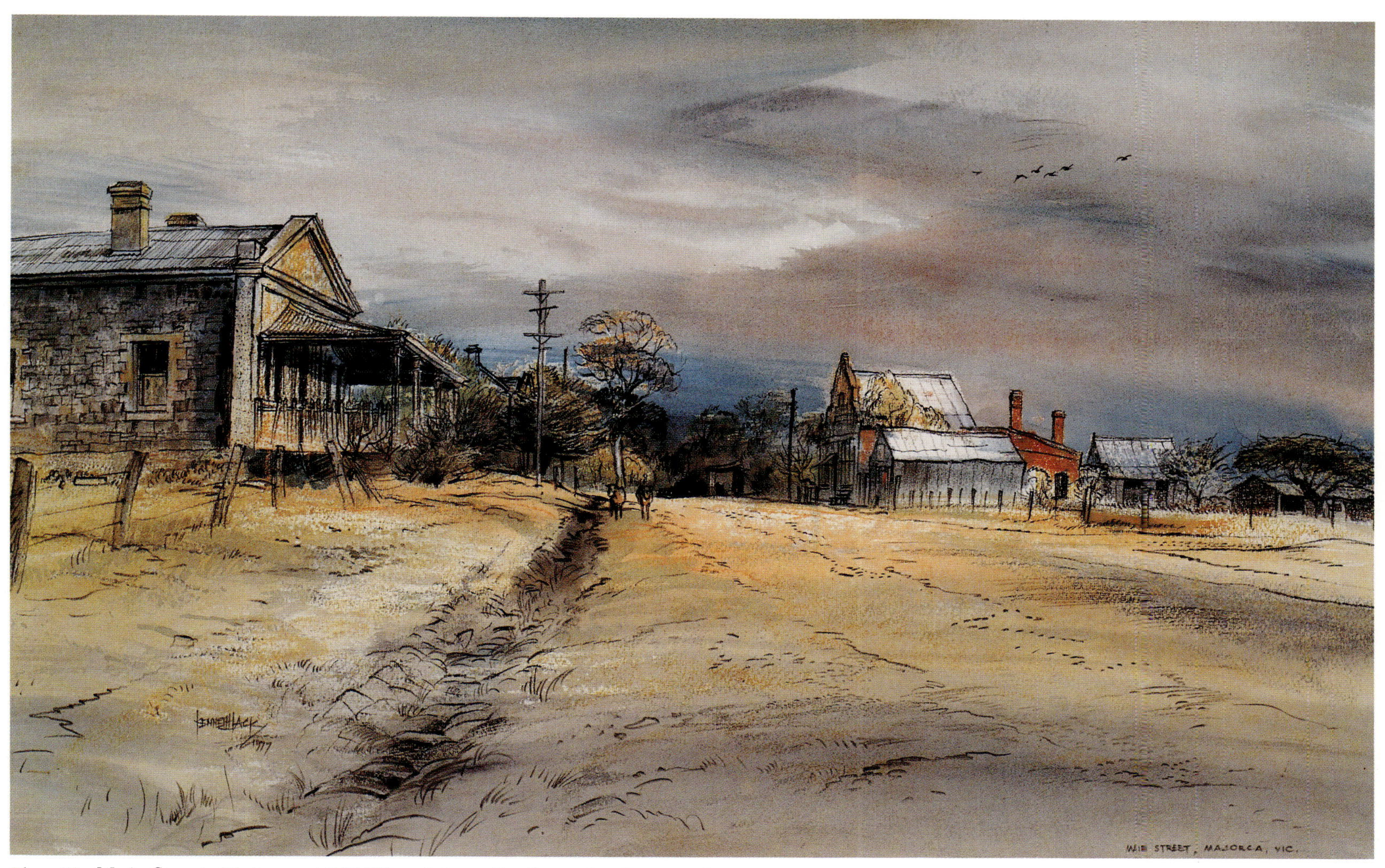

Plate 22 *Main Street, Majorca* 1977 (Victoria) pencil, oil pastel and watercolour, 33.5 × 54 cm

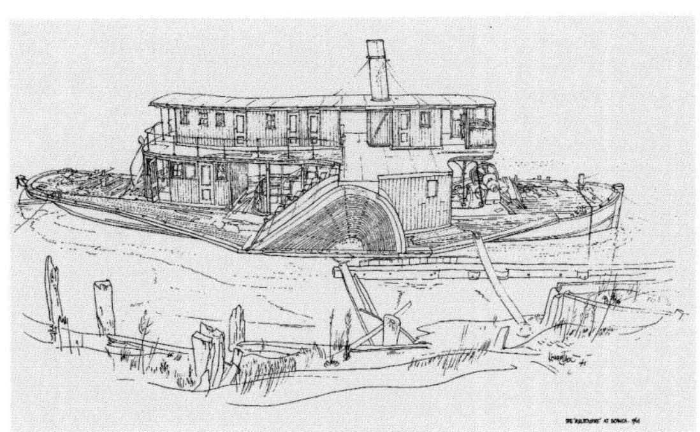

Fig. 10 *The 'Melbourne' at Echuca*
1963, pen line, 44 × 64 cm

The direction taken by painting in the 1950s was away from figuration. Abstraction had taken a leading role in modern American painting as well as in Europe but its full effect was not quite so sudden in Australia. Nevertheless, a striving to be contemporary was reflected in the work of most of the painters of the time. Those who were reluctant to embrace total abstraction introduced a strong emphasis on design to counter figurative elements. During the middle 1950s Bernard Buffet's thick formalised drawings, creating a scaffolding-like grid of the image, showed their influence in the work of John Brack, Michael Shannon and Kenneth Jack. This was most obvious in Jack's case in a large mural he made directly on plaster for the office of the Walter J. Ham Investment House in Queen Street, Melbourne. The work was destroyed when the building was taken over and remodelled.

Art books were in short supply during the war and remained so well into the 1950s. The series of small Penguin volumes already mentioned accordingly made an impact on younger artists. The one published on Paul Klee in 1949 and repeatedly reprinted had a particularly strong influence on painters born between 1925 and 1930. Leafing through this little book today it is easy to see which Australian artists derived inspiration from it when they first began to paint. Kenneth Jack remembers taking an interest both in it and the other volume on a non-British artist, American Ben Shahn.

This was a period when Australian artists looked for models and for confirmation of the direction of their work. Kenneth Jack found a useful model in Lyonel Feininger, whose work had a considerable influence on him both as a painter and a printmaker. The principal element he absorbed was a tendency for images to be reduced to the flat picture plane, abandoning the illusions of space and light to conform to the contemporary canon of picturemaking.

In many cases this seemed a big sacrifice to make in order to be or to look modern and at the same time the innovation in art was something of a shock to the Australian art public, which had always expected a picture to resemble the subject. There was an important clearing away of many misconceptions about art during the decade and though much of the work produced then looks decorative and rhetorical now, it provided a serious basis on which to build. Australian painting was revitalised in the 1960s because of it.

Determined to master drawing from the beginning, Jack copied drawings he admired and searched out various ways of representing light and shade and depicting trees, leaves, buildings, windows, clouds and so on. He acquired such skill that by the time he was fourteen his drawings looked like those of a professional artist. By the time he was attending evening art classes at the age of fifteen he could letter as well as any of the teachers at Melbourne High School. When the names of students had to be lettered on Proficiency Certificates to be given out at the end of the school year, the fifteen-year-old Jack was co-opted into the staff room to join a group of teachers writing out names.

His rapid development as a draughtsman was also aided by his father's interest in his work. He kept the boy's early drawings and encouraged him to submit work to the Saturday children's pages in the *Sun* newspaper, which published a number of his drawings between the ages of nine and about fourteen.

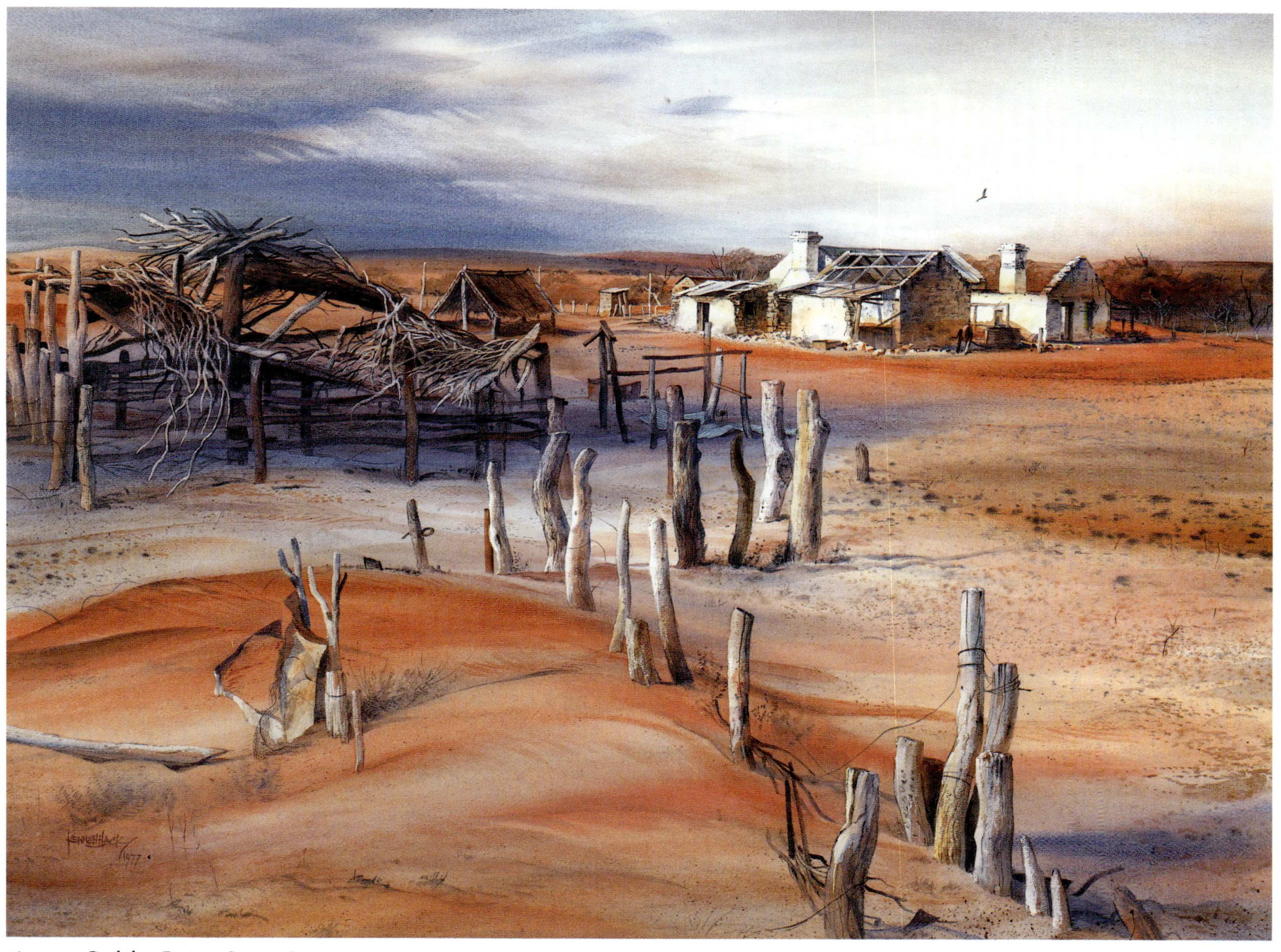

Plate 23 *Cadelga Ruins, Sturt's Stony Desert* 1977 (South Australia) watercolour, 76 × 102 cm

*These ruins stand in desert country near the corner
of South Australia where it borders on the south-
west corner of Queensland. Cadelga used to be an
outstation of the huge station Cordillo. To the
north-west of Cadelga lies the famous outback town
of Birdsville. The old ruins are paintable from any
angle and the white-washed walls contrast with the
apricot-coloured sand drifts.*

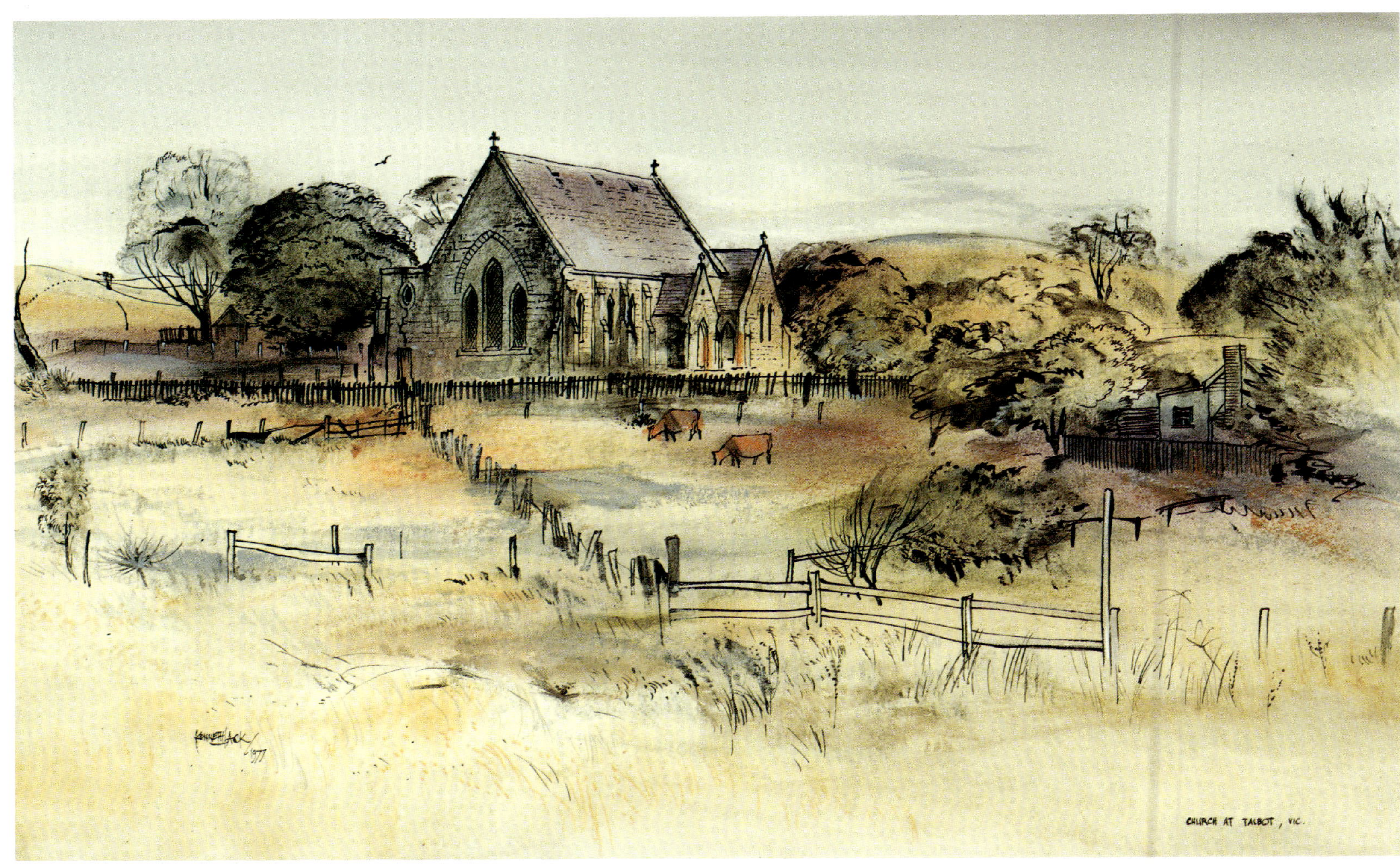

Plate 24 *Church at Talbot* 1977 (Victoria) pen and smudge, pastel and watercolour, 30 × 49 cm

At thirteen he won first prize at the Melbourne Royal Show, for a pastel drawing of a horse. (His sister was awarded second prize in the same competition.) He also won a bicycle in a competition in which he had to sort out the jumbled phrase 'Panther cycles are the best.' He sent in an entry in pictorial form, showing a panther lying on the top of block letters drawn in perspective. The bicycle was very useful because it allowed him to go to places like Keilor, Bulla, Ferntree Gully and Lysterfield — now all outer suburbs of Melbourne — with a pencil and a small sketch pad to do outdoor sketches: '. . . this was the way things started and I've never regretted this early acquaintance with Nature. On a bike with much walking up steep hills, and ploughing into head-winds one is in fairly close contact with the whole of natural things. A few years later I was occasionally allowed to cycle further to stay overnight in a hotel.'[10]

He sold his first watercolours while still at school. His father regularly supplied attractively lettered mottoes to a lady who ran a framing business; he told her that his son made watercolours and was asked to bring some in. From then on she took whatever he could do at five shillings, seven and sixpence and ten shillings for the larger ones (28 cm × 38 cm). It was in this way that he taught himself the technique of watercolour.

Although Jack first thought he would have to follow his father and become a commercial artist if he wanted to pursue his love of painting and drawing, he realised later that if he became an art teacher the longer holidays would give him much more free time to follow his real bent. Art as art was a distant idea at first. It was his natural ability and his father's profession that directed his choice of a career. It was fortunate for him that the art room at Melbourne High School had some original paintings by artists such as W. D. Knox but he had to find out his talent alone. He was not noticed by any practising artist or perceptive person who might have introduced him to the work of artists he did not discover for himself until much later. When as a young man he visited the National Gallery of Victoria he was attracted by works by Hans Heysen, Harold Herbert, and of course Streeton.

Jack was not so lucky as the sixteen-year-old John Perceval, who was given his first box of paints by Arnold Shore. He had to beat a path alone all his life, as his stubborn determination in his own direction shows. It is remarkable how many things which were technically useful to him he discovered on his own. A great interest in the drawings of Muirhead Bone and his own interest in drawing buildings attracted him to a small but brilliant publication produced by Hal Missingham in 1946. This was a diary interleaved with drawings of Sydney buildings by Missingham, Paul Beadle and Roy Jenkins and given away as an advertisement for Berger Paints. Missingham had done similar diaries in England before the war. When he was Director of the Art Gallery of New South Wales in 1945, he had little spare time and so enlisted the help of two artist friends to help him draw the illustrations. The shape, design and execution of the drawings are all very fine, particularly those by Paul Beadle, who drew in a thin pen line with perfect control. Beadle had been a student of Missingham's at the Central School in London and came to Australia during the war in the Royal Navy as a member of a submarine crew, despite his eighteen-stone weight. When these drawings were made in 1946 he was teaching at East Sydney Technical College.

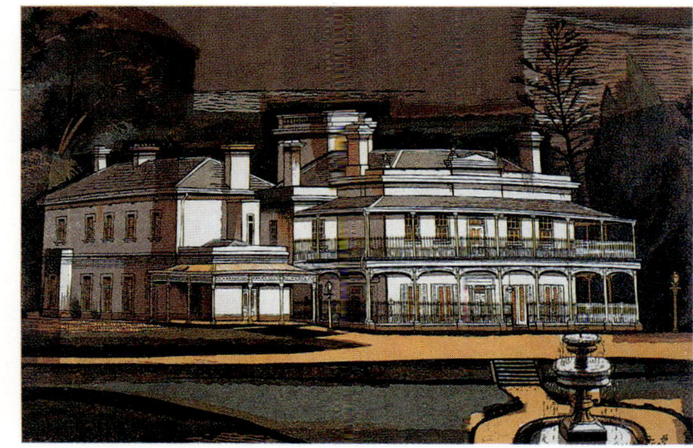

Fig. 11 *'Como', South Yarra*
1963, linocut, 29.5 × 46 cm

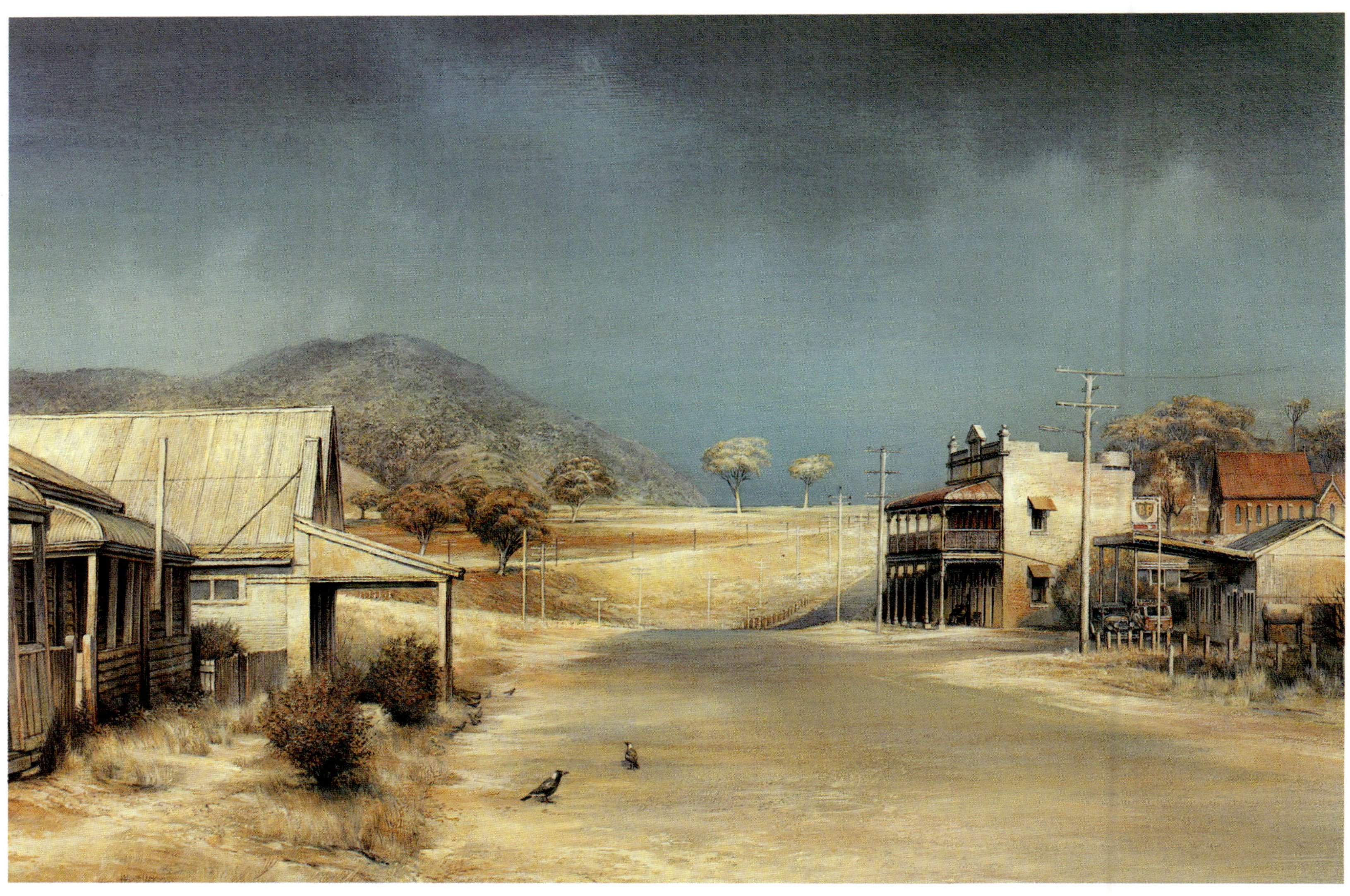

Plate 25 *Currabubula* 1977 (New South Wales) acrylic, 61 × 91 cm

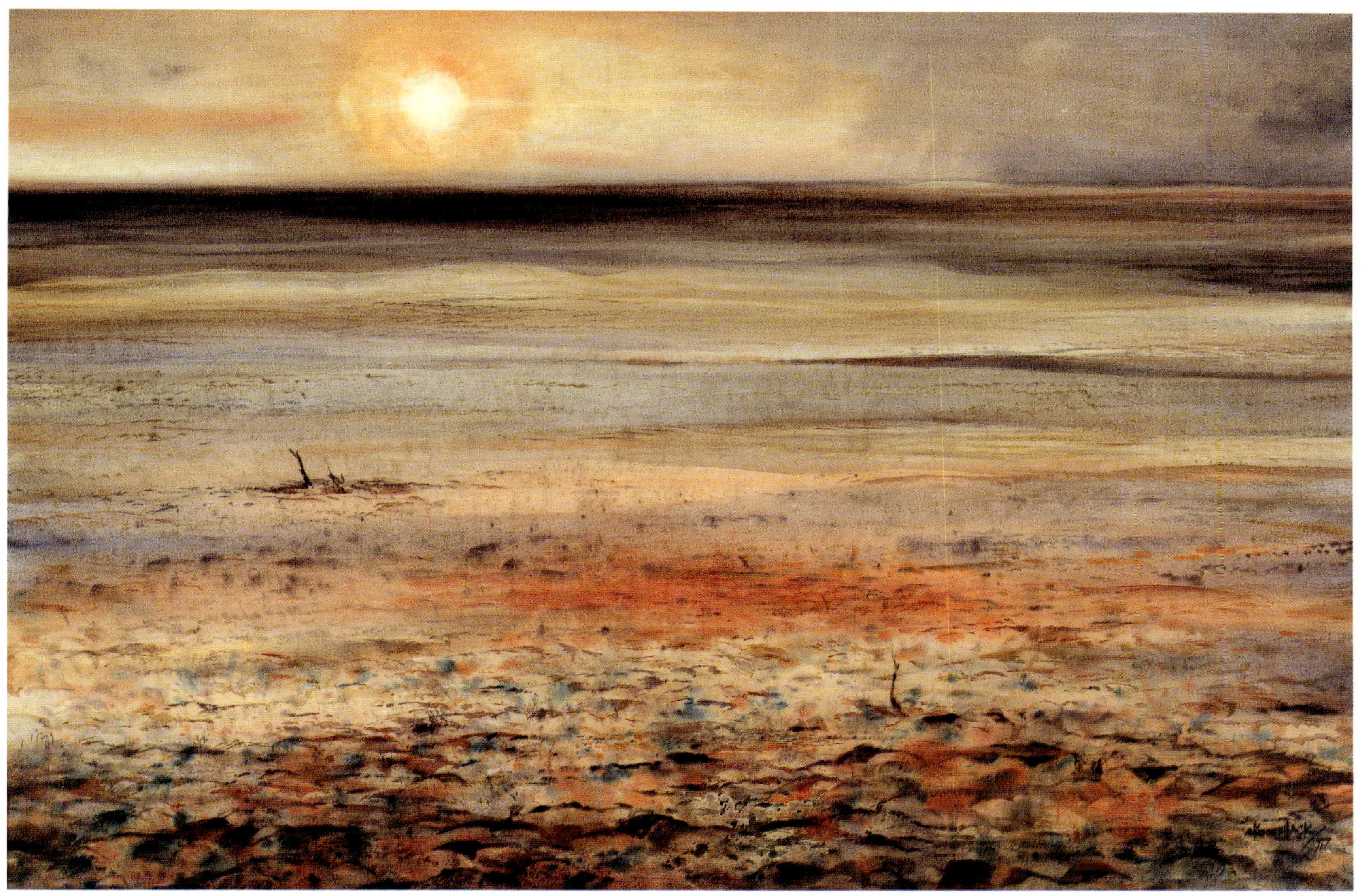

Plate 26 *Gibber Plain* 1977, watercolour, 69 × 102 cm

*The idea for this painting came from a trip across
Sturt's Stony Desert — one of the harshest and most
desolate places on earth. This Gibber plain lies north
of Innamincka, which is on Coopers Creek, in the
north-east of South Australia. Birdsville is on its
northern edge.*

*A gibber plain is characterised by a surface of
stones which stretches to the horizon. On a hot day
the heat is like an oven. The stones have broken
down to rounded shapes glistening in the sun, due to
extremes of heat and cold and have been there for
countless millions of years. Gibber plains are
occasionally cut across with red sand dunes. There
is very little vegetation in these harsh inland areas.*

*The composition of this watercolour is imaginary
— painted in the studio from memory. I chose to
place the sun in the painting for I find it difficult to
imagine a gibber plain without a blazing sun. I have
attempted to make a visual statement out of what
most people would consider to be a non-subject.*

This now forgotten publication revealed to the young Kenneth Jack the means by which architecture could be delicately rendered in pure line. He still has a drawing he made in 1949 of 164 Phillip Street, Sydney, inspired by one made by Paul Beadle. It reveals how readily Jack absorbed those elements which were useful to him.

Like so many Australian artists, Jack had a strong urge to go overseas after the war. He longed to see the great cathedrals and the masterpieces in the famous art galleries but when in 1947 he applied for a British Council Scholarship to study in London he was not successful. Shortly afterwards he and a friend actually booked to go overseas but Jack got married and his friend went alone. Three young children then kept the family in Australia until they grew up and left home. Kenneth and Betty Jack went overseas for the first time in 1973, when he was already a formed and established artist. Meanwhile, the means of his exploration of art remained the art book. He became interested in Van Gogh's reed pen drawings and he liked the freedom and exuberance of Dufy's drawings, partly no doubt in reaction to his own disciplined style.

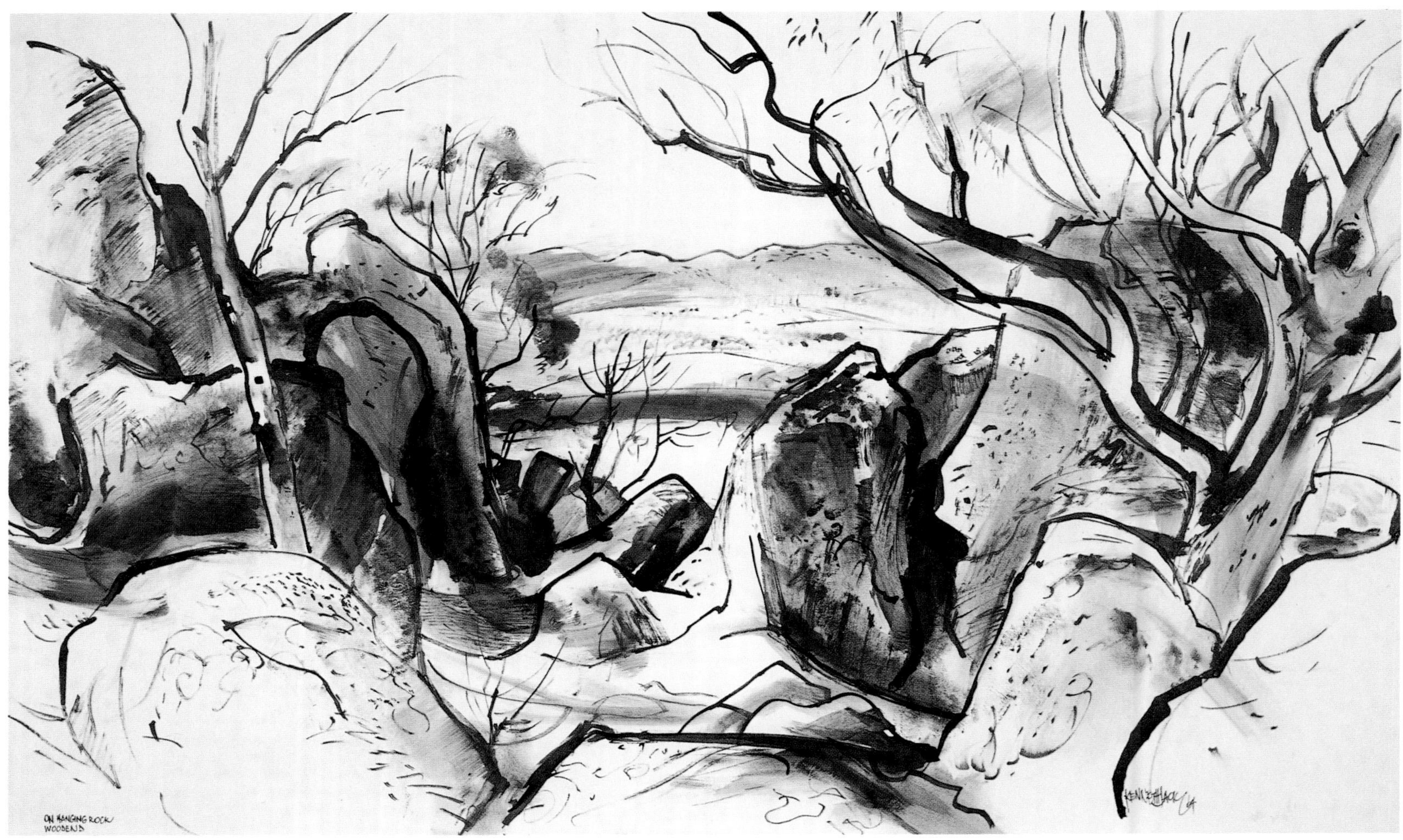

Fig. 12 *On Hanging Rock, Woodend* 1964, quill, ink and smudge, 34 × 57 cm

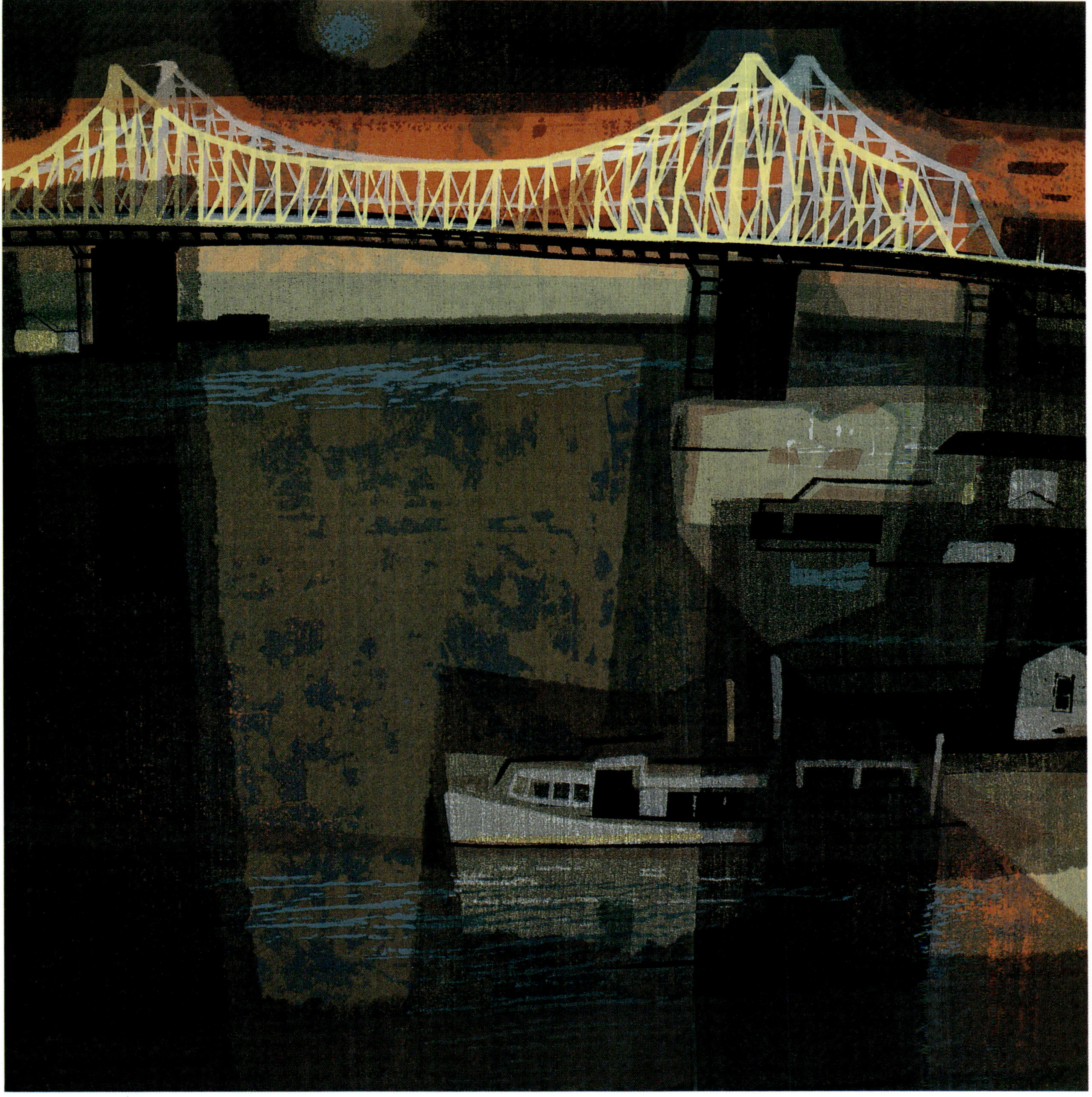

Fig. 13 *The Story Bridge, Brisbane* 1964, silkscreen, 38 × 38 cm

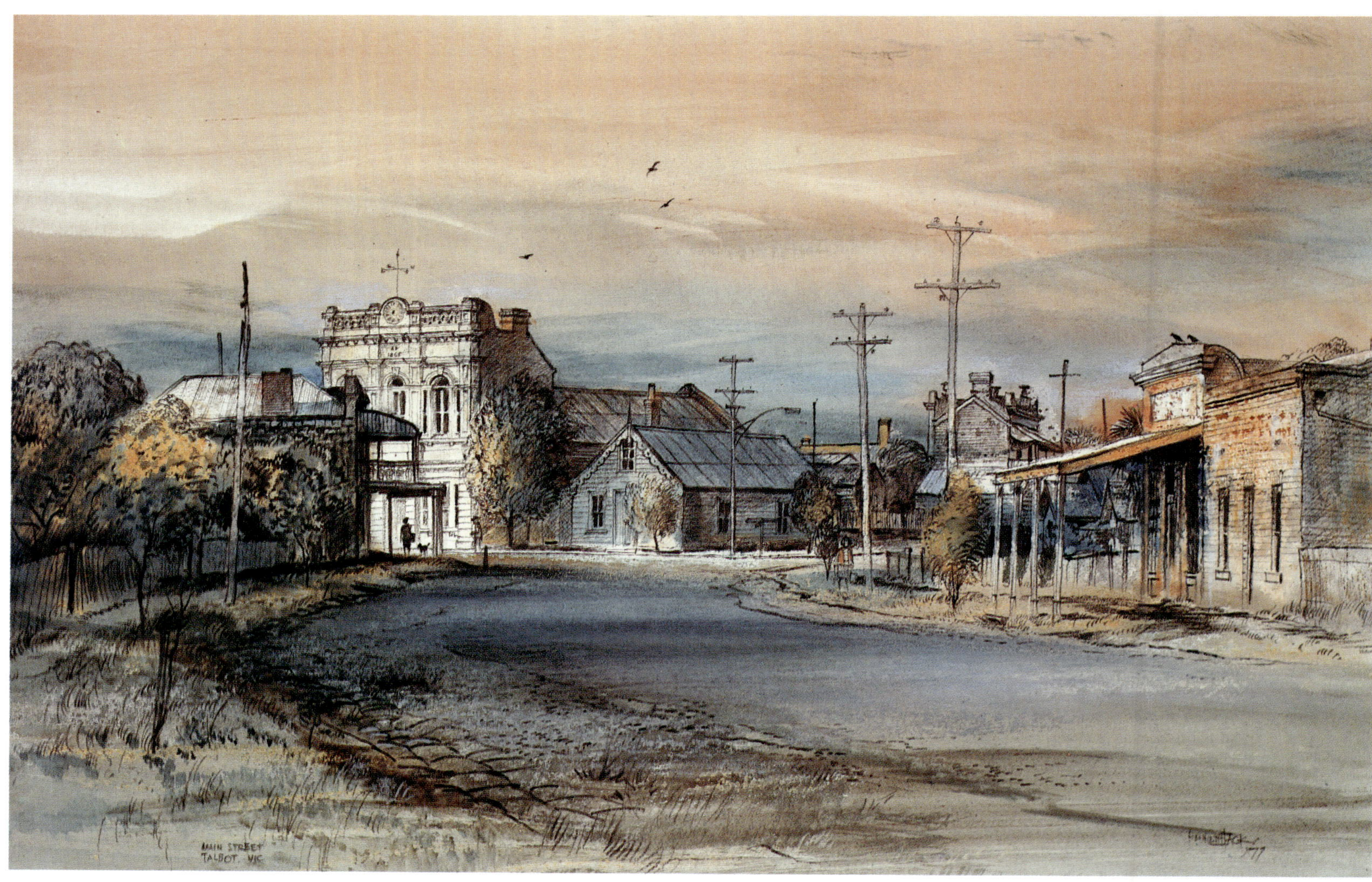

Plate 27 *Main Street, Talbot* 1977 (Victoria) pencil, oil pastel and watercolour, 30.5 × 49.5 cm

*This is a drawing of one of my favourite small towns
— an old Victorian goldmining town between
Clunes and Maryborough. Its main street makes
several turns and one is able to see buildings closing
off the composition in a more limited depth than is
the case with most long, straight, Australian main
streets.*

*The old town hall once had a quite lofty
hexagonally-shaped tower in the centre of its ornate
front facade; but it was pulled down in the 1950s.
Still visible at the centre of the top of the parapet is
a clock face which is only painted on. It has never
had any clock behind it! This has always seemed to
me to be a rather peculiar thing. However, it's one
of the eccentricities of the Victorian era and I like
drawing it. I have made many drawings, paintings
and prints of this subject from different angles over
the years.*

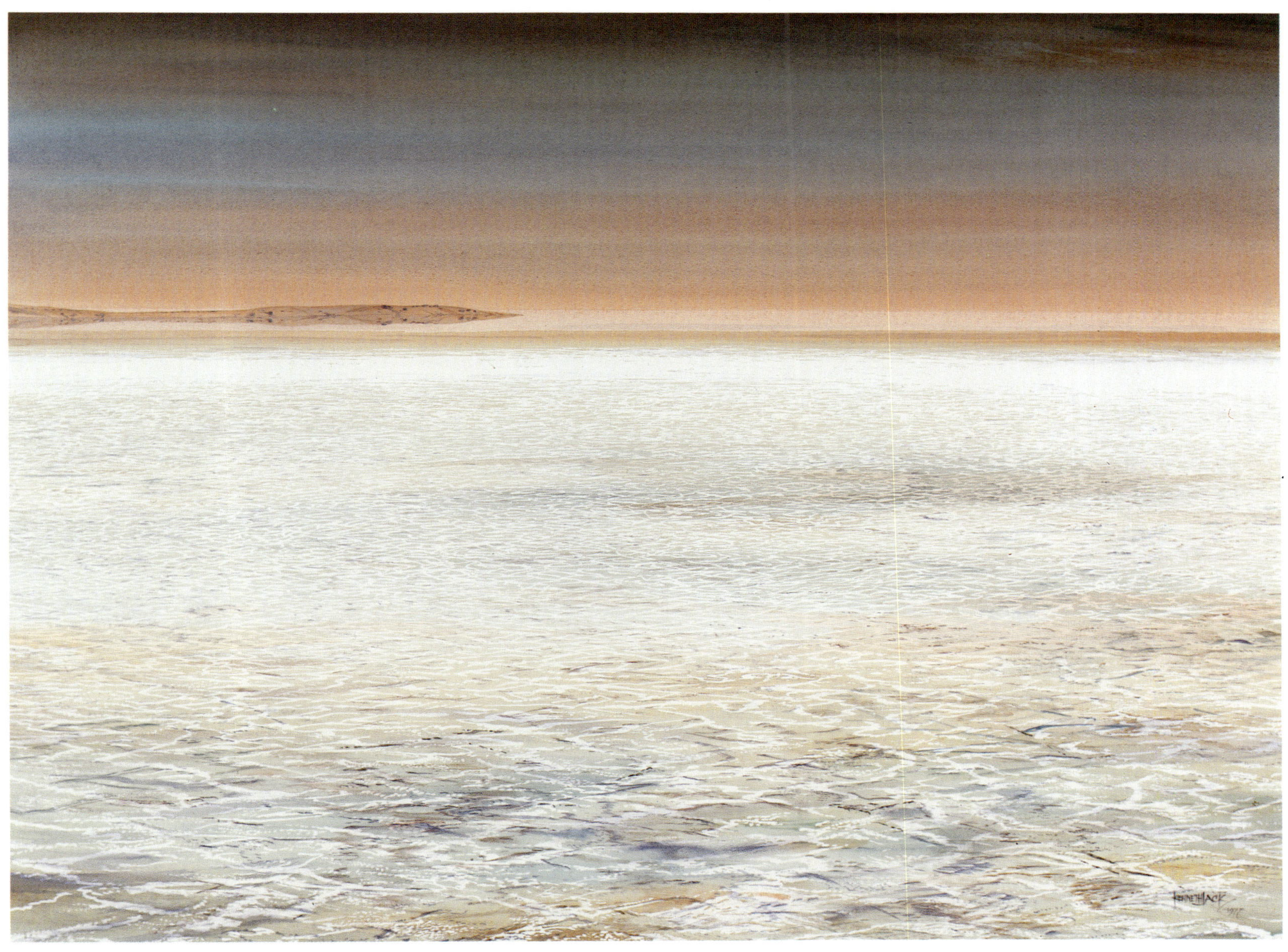

Plate 28 *Mirage, Lake Eyre* 1977 (South Australia) watercolour, 76 × 102 cm

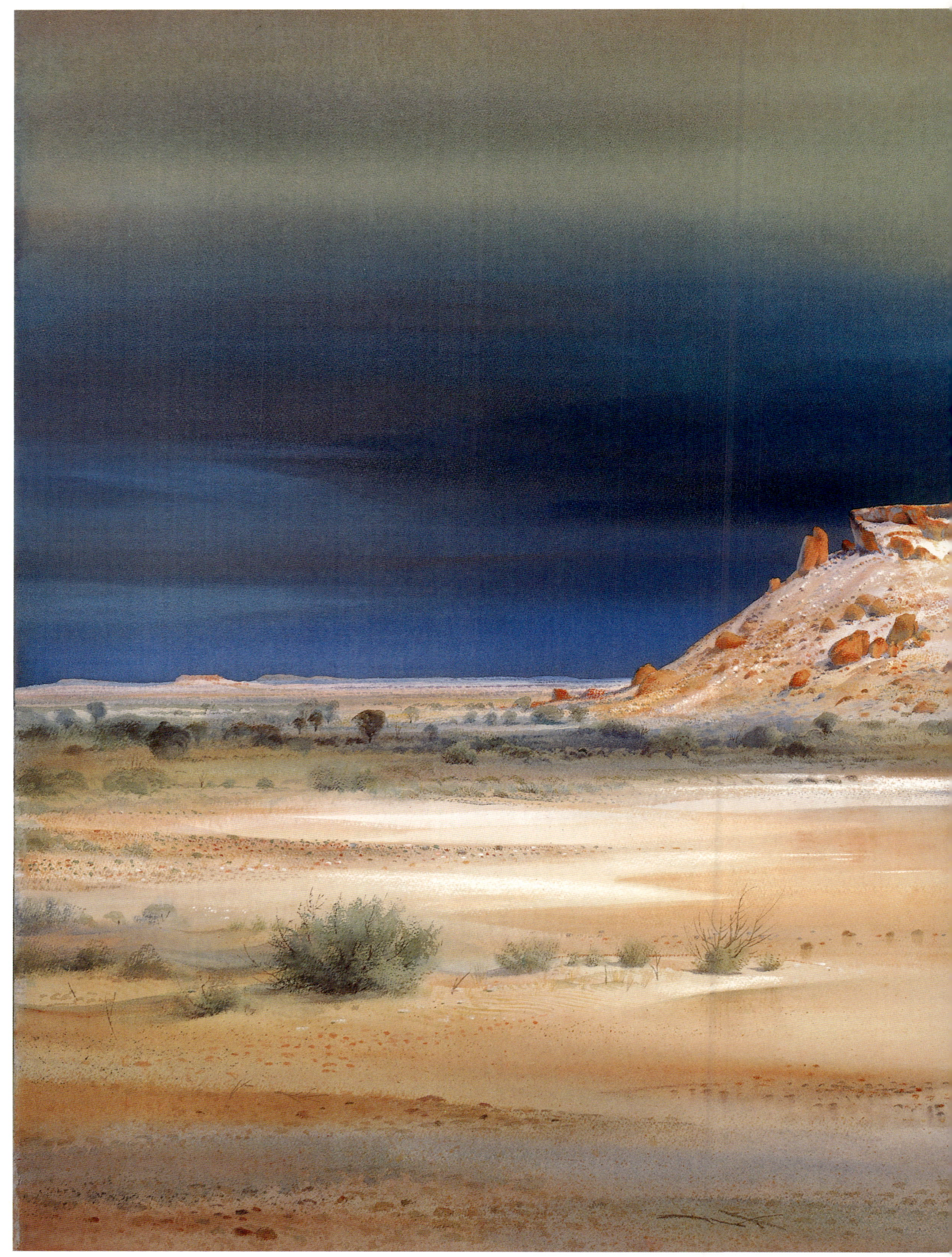

Plate 29 *Mesa and Rain Pool, Great Western Plateau* 1987 (Western Australia) watercolour, 101 × 152 cm

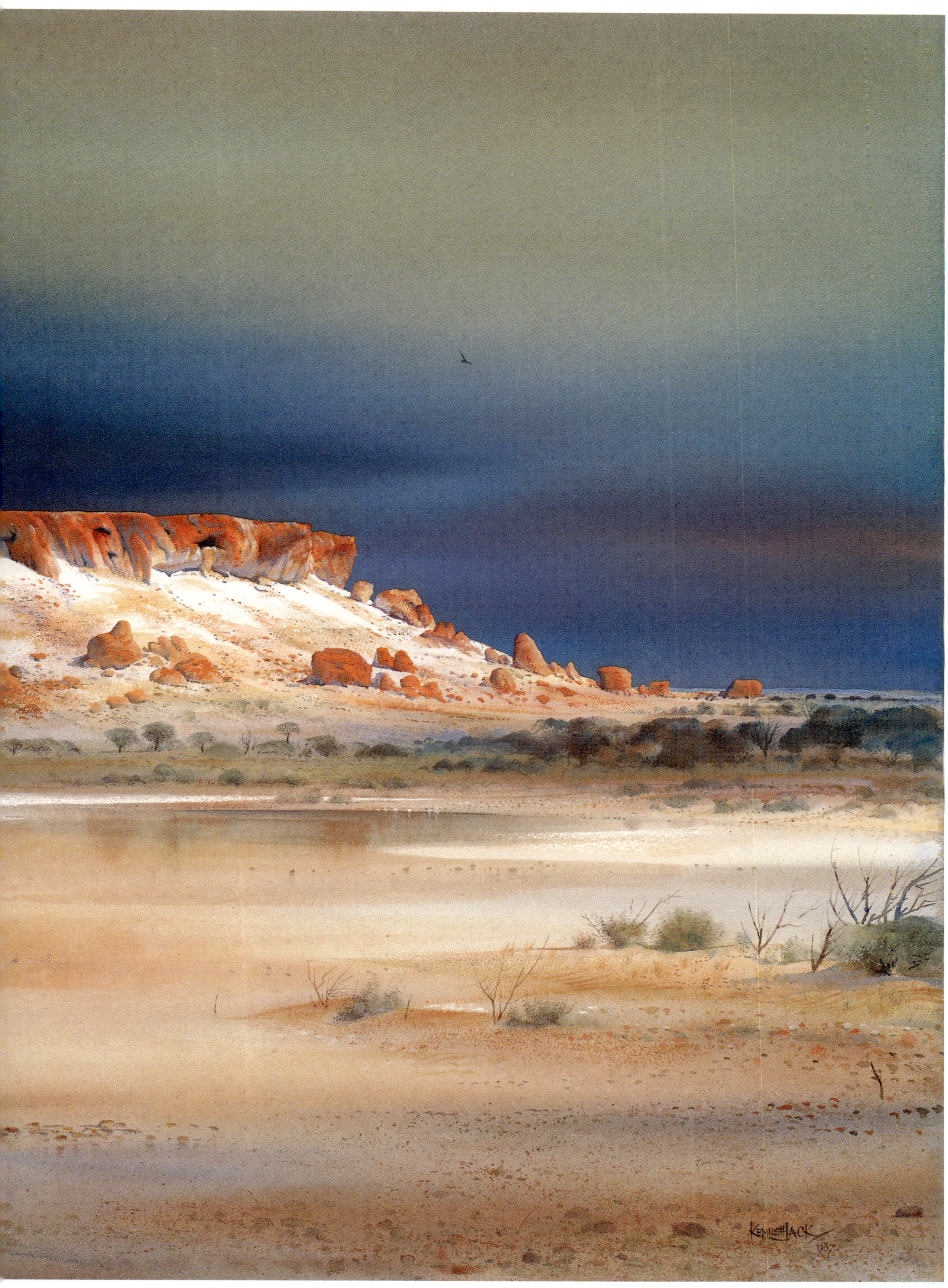

In 1956 he was appointed senior lecturer in painting and printmaking at the Caulfield Institute of Technology. He continued to experiment with printmaking and kept an open mind to all kinds of technical and stylistic developments because he felt that a teacher should be broad minded and impart a wide range of possibilities rather than a narrow polemical view. He also took classes in art history and tried to interest his students in some of the great painters of the past like Rembrandt. But much of the work was repetitive and he longed to get on with his own. After a day's teaching he would often feel drained when he finally got to the studio to begin to paint or to work on an etching or linocut. Yet he kept going, year after year, with the set minimum teaching load of twenty-six hours per week of a full-time teaching appointment. He bought a house in which to live close to the college so that he was home at his easel by a quarter past four in the afternoon, but he was obliged to sacrifice almost all social life.

When the Art Gallery of New South Wales sent him another biographical questionnaire in 1957 after they had acquired another watercolour, Jack stated some of his views:

> Broad minded, shunning the insincere and spectacular . . . Interested in the modern movement as well as the great painters of the past . . . My own art has many influences, but am striving to interpret principally the Australian scene as I see it — am always interested more in the subject seen than imagined, preferring to use my imagination upon the designing of the subject into the picture plane. Prefer to work in a fairly tight manner at the moment but with a broad sweep to the design, countering the interest I have in details.[11]

He remained passionate about printmaking and exhibited his works in both one-man and group shows. In 1956 and 1958 he sent works to the Giles Bequest Exhibitions of Contemporary Woodcuts and Linocuts at the Victoria and Albert Museum in London, both of which were acquired for their collection. The Cincinnati Art Museum also purchased one of his lithographs from its 1958 Colour Lithography Biennial. Between 1955 and 1965 he was awarded many prizes and his prints and paintings began to sell steadily but at the same time he began to feel dissatisfied with his work and the direction in which it seemed to be going.

Two main factors influenced the direction of Kenneth Jack's art. The first was that his ability as a draughtsman was recognised and appreciated mainly by older artists who had grown up with the traditional respect for skill in drawing, while the younger generation, influenced by an anarchic reaction to traditional values and the fashionable trend for abstract expressionism, was beginning to neglect drawing altogether. In fact the teaching of drawing suffered great neglect in most Australian art schools for the next two decades. It was maintained in a few places through the eminence and persistence of people like Dorothy Dundas, who taught it at East Sydney Technical College, and the enthusiastic support of Alan McCulloch, in Melbourne, who has devoted his life to this vital element of art, and of course through Kenneth Jack, who stressed its importance to his students.

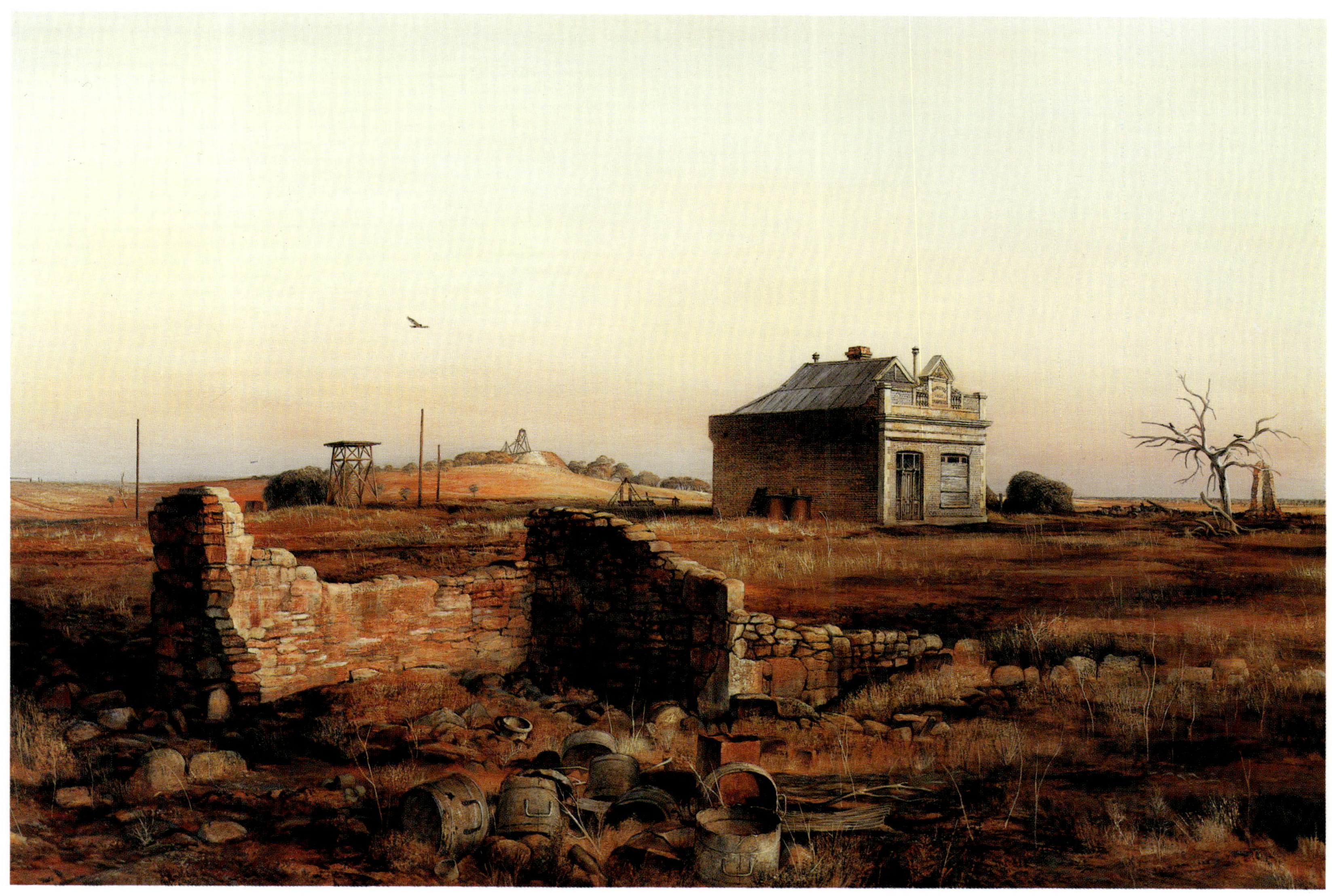

Plate 30 *Mt. Morgans* 1977 (Western Australia) acrylic, 81 × 122 cm

This is about all that is left of a once thriving gold mining centre inland of Western Australia. Mt Morgans is a few kilometres south of the road running between Leonora and Laverton. The building is the only one left and used to be the council chambers. No one lives in the place nowadays.

There are some mine ruins on the hill and broken mine poppet heads, otherwise all one can find are the remains here and there of a broken wall and household utensils lying about. A dead tree and a wedge-tailed eagle give this desolate and remote place an atmosphere which I could not resist. The absolute feeling of loneliness and of being far from anywhere is quite overwhelming — the lone building seems to intensify this isolation.

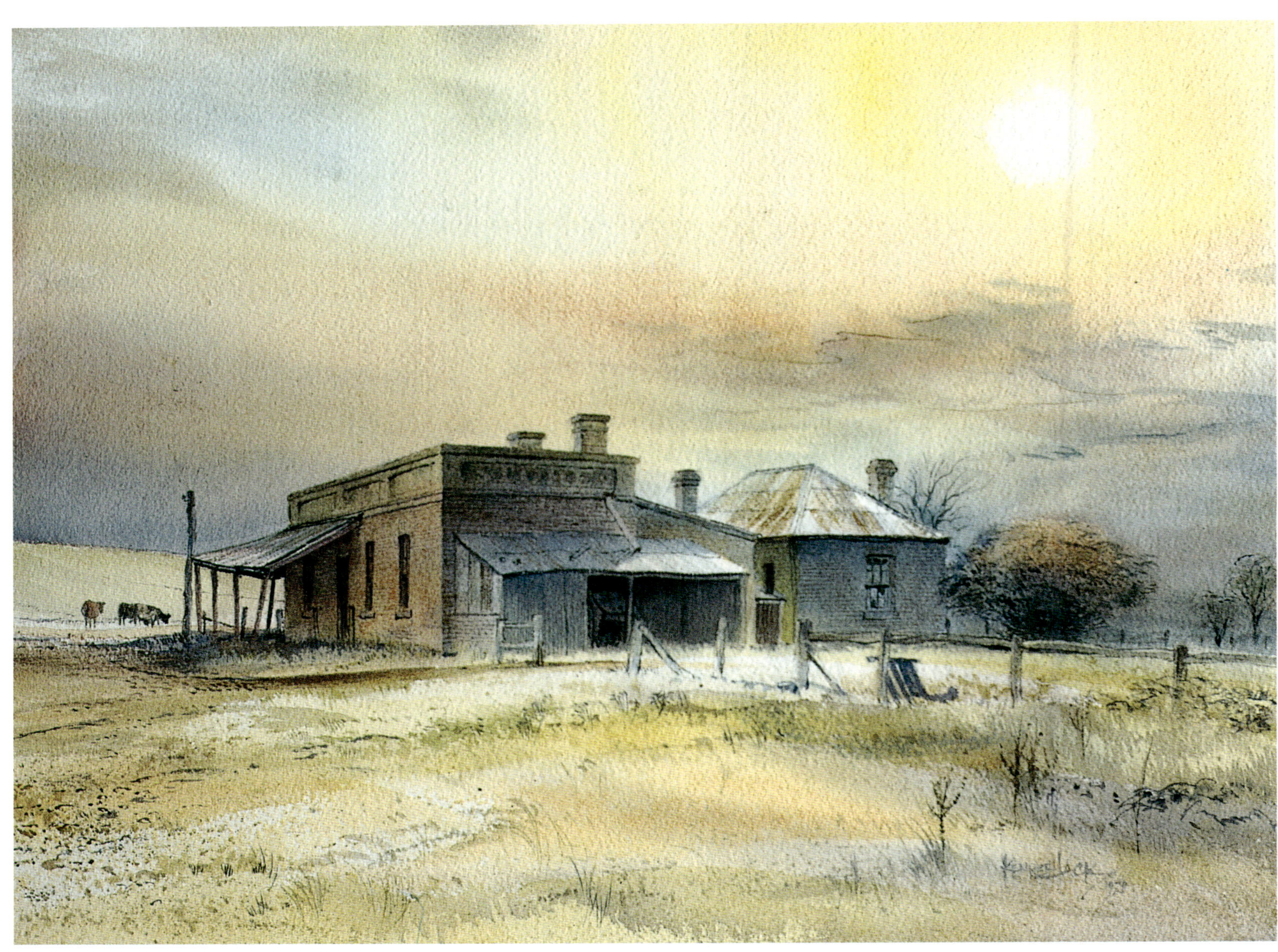

Plate 31 *Abandoned Store, Franklinford* 1978 (Victoria) watercolour, 28 × 38 cm

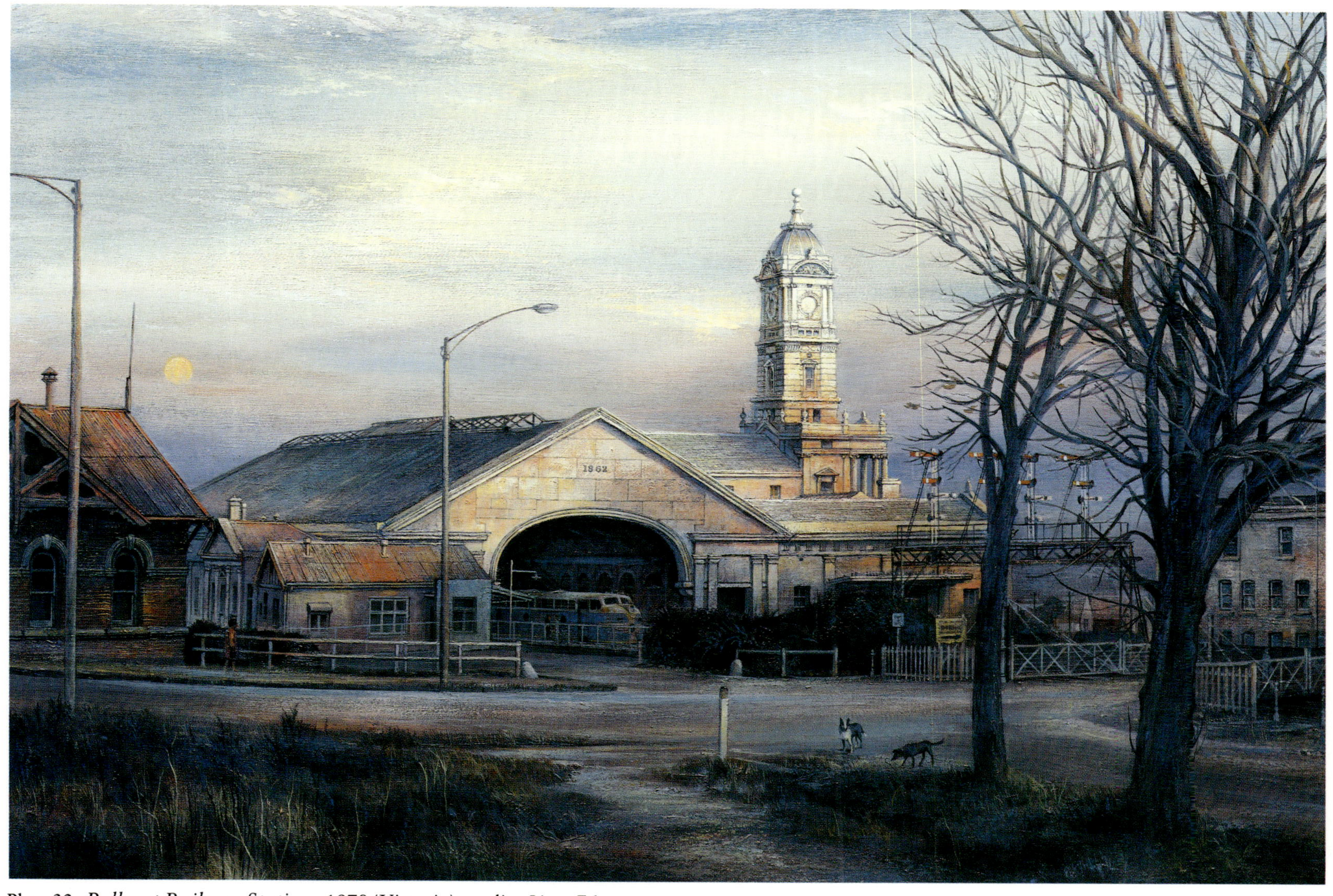

Plate 32 *Ballarat Railway Station* 1978 (Victoria) acrylic, 51 × 76 cm

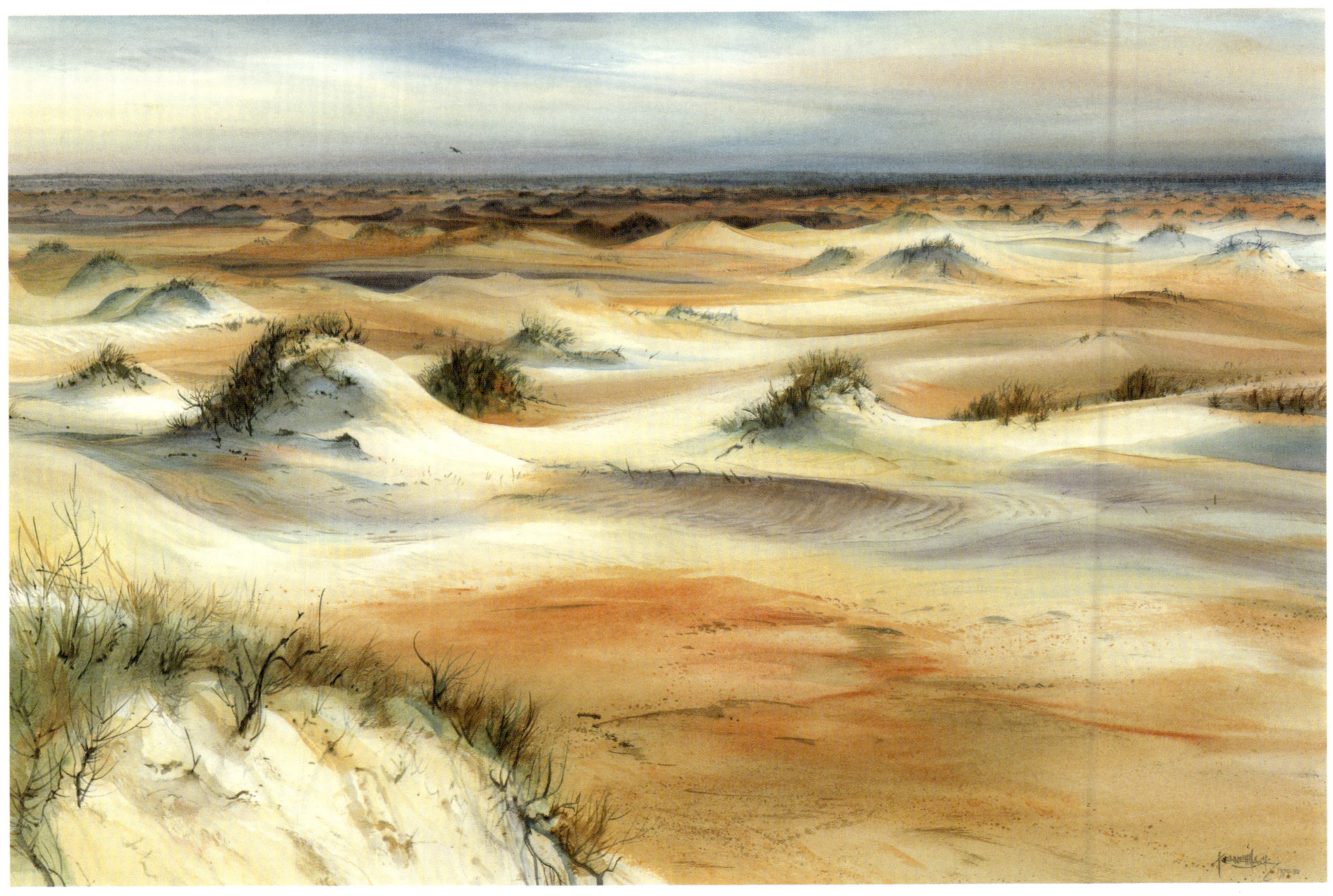

Plate 33 *Cobbler Desert — Strzlecki Track* 1979–80 (South Australia) watercolour, 68 × 101 cm

*This particularly grim and desolate desert is south-
west of Innamincka and north of the Flinders Ranges
near where natural gas has been found. It has a
strange and eerie beauty unlike any other area
I know. It is a place where one hopes one's vehicle
will not break down. The desert consists of
kilometre after kilometre of sand hillocks, each one
being topped by a saltbush. The sand between the
bushes has been blown away over many years. If one
has an eye for it, it can be a most beautiful place.*

The other factor, and probably the decisive one, was that unlike most artists of his generation Jack was unable to go overseas during his formative years. His experience and artistic loyalty remained totally Australian and this reinforced his bond with the artists who had painted the Australian landscape in the past and eventually made him less interested in the international fashions which were sweeping the art schools. It also made him intolerant of painting which was not based on sound, solid training.

This restriction had the benefit of intensifying an important element in the make-up of a landscape painter. Anyone who drives through the Victorian landscape in the direction of Castlemaine, calling at the various small country towns on the way, will be surprised at how everything looks like the paintings of Kenneth Jack. The general colour of the trees seen in the changing light, whether clear or overcast, the pinkish colour of the earth at the side of the road, the blue haze of the distant mountains, the character of the buildings — everything is just Kenneth Jack.

The perception of regional characteristics and the subtle variations in the dominant tone of a region — as obvious as a local dialect to those who can perceive them — results from the bonding of the artist with the world he paints. Artists who are active in particular places invariably introduce the specific qualities of their world into their paintings. Piero della Francesca, Vermeer, Constable, Cézanne and Morandi, besides achieving a profound synthesis of vision, have all accurately captured the character and light of the places with which they are especially associated.

Australia, being so vast, has many regions characterised by subtle as well as obvious differences.

The works of just three Australian landscape painters, Arthur Streeton, Hans Heysen and Lloyd Rees, show how accurately each has captured the subtleties of light and atmosphere of the region where he painted. Though born in Brisbane, Lloyd Rees has lived most of his long life in Sydney and it is the light and colour of Sydney that one sees when one looks at his paintings. Out of any window in Sydney one sees a Lloyd Rees. This partly explains why certain artists are neglected in some States. It is not merely regional jealousy but simply that Victorians, for example, can recognise their world in Streeton and do not find it in Lloyd Rees. Streeton is popular in Sydney, but what collectors there respond to most is Streeton's paintings of the harbour. Heysen is loved everywhere, no doubt because he paints a cosy and comforting world and gum trees. But his work looks best and is most alive to those who know South Australia very well. As Lloyd Rees's work became more profound and his vision moved onto a unique spiritual plane he was able to conquer not only Victoria but all other States as well. Yet on the opening day of his exhibition in Melbourne in 1925 the artist and Harold Herbert, who came to review it, were there, and not another person. If one disregards the financial aspect which has become such an important factor in the art world, one can see that Australians in various parts of the continent collect and acquire what makes them feel comfortable. They feel most comfortable with what is familiar, and this includes the atmosphere and colour in the landscapes they buy. The inherited differences between the States since before Federation have also played a part in the appreciation or neglect of our great

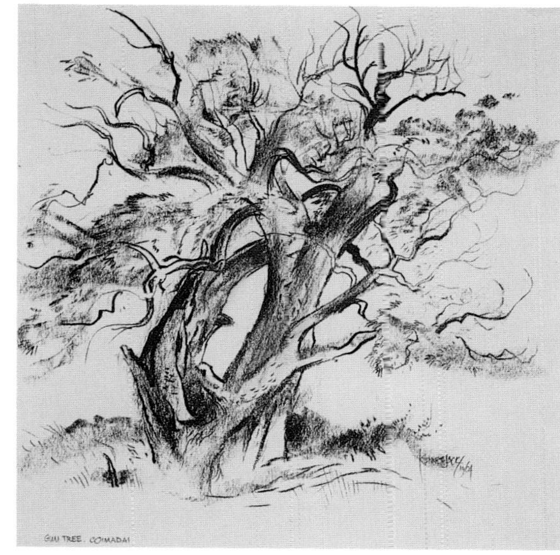

Fig. 14 *Gum Tree, Coimadai*
1964 (Victoria) Conté crayon, 33 × 34 cm

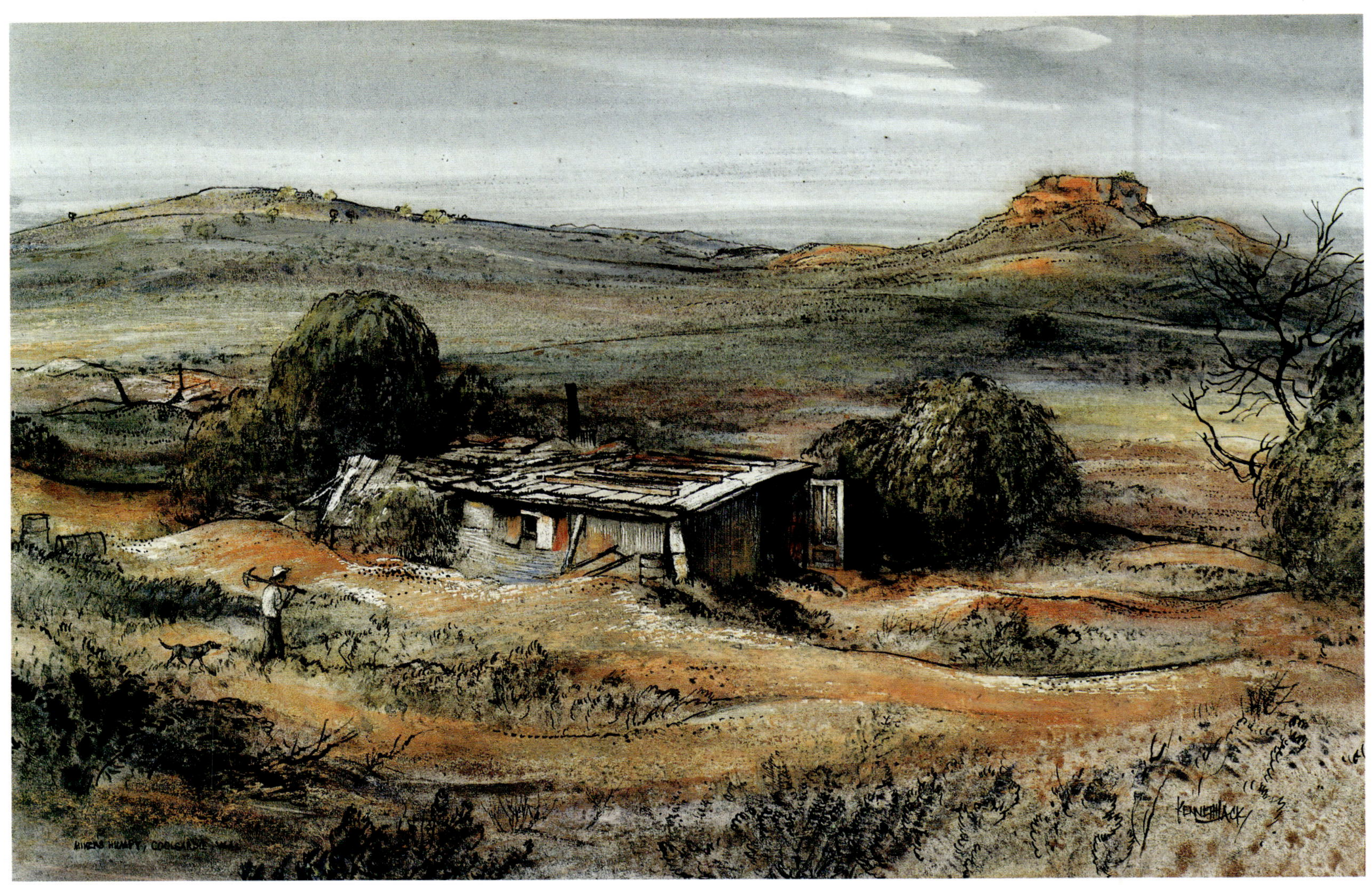

Plate 34 *Miner's Humpy, Coolgardie* 1979 (Western Australia) pencil, oil pastel and watercolour, 21 × 33 cm

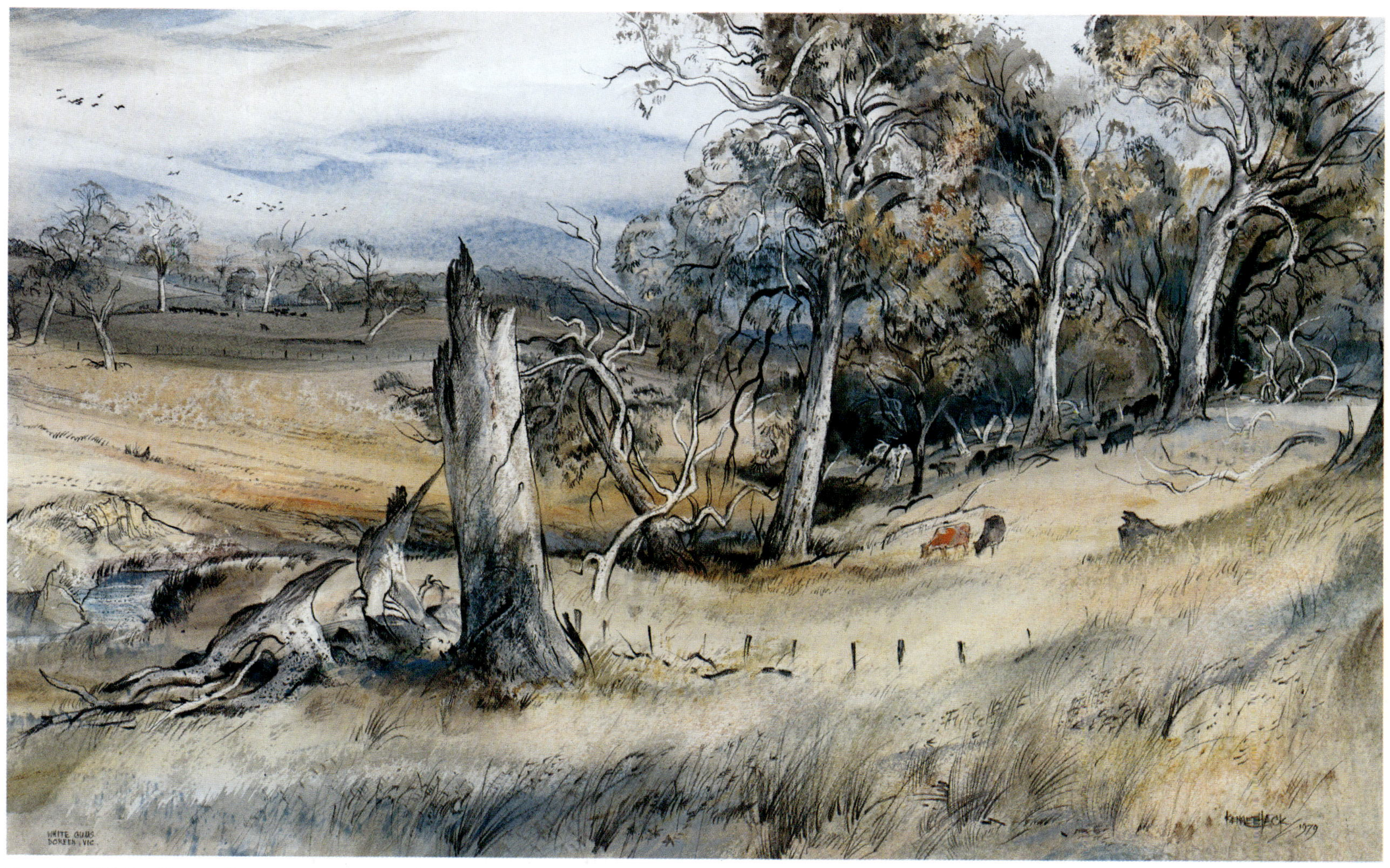

Plate 35   *White Gums, Doreen*   1979 (Victoria) pencil, oil pastel and watercolour, 30.5 × 50 cm

*The landscape depicted here is on my neighbour's
property 'Hazel Glen' — still owned by the same
family which settled there in 1843. The interesting
variety of gum tree shapes, and the stump of the
dead one form a key element in the overall design.
The drawing was made outdoors and I am
looking towards my own block of land (in the
far background) before I built our home on it.*

painters in particular States and are reflected in their representation in the various public collections, but much is due to unconscious reactions to certain basic elements in the art itself.

Formed artists who leave their native regions often retain their original 'bonding' for the rest of their lives, like Sidney Nolan and Arthur Boyd, who have been painting Australia but living in England. Landscape is an art which develops from persistence. Claude would not have been Claude if he had not lived in Rome most of his life.

Kenneth Jack was lucky that his parents took him on frequent trips into the Victorian countryside which he got to know so well. They went by train and later by car as far as Warrnambool, Sale and Echuca. The trips were important to the city-born boy, and they remained ingrained in his memory as happy experiences. Besides the trips with his parents and his own explorations by bicycle he also made good use of his father's staff travel pass on the railways before his sixteenth birthday (after which he was no longer permitted to use it) to see as much of the Victorian countryside as he could. When his father bought a car, he established the habit of frequently getting away from the city, a tradition Kenneth Jack continued with his own family.

While stationed at Victoria Barracks, Jack made occasional trips by bus, such as one to Yea, some seventy miles from Melbourne. As he wanted to find subjects to draw and could not get about easily, he called on the local policeman and asked him for the loan of his bicycle. The policeman did lend him his bicycle but Jack recalls that he seemed rather uncertain whether he would ever see it again. A drawing of the main street of Yea, made in pen and ink on some cheap butcher's paper, with no blocking in in pencil, shows the young artist's sureness of touch. After the war Jack included the drawing in his thesis 'On the Drawing of Architecture', where it is preserved still.

During the 1950s Kenneth Jack painted and made prints in which he adopted a formalised decorative design somewhat in the manner of Feininger, whose work he knew from books on contemporary art. It was a mixture of well-drawn subject matter imposed on to a non-realistic flat colour scheme which was the acceptable contemporary trend. It created a dramatic effect but it flattened space, and light had to be sacrificed to decorative effects. The prints were very accomplished and beautifully cut in wood or lino. As always, he was meticulous about the technical side of his art.

During the early 1960s it became possible for the Jacks to acquire a more reliable car, which made it possible for them to venture further inland as far as Mildura and Broken Hill, though one still had to drive on gravel roads and across sand dunes to get there. This new experience of the immense inland of the continent made him question the way he had been treating space in his paintings and prints. He came to feel that he did not have to conform to what he felt was limiting the scope of his work and began to paint in the way he felt was natural to him and was best to express his experience. The landscape, he felt, demanded it, and if it felt right then it was right. This was not, however, what the students or his colleagues at the college were interested in. One of them told him that painting was quite dead and would be replaced by something halfway between painting and sculpture. Jack could see no way of painting being dead, but

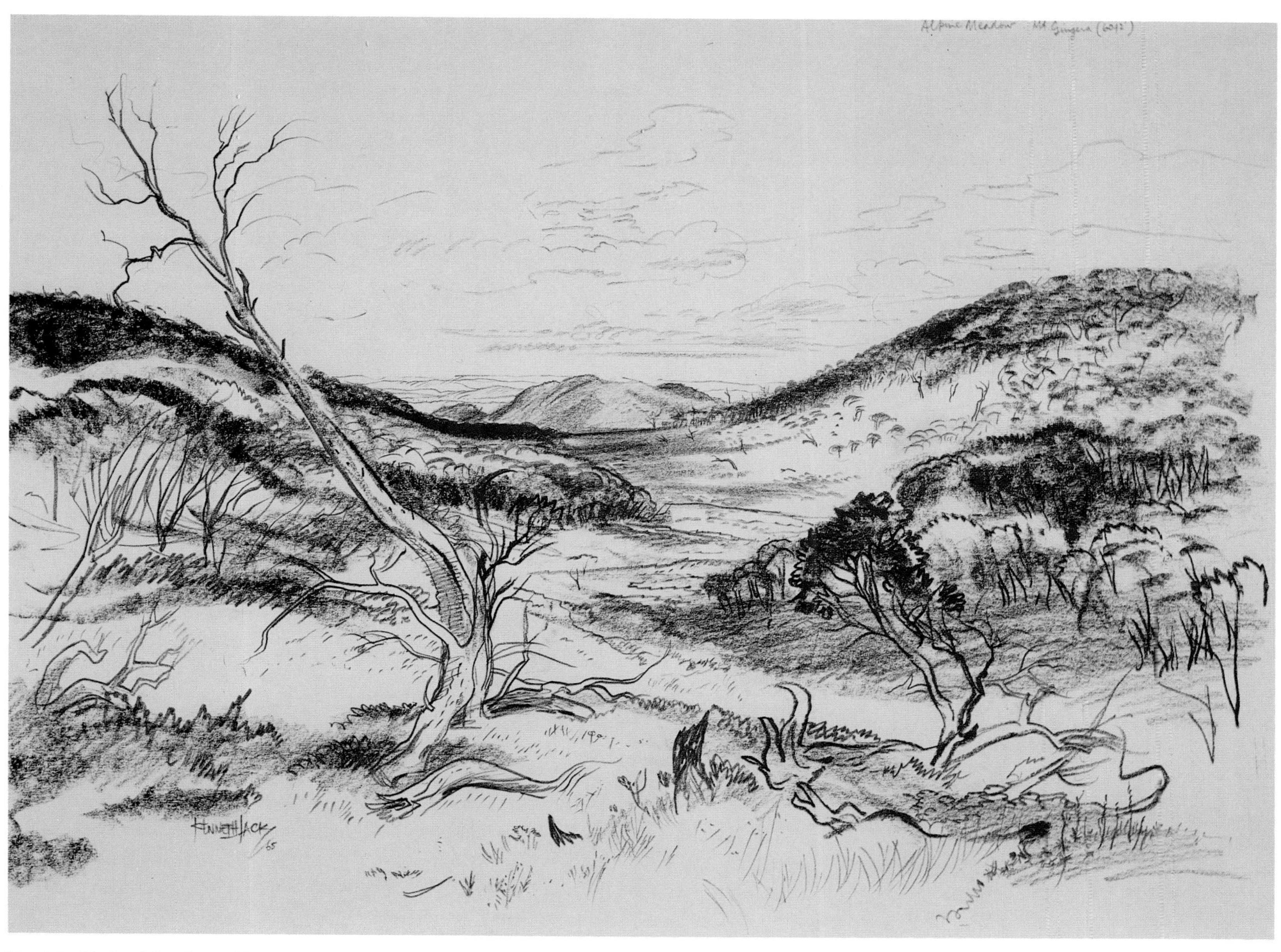

Fig. 15 *Alpine Meadow, Mt. Gingera* 1965 (Australian Capital Territory) carbon pencil, 35 × 50 cm

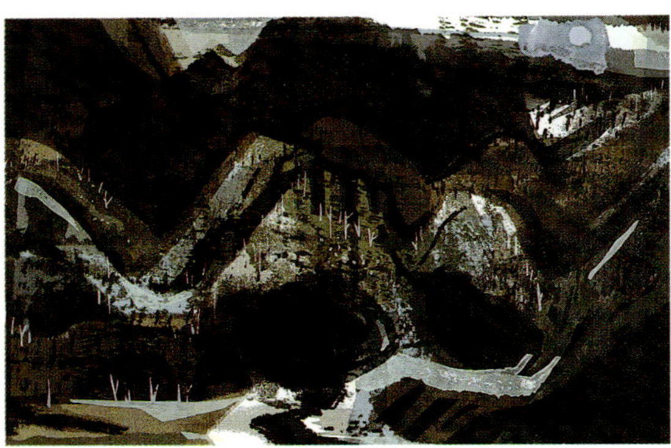

Fig. 16 *Cave Country*
1965, silkscreen, 24 × 38 cm

the comment made him feel all the more isolated from the general trend of Australian art.

There was no question that there was a public for Jack's kind of painting, but critics began to be very uninterested in anything which was representational. He had won some forty or so prizes but he decided he would not enter any more competitions. The one exception was the Art Gallery of New South Wales's Wynne Prize for landscape painting. He had first sent a work there when he was twenty and has continued to do so ever since. Only once did he miss, when the carriers delivered the painting to Tasmania by mistake and it got to Sydney too late.

When he reached his early forties he began to feel that teaching was not proving as rewarding as he had hoped. More and more he longed to be out painting and he began to consider giving up teaching to paint full time. His father, who had lived through the Depression, advised him against it, but John Brackenreg, who was his Sydney dealer as well as a friend, told him that if he didn't do it before fifty, he would never do it. That is what he did. To be doubly sure, he carefully saved a year's salary and one month before his forty-fourth birthday he became his own boss. The year before, 1967, he had taken his six months' long-service leave to try out life as a full-time artist. He did not regret the years spent teaching nor the period spent making semi-abstract prints, he felt it had been important training:

> . . . working semi-abstractly and at times decoratively, I was able to dispense with perspective and the more realistic treatments, concentrating on design, line, texture, tone and to think abstractly about them. This long training enabled me to slowly improve the realistic pictures that I kept going back to draw and sometimes to paint.[12]

Kenneth Jack's art is based primarily on strong draughtsmanship. He recalls that he was taught to draw but not to paint. Perhaps it was the insistence on drawing when he first went to art classes which predisposed him against the loose painterly style of abstract expressionism. It was also his nature to prefer the controlled logic of drawing to the wild search for form through gesture.

A different painter might have been quite happy to stay in the studio, absorbed in painterly intricacies and exploring abstract colour but Jack preferred drawing and this created a need for specific subject matter. This need inspired his travels and stimulated him to go to out-of-the-way places. The search introduced him to a sense of adventure well beyond that of going camping or on a weekend picnic.

During his long-service leave in 1967, just before he officially resigned from teaching, he went on a five-week bus tour across Australia to try to see some of the most inaccessible country. In the company of twenty-one passengers he travelled some six thousand miles, much of it through most difficult country. The bus went through flood-bound Central Queensland to Darwin, across the north-western coast to Port Hedland and Wittenoom and back to Hall's Creek. From there they made their way to Alice Springs via the Tanami Desert, experiencing holdups such as that caused by a broken spring. A replacement had to be air freighted from Adelaide to Alice Springs and then by air taxi to Mongrel Downs station before they could go on.[13]

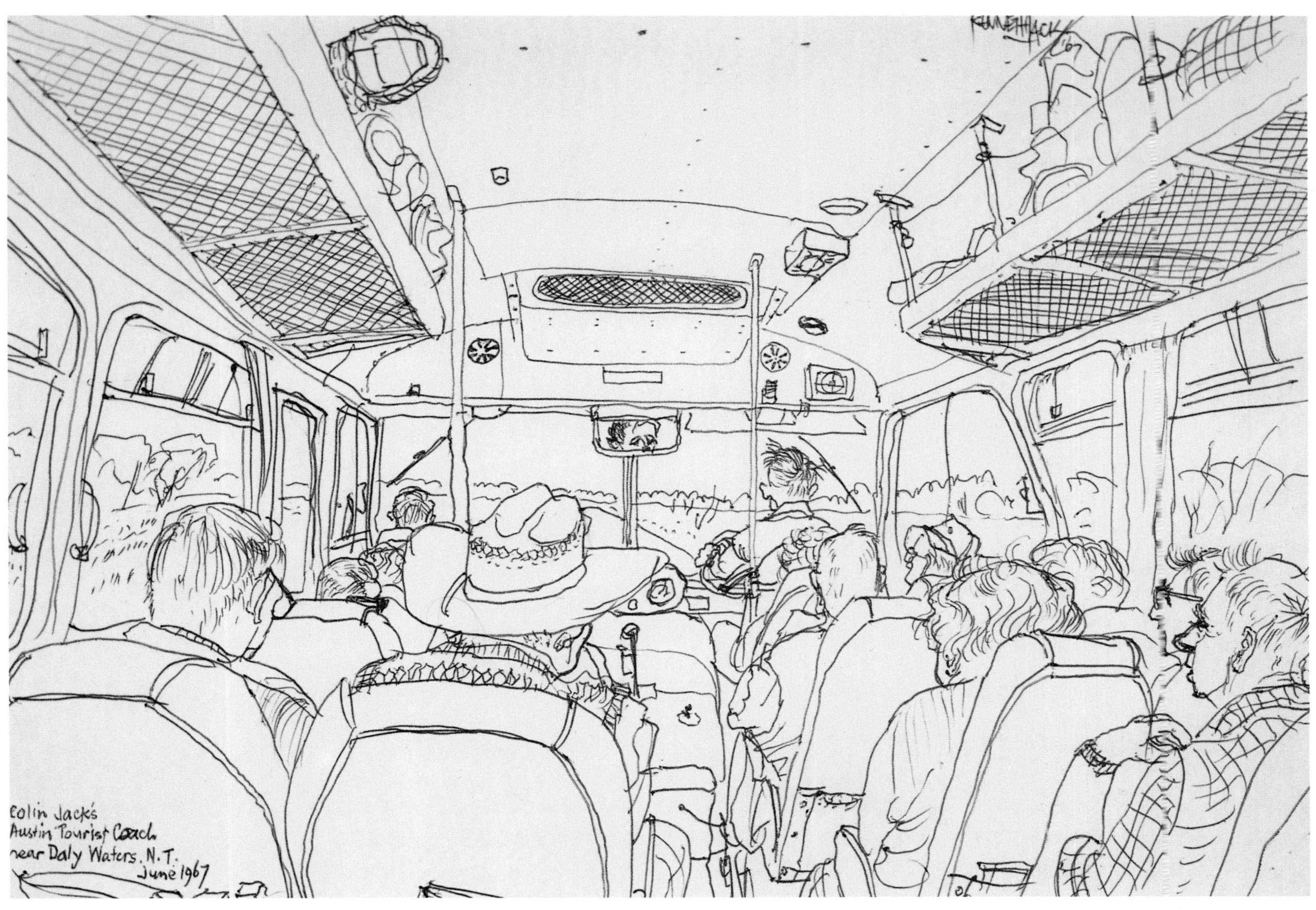

Fig. 17 *Colin Jack's Bus Interior* 1967 (Northern Territory) pen line, 18.4 × 27.5 cm

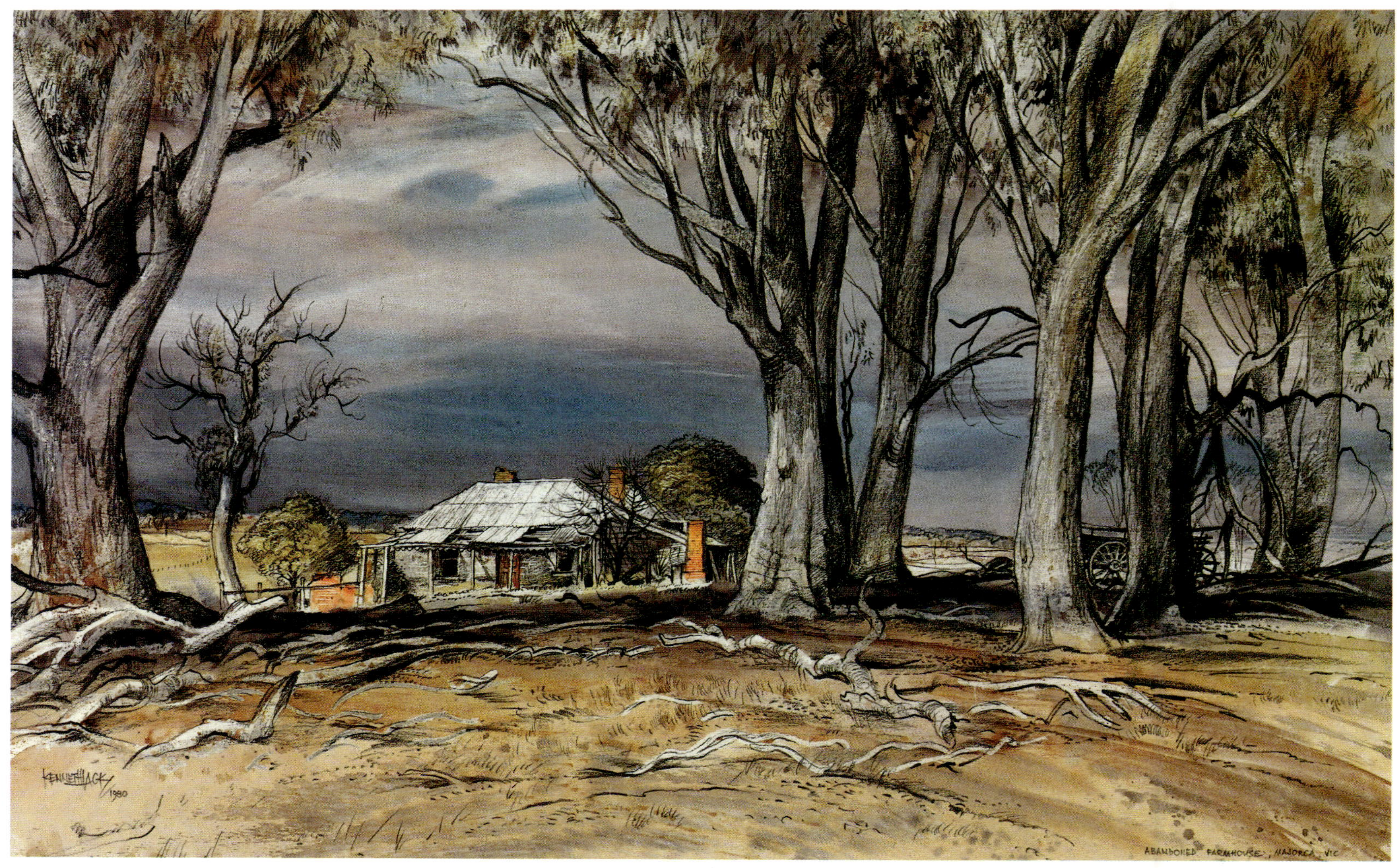

Plate 36 *Abandoned Farmhouse, Majorca* 1980 (Victoria) pencil, oil pastel and watercolour, 30 × 50 cm

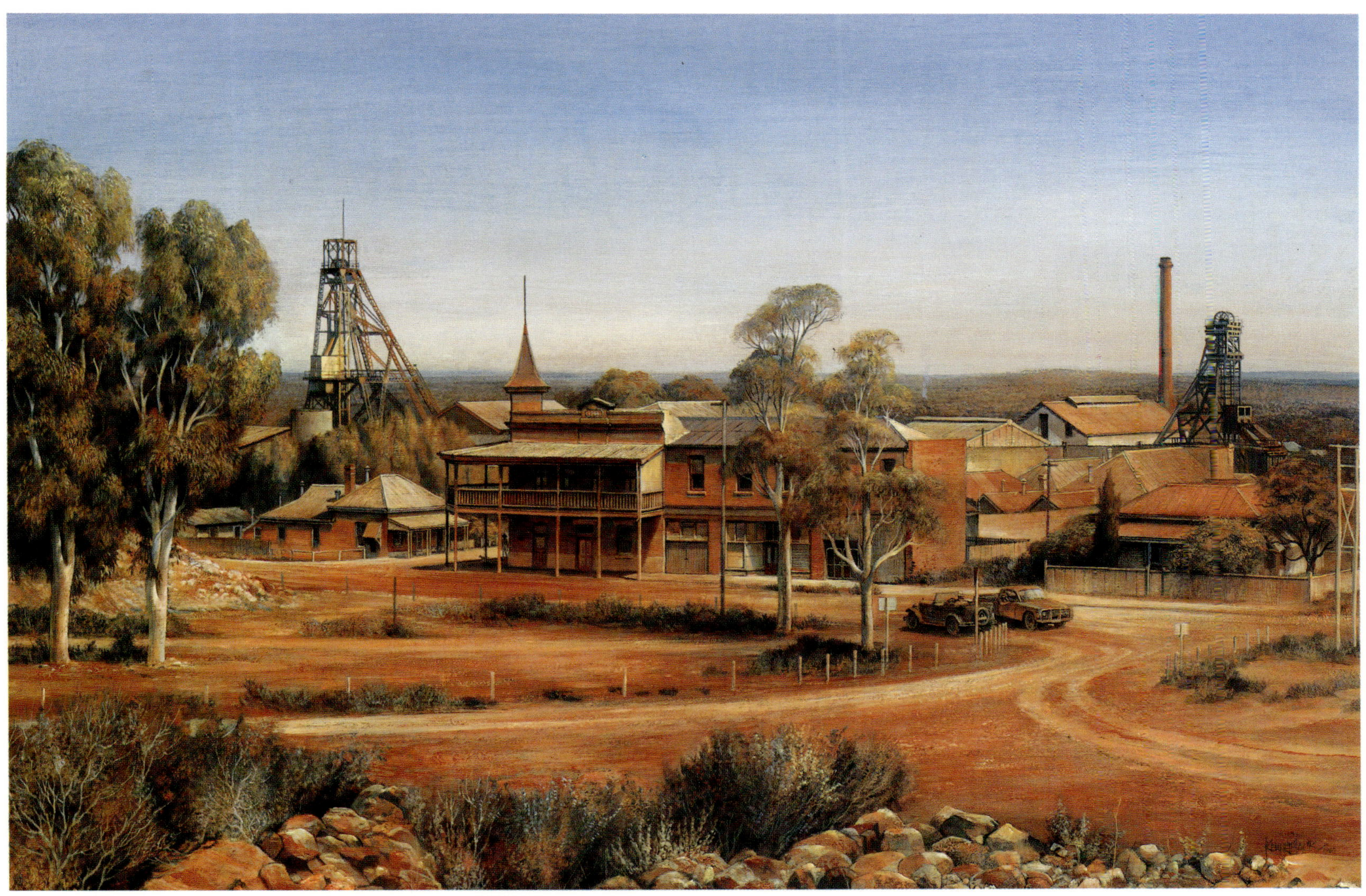

Plate 37 *Boulder* 1980 (Western Australia) acrylic, 61 × 91 cm

*Boulder is part of the Kalgoorlie Golden Mile which
is reputedly the richest square mile in the world and
from which gold is still being extracted. All over the
area there are poppet heads at the tops of many
mines. On a recent visit to Boulder I found that the
old hotel building in this painting has been
demolished. The small building on the left across the
road is the post office.*

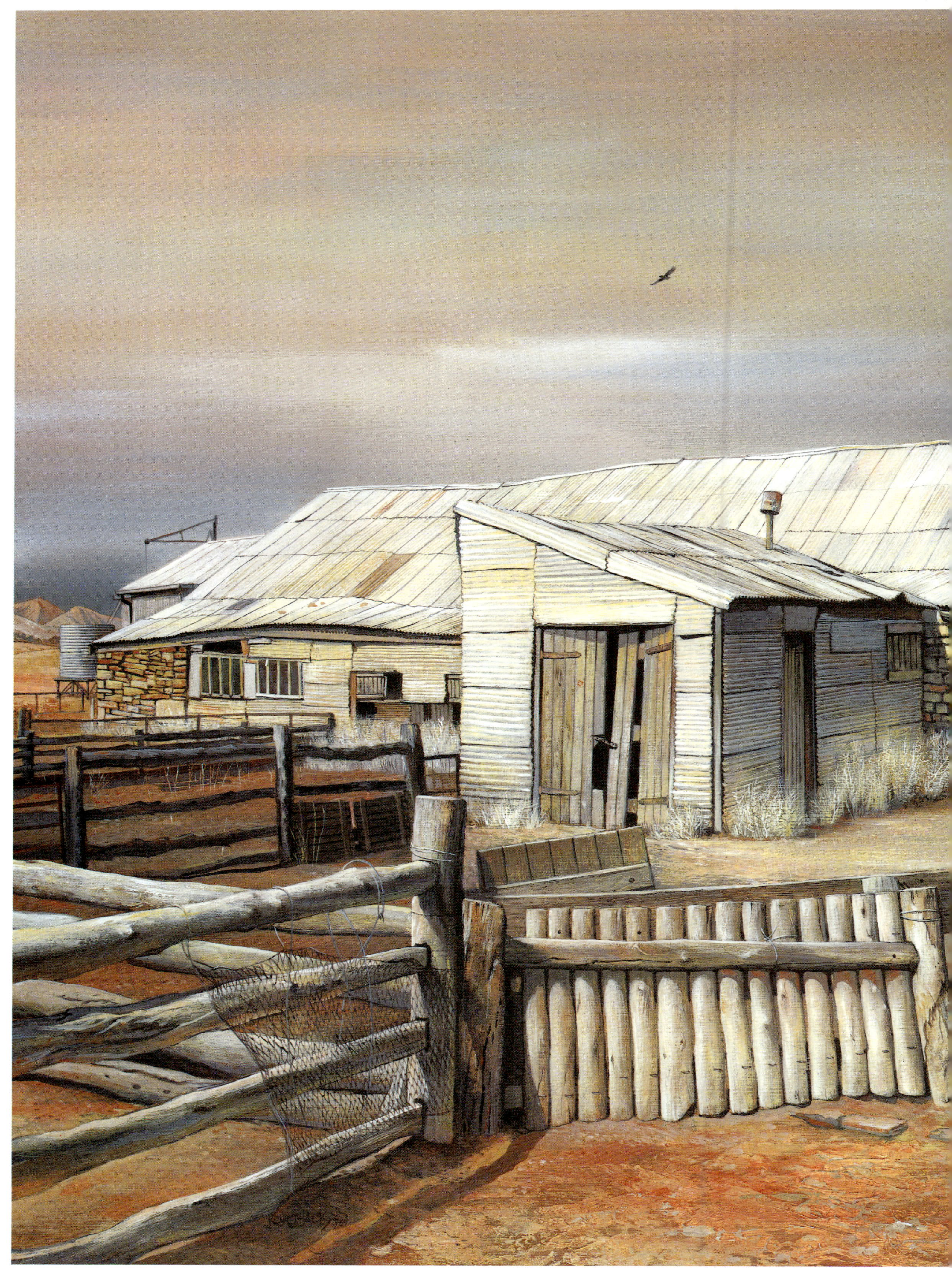

Plate 38 *Moolooloo Woolshed* 1984 (South Australia) acrylic, 51 × 76 cm

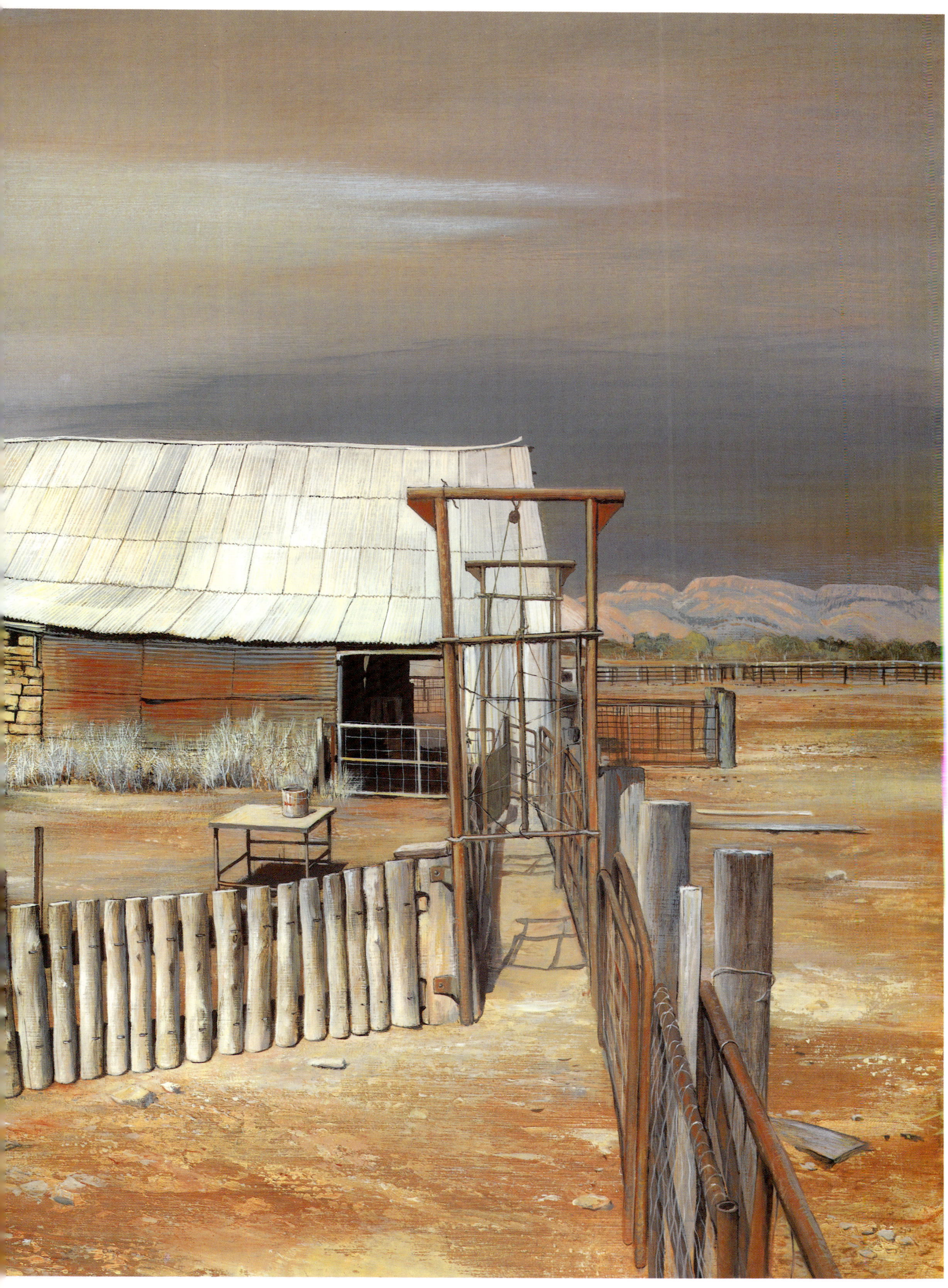

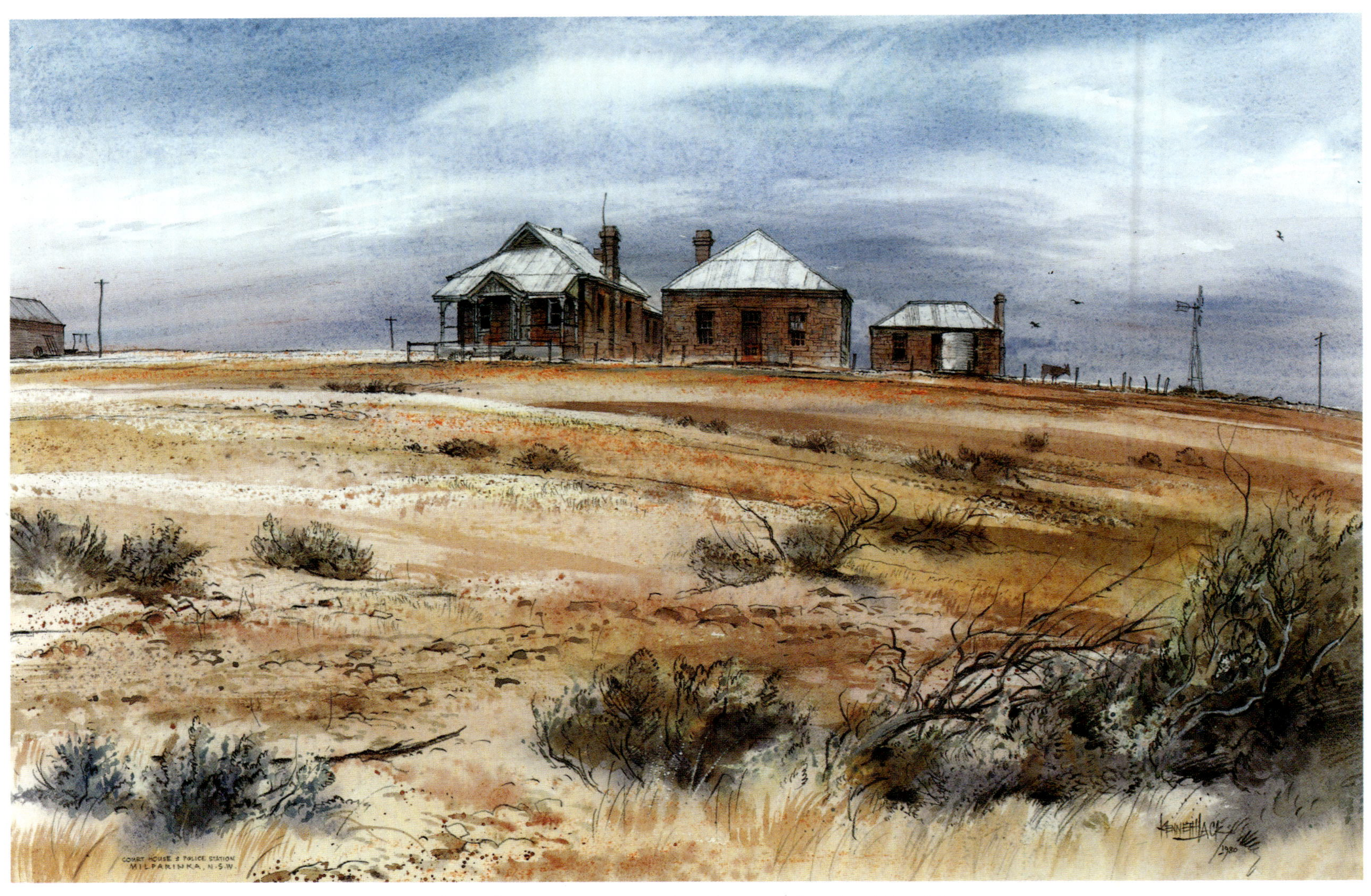

Plate 39 *Court House and Police Station, Milparinka* 1980 (New South Wales) mixed media, 36 × 55 cm

Even when he could afford a four-wheel-drive vehicle, he occasionally got into difficulties. In 1971, driving more than 200 miles north-west of Broken Hill out through the world's longest fence, the dingo fence, he found himself in the no-man's land between the large salt lakes of Frome and Callabonna, trying to reach the northernmost point of the Flinders Ranges to the west. They encountered such bad ground — floodwaters and boggy sand between sand dunes — that for a while he began to wonder if they would get through. They had to camp out in this desolate and lonely area after managing to cover only thirty miles. All night he couldn't sleep, wondering if he would ever be able to get his family back to civilisation again. At such times survival took precedence over making drawings.

> The gradual move I made to explore further inland in the Australian continent, and the buying of a four-wheel-drive vehicle, changed my outlook on the semi-abstract methods. The great inland or dry outback of Australia cuts one down to size — out there one is a dot in a vast space which Nature alone controls — one feels that man is there by the Grace of God . . . Nature is supreme, and it is really awe-inspiring and continually draws one to it . . . a marvellous sense of adventure is still possible in Australia . . . The space in Nature is far too compelling for me to ignore and to continue to treat with very shallow semi-abstractions. I have gradually felt the urge to get to grips with the space, depth, earthiness, texture, colour, structures and rhythms of the inland.[14]

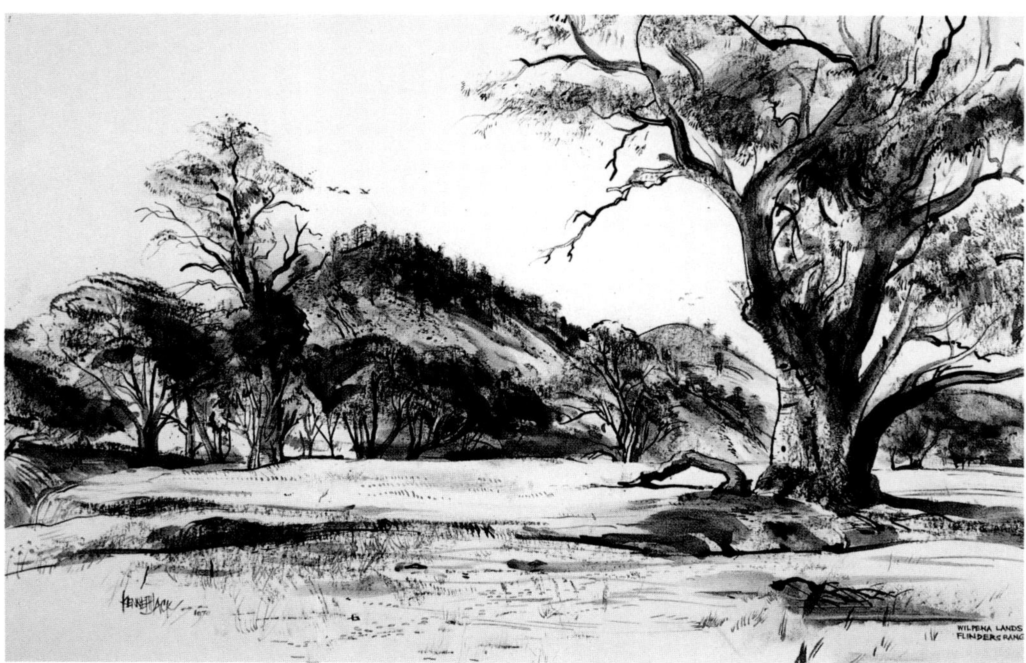

Fig. 18 *Wilpena Landscape, Flinders Ranges* 1970 (South Australia) quill, wash, ink and green chalk, 30.5 × 49.5 cm

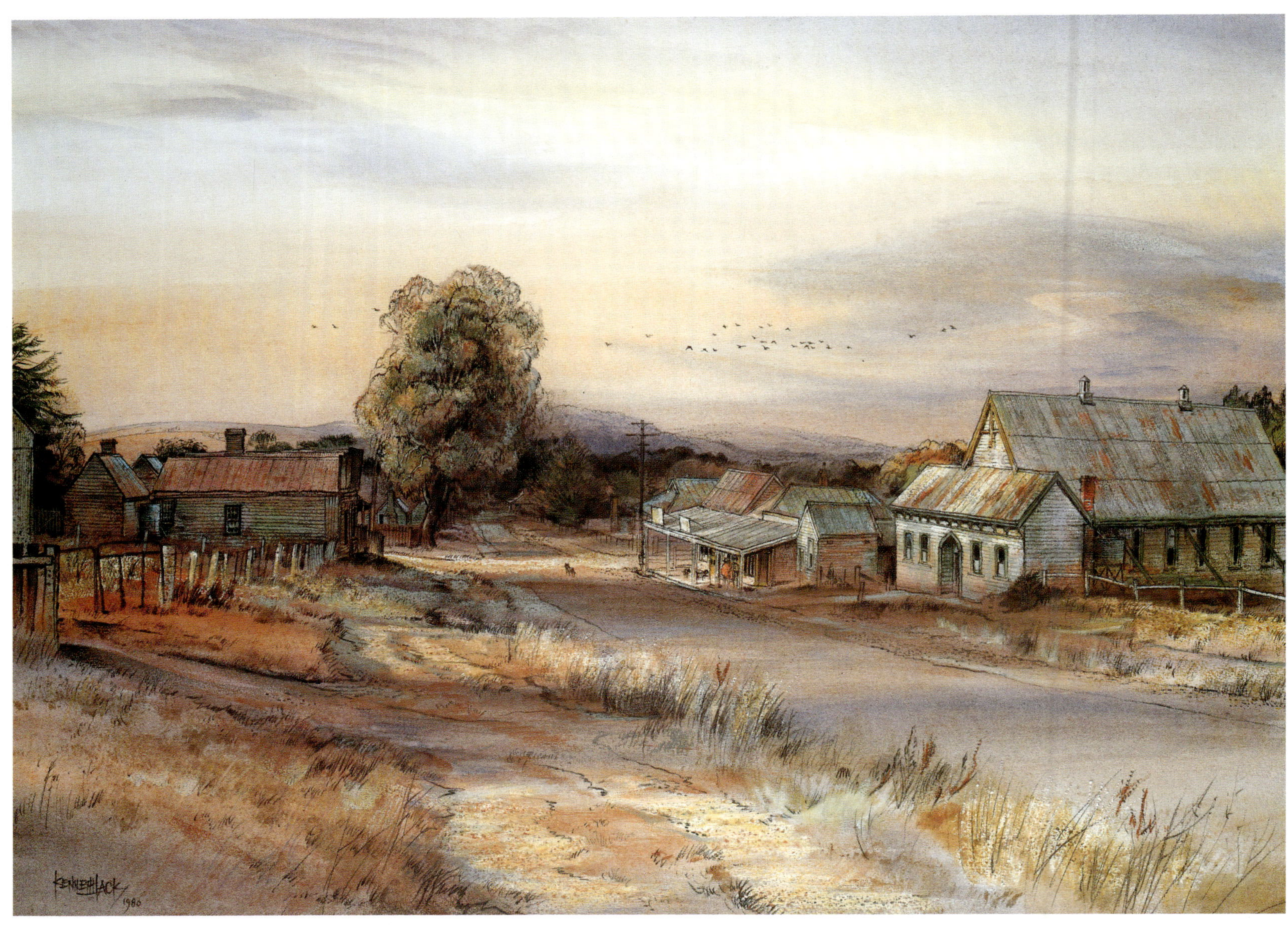

Plate 40 *Evening Shadows, Mt. Egerton* 1980 (Victoria) pencil, oil pastel and watercolour, 46 × 64 cm

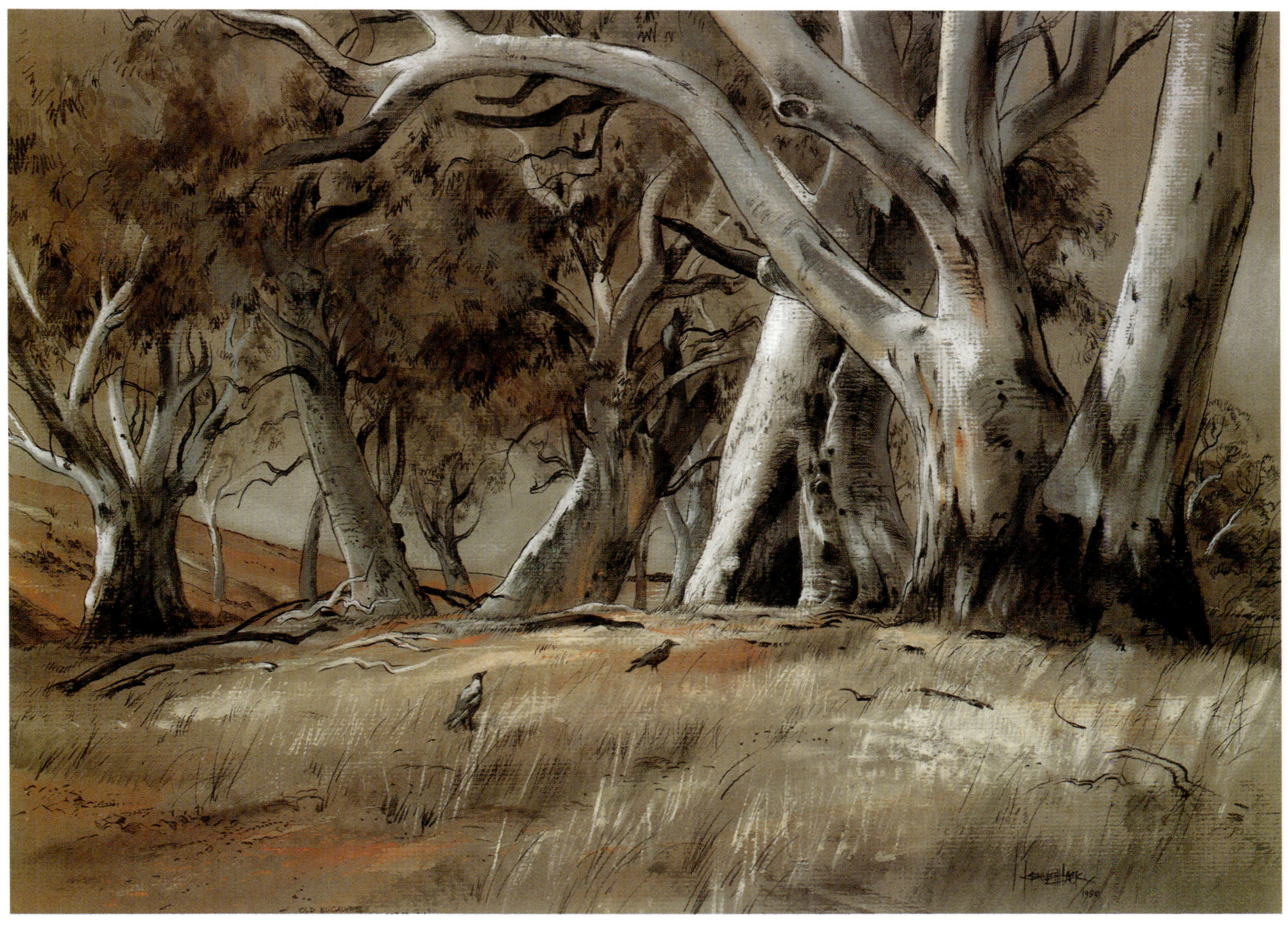

Plate 41 *Old Eucalypts, Buckaringa Gorge* 1980 (South Australia) pencil, oil pastel and watercolour, 39 × 55 cm

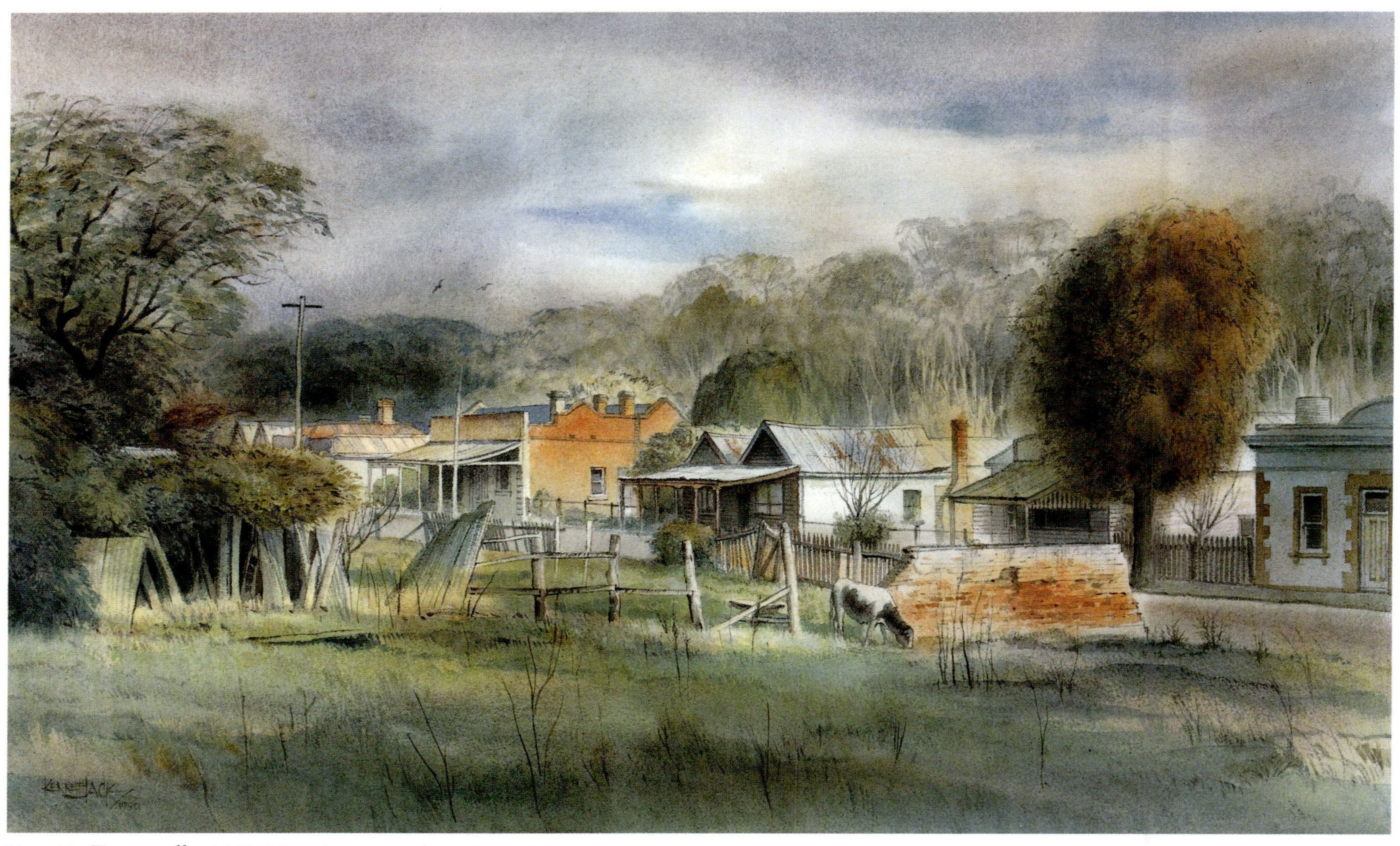

Plate 42 *Tarnagulla* 1980 (Victoria) watercolour, 34 × 56 cm

THE PROFESSIONAL

After he became a full-time painter Kenneth Jack's trips into the outback were no longer restricted to college holidays and he could travel whenever he wanted to and wherever he needed to find new subjects. He embarked on a series of journeys which over the next twenty-five years made him familiar with every corner of the continent, returning again and again to places which have become important to him. Few Australian painters have travelled so widely and fewer still have such a passionate love and concern for the subject matter of their art.

In 1987 a major exhibition of photographs by Russell Drysdale mounted by the National Gallery of Victoria and a book on the same subject by Jenny Boddington revealed the remarkable colour photographs the artist took during a six-months' trip with his son to the remotest parts of the continent. Drysdale loved to be out in the open gathering first-hand experience, yet during the six months he filled only one sketchbook with notes and drawings. He was interested in the typical rather than the specific. Kenneth Jack has always been concerned to capture the particular character of a place or building and it is this interest in the specific which has gained him many admirers while causing him to be neglected by the critics. The subject matter which attracted the interest of so many of our earlier painters has during the last twenty years been generally neglected by professional artists.

It was probably the sense of being out on a limb, alienated from the mainstream, which led Jack to take an interest in the work of Andrew Wyeth. He had known of him vaguely, but it was only when he saw a lavish book on Wyeth's work that he felt that here was a painter following a similar direction to his own, yet he was far from neglected in the United States.

Jack did not like all Wyeth's work he saw, but it made him aware of two things: first that there was at least one other painter pursuing a similar type of subject matter, and second, that he should become more exacting in his detail. For a time Kenneth Jack's work showed some influence from Wyeth, mostly in the choice of subject matter, such as abandoned carts by old farm buildings or a much more detailed treatment of corrugated iron, but this influence lasted only a short time. What he saw and experienced during his travels was much more important.

A more lasting influence arose from an experience during his first trip to the Flinders Ranges in 1965. He had long been interested in the area from work he had seen and admired by Hans Heysen and he could not wait to get there. The Jacks stayed at Wilpena Chalet and soon after their arrival he saw in the dining room a man whose face was very familiar. It intrigued him during the meal until he realised that he had seen a bronze of that head by Daphne Mayo reproduced in one of Ure Smith's publications — it was Lloyd Rees. After the meal Jack went over and introduced himself; Rees already knew him by name, having awarded him several prizes in art competitions he had judged.

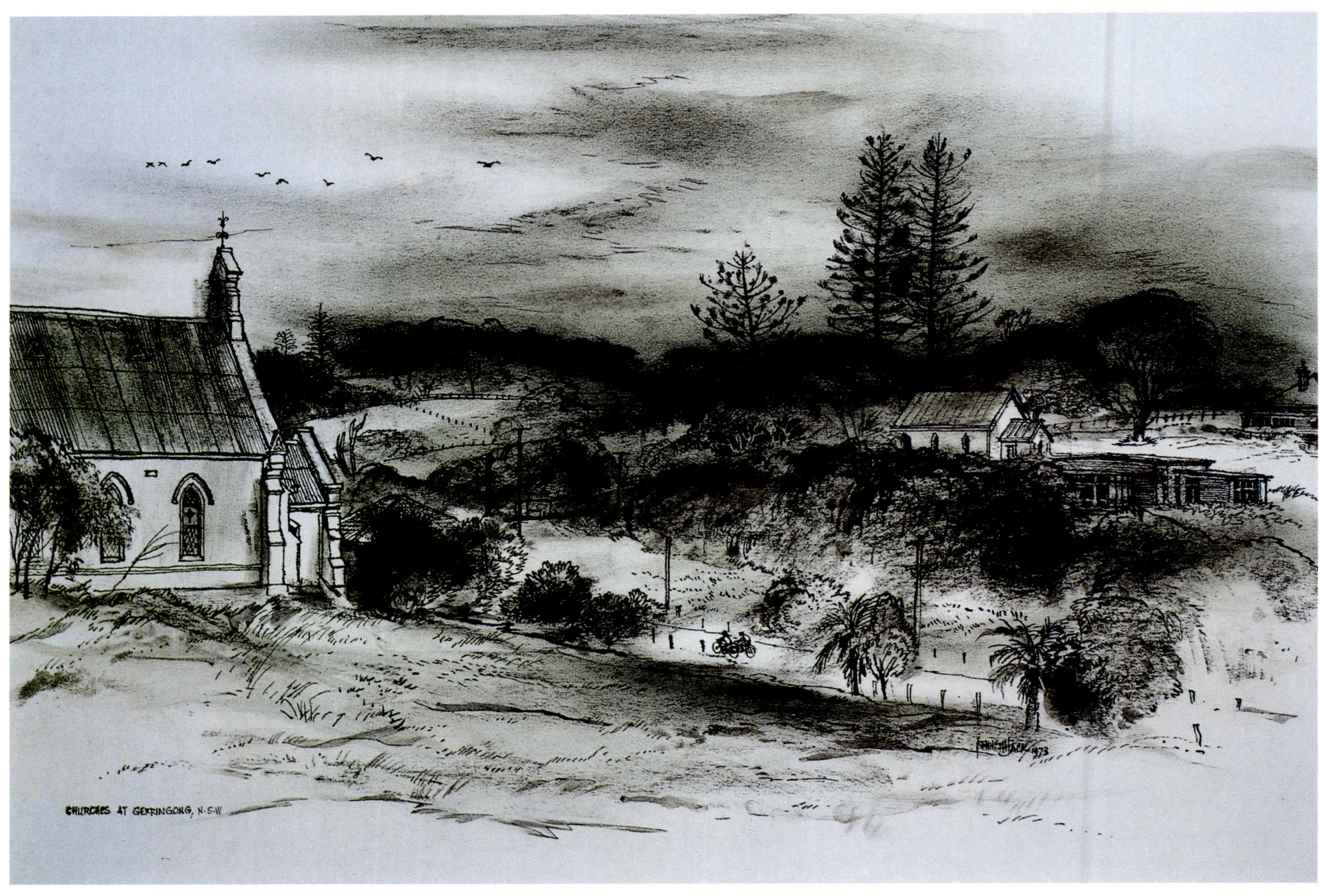

Fig. 19 *Churches at Gerringong* 1973 (New South Wales) pen, ink and green chalk, 30.5 × 45.5 cm

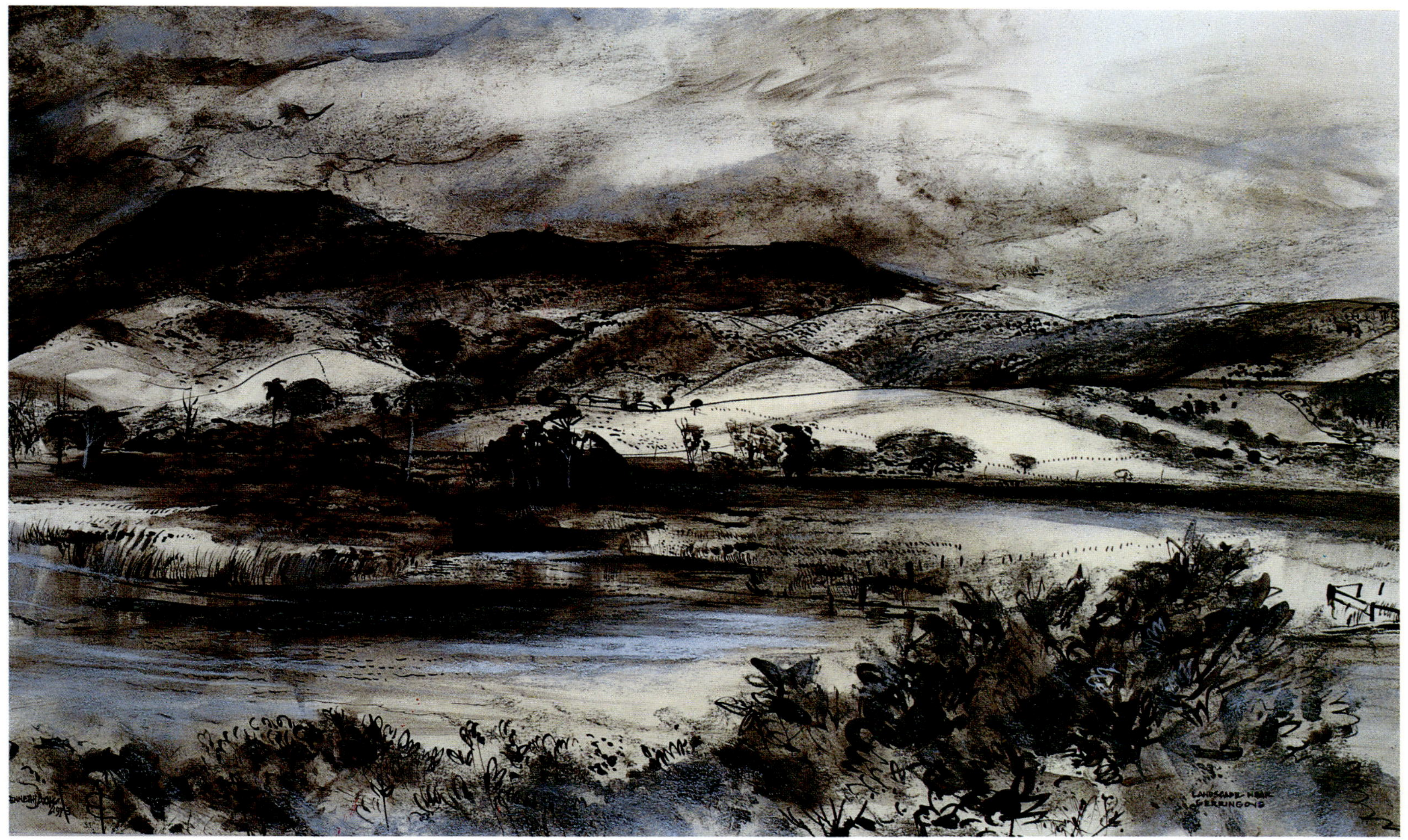

Fig. 20 *Landscape near Gerringong* 1973 (New South Wales) quill, ink and wash; white and grey chalk, 30 × 52.2 cm

Lloyd Rees was there with his wife and her brother and his wife. By coincidence they occupied the cabin next to the Jacks and each evening, after having gone their own way to work, the two artists exhibited their day's work for their families. During this first trip to the Flinders, Jack found it very difficult to get to grips with the subject and was quite heartened to find Lloyd Rees equally concerned. Rees complained that everywhere he looked he kept seeing Hans Heysen . . . 'this of course is a fact. Heysen had so thoroughly moved all over the area and captured its character in charcoal and watercolour. Yet Lloyd Rees produced some entirely original versions of the landscape that could only have been done by his hand, and it was quite a revelation to see that, although he said he struggled over them, how simple and right they seemed to be.'[15]

The meeting with Lloyd Rees, the sharing of ideas and tackling similar subjects was particularly important to Jack, who had had no close connection with any major figure in Australian art other than John Rowell, who had been his teacher at Melbourne Technical College. Here was one of the giants of Australian art whom he admired, and he also knew Kenneth Jack's work. They had a mutual friend in John Brackenreg but there was another important connection between them which may not have occurred to either of them at the time.

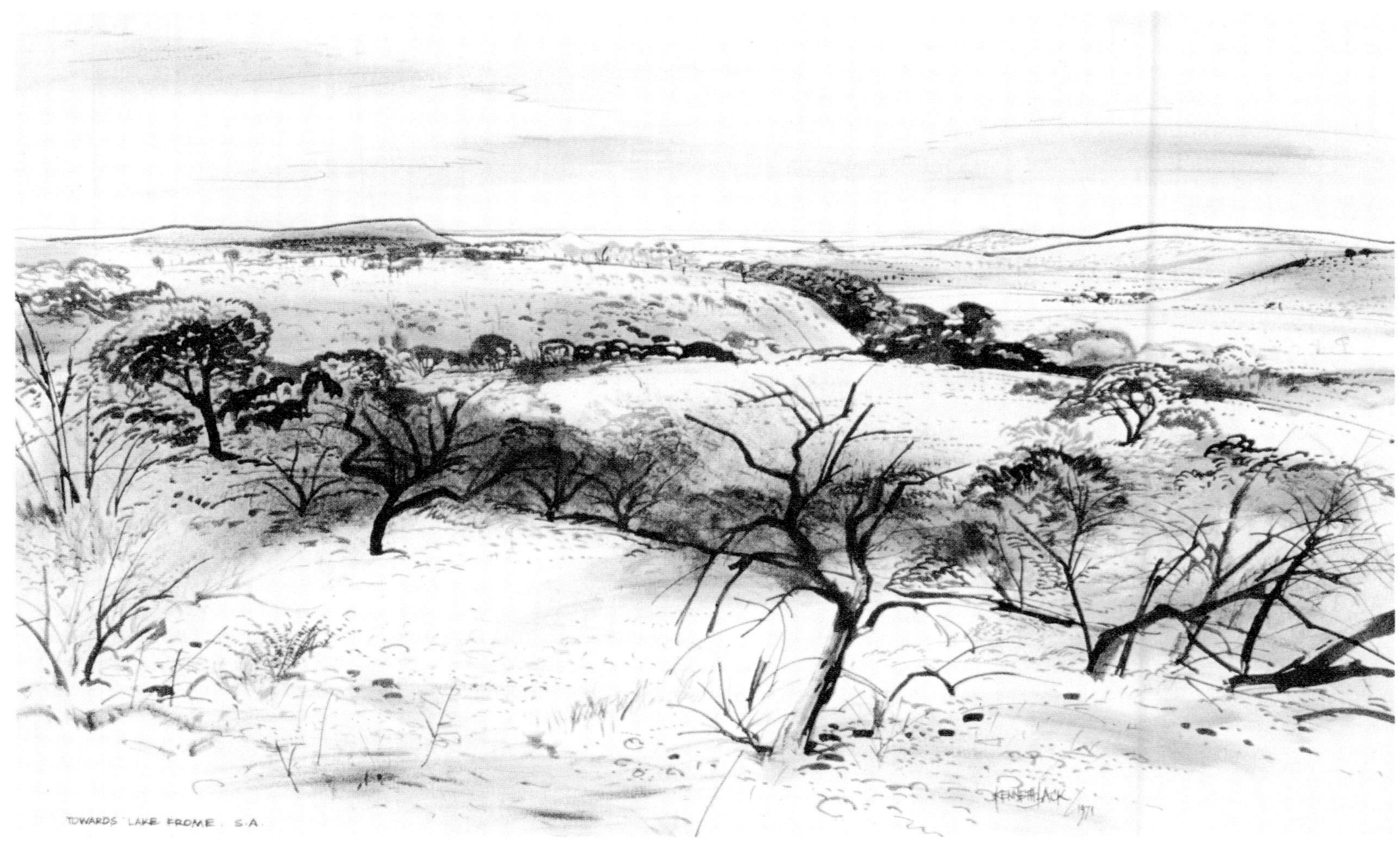

Fig. 19 *Towards Lake Frome* 1971 (South Australia) pen and wash, 30 × 50 cm

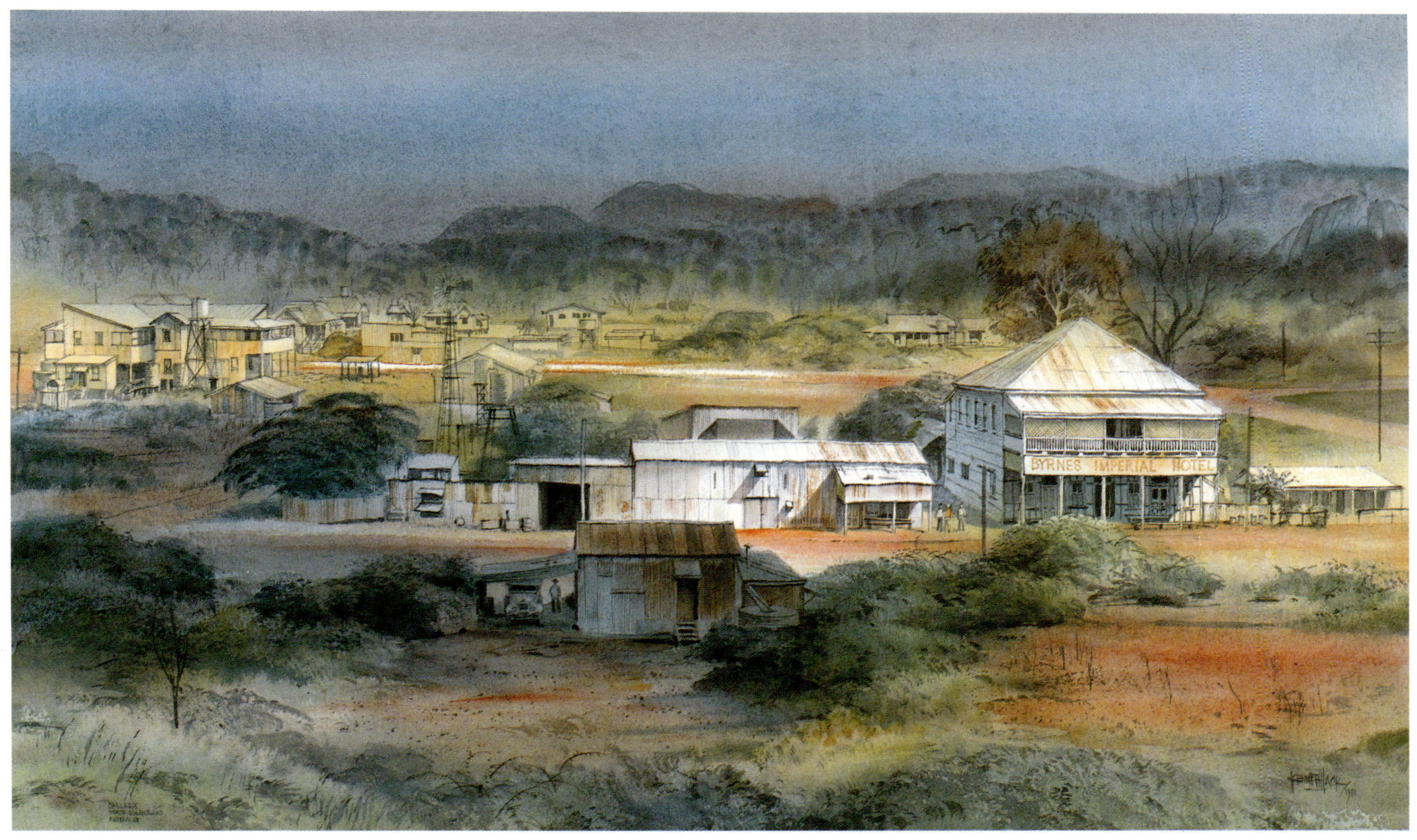

Plate 43 *Chillagoe, North Queensland* 1981, watercolour, 33 × 55 cm

I think the first time I became aware of this small mining town in North Queensland was through the paintings of Ray Crooke. When in the Cairns area I have always made a point of travelling west the 200 or so kilometres to visit Chillagoe again. The journey is fascinating, passing through very small, tired-looking places such as Lappa Junction, Petford and Almaden. And as one nears Chillagoe the country takes on a strange appearance with weird-shaped hills like castles which pop up here and there. It is limestone country with caves and eroded, rocky outcrops weathered into grotesque shapes.

The town itself is not really a tourist place, but one of those 'non-architectural' places which strangely attract me. This watercolour shows the old two-storey Imperial Hotel which sadly has been replaced by an uninteresting one-storey modern hotel. Next to it is an open-air movie theatre. The larger building to the left is the back view of another hotel on main street. To obtain this view I climbed one of the limestone outcrops.

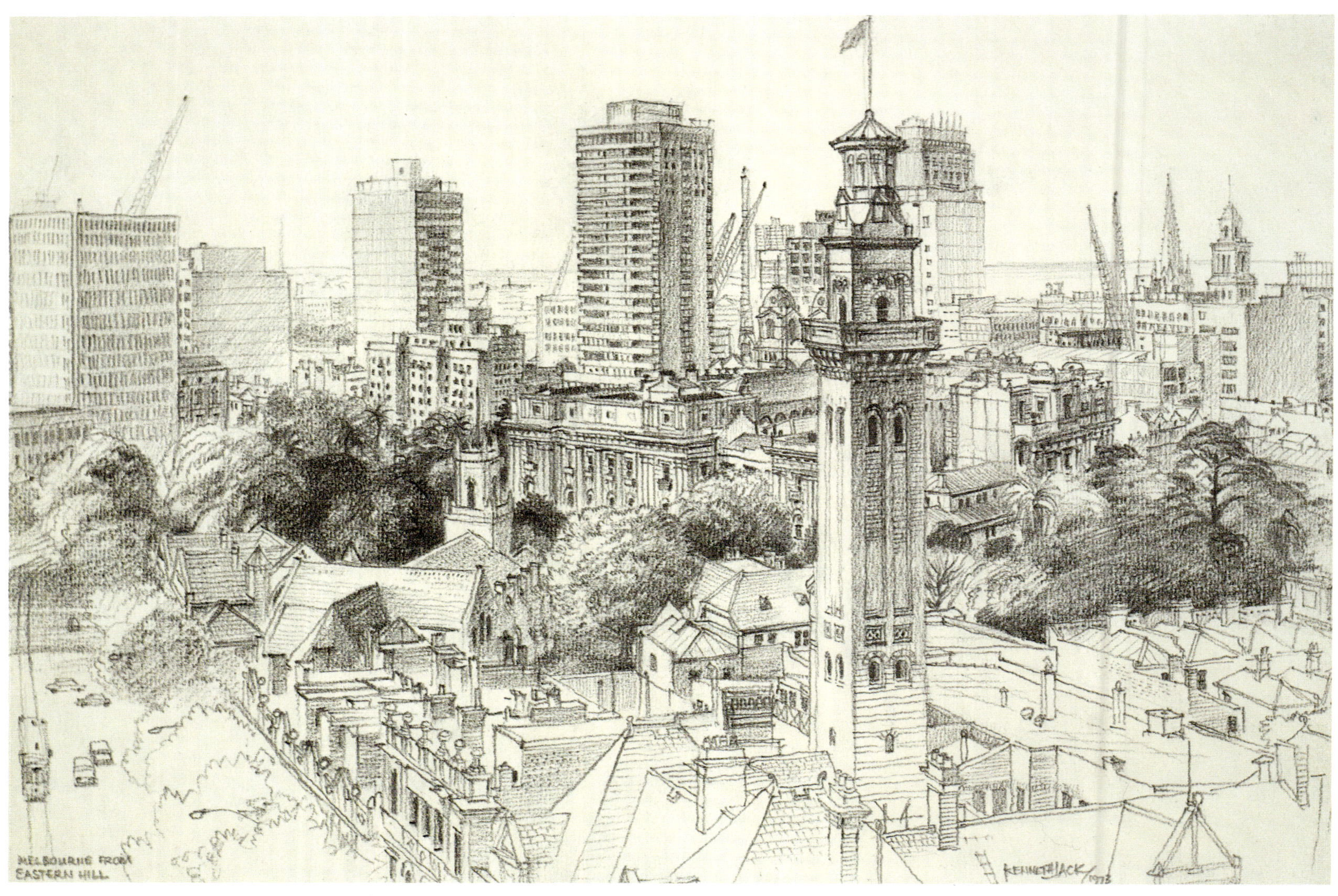

Fig. 22 *Melbourne from Eastern Hill* 1973, pencil, 18.5 × 24.7 cm

Although they belonged to different generations, both were precocious and gifted draughtsmen, both were interested in drawing architecture, and both drew well-known European buildings from photographs long before they went there. Both were interested in the great cathedrals; Lloyd Rees drew them while still in Brisbane before he went to live in Sydney and Kenneth Jack, inspired by Turner, made a pilgrimage to see and draw many of the English cathedrals just as Rees had done some fifty years before him in London, Paris, Chartres and Rome. Both loved the Australian landscape, but perhaps most important of all, the early talent in each had been discovered and fostered by Sydney Ure Smith. Ure Smith gave Lloyd Rees a steady job with Smith and Julius in 1917, introduced him into the Society of Artists and supported his work; and in the same way Ure Smith discovered Kenneth Jack and promoted his work nationally by illustrating it in his publications and commissioning him to do the drawings for *The Melbourne Book* and *The Charm of Hobart*.

This chance meeting, where Kenneth Jack met a man he considered one of the greatest Australian artists of any time, led to other encounters and developed into a warm friendship. Great as he was, Lloyd Rees was still considerably neglected at the hands of critics who could not see beyond the subject matter of his paintings to the power and impact of his unique vision. The interest in his work by a younger man, and an artist, was therefore equally rewarding to him.

When Kenneth Jack had an exhibition at the Artarmon Galleries in 1972 it was Lloyd Rees who opened it:

If I might express a preference, because I am often asked, have you a particular picture in an exhibition you like beyond all others, this is an exhibition in which I have a very positive feeling towards one picture. It's a picture of a town in that early early hour that not many city folk know about — I am referring to that hour when you are in the country place and you're itching to explore and get up very early. There is no life about, there is even more sense of people sleeping in the very early dawn than there is at mid-night when the sleepers seem to be alive. But very early dawn you get that wonderful feeling of just a stray person, as happens in this picture — I understand the stray man is a butcher — but I don't think he comes from that town; there you are, there is a surrealistic man coming into that picture.

He has captured that wonderful feeling of early morning with the mist just rising and an extraordinary feat of draughtsmanship and feeling, not just draughtsmanship, on the old bandstand right in the centre with its filigree work. Now all that filigree ironwork, the old balcony, now that is all something that is validly Australia and although Kenneth Jack has no, I think, ulterior purpose whatever in his work, it is irresistible, but then he could not help it as he was born to do it. But he is also revealing to us something that a lot of us are now becoming conscious of, the need to conserve some of these things so that we have a humanistic basis to our lives, because the wonderful thing about the Australian town with all its ramshackledness and so on, is the humanism of it.

I cannot look at one of these pictures of the old hotel without feeling the excitement of the travellers arriving at night, before the days of the motor car when it was a real journey, and you were looking forward to the warmth and hospitality, the life that was in these old towns, and particularly in the country pub.[16]

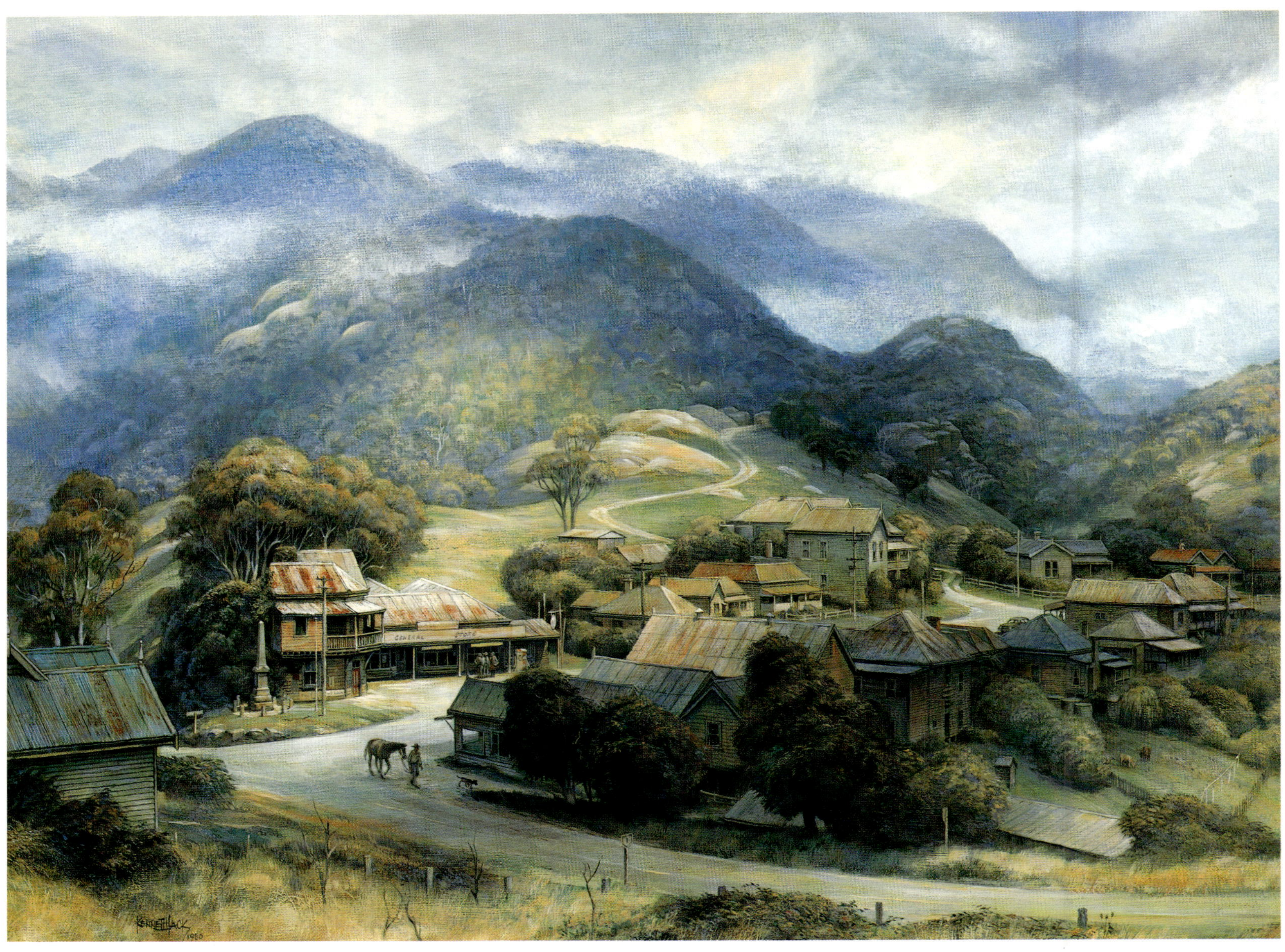

Plate 44   *Tilba* 1980 (New South Wales) acrylic, 42 × 57 cm

This marvellous small town has often attracted me.
It is interesting from almost any angle — this
painting shows the town from a high viewpoint and
gives a very good idea of its picturesque mountain
setting. Nearly all the buildings are timber with iron
roofs.

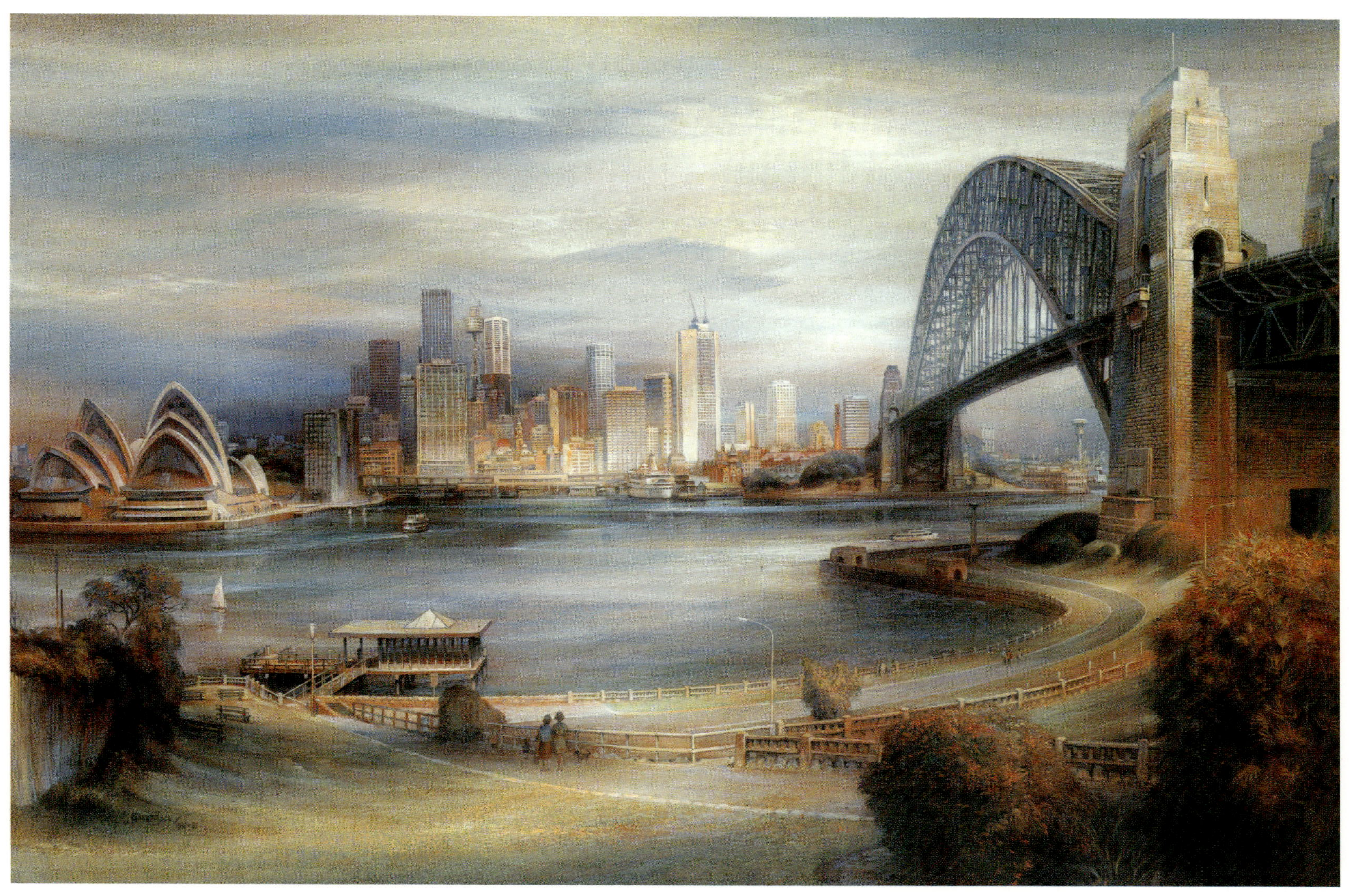

Plate 45 *Sydney from Kirribilli* 1980–81, acrylic, 81 × 122 cm

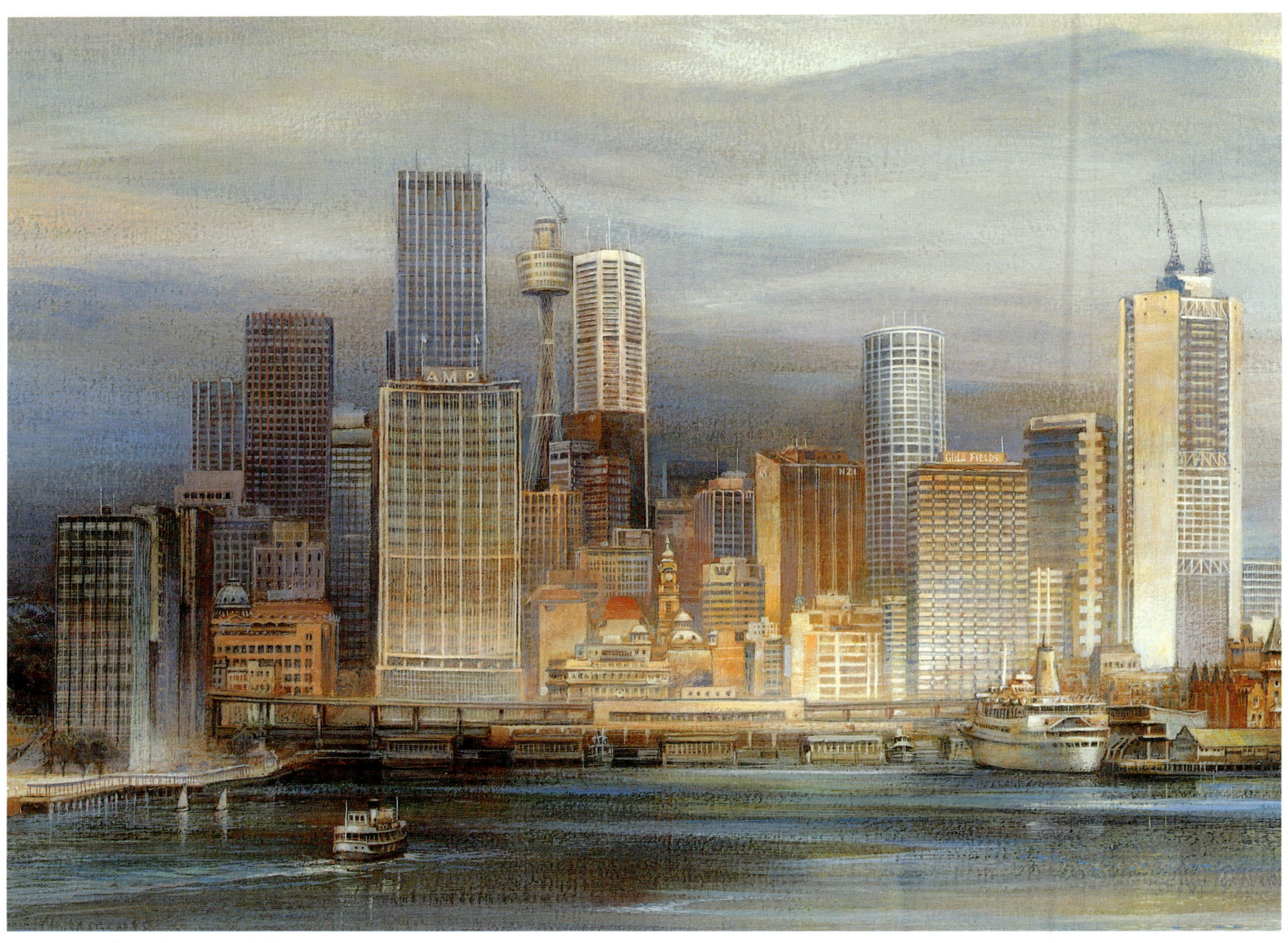

Detail of *Sydney from Kirribilli* (Plate 45)

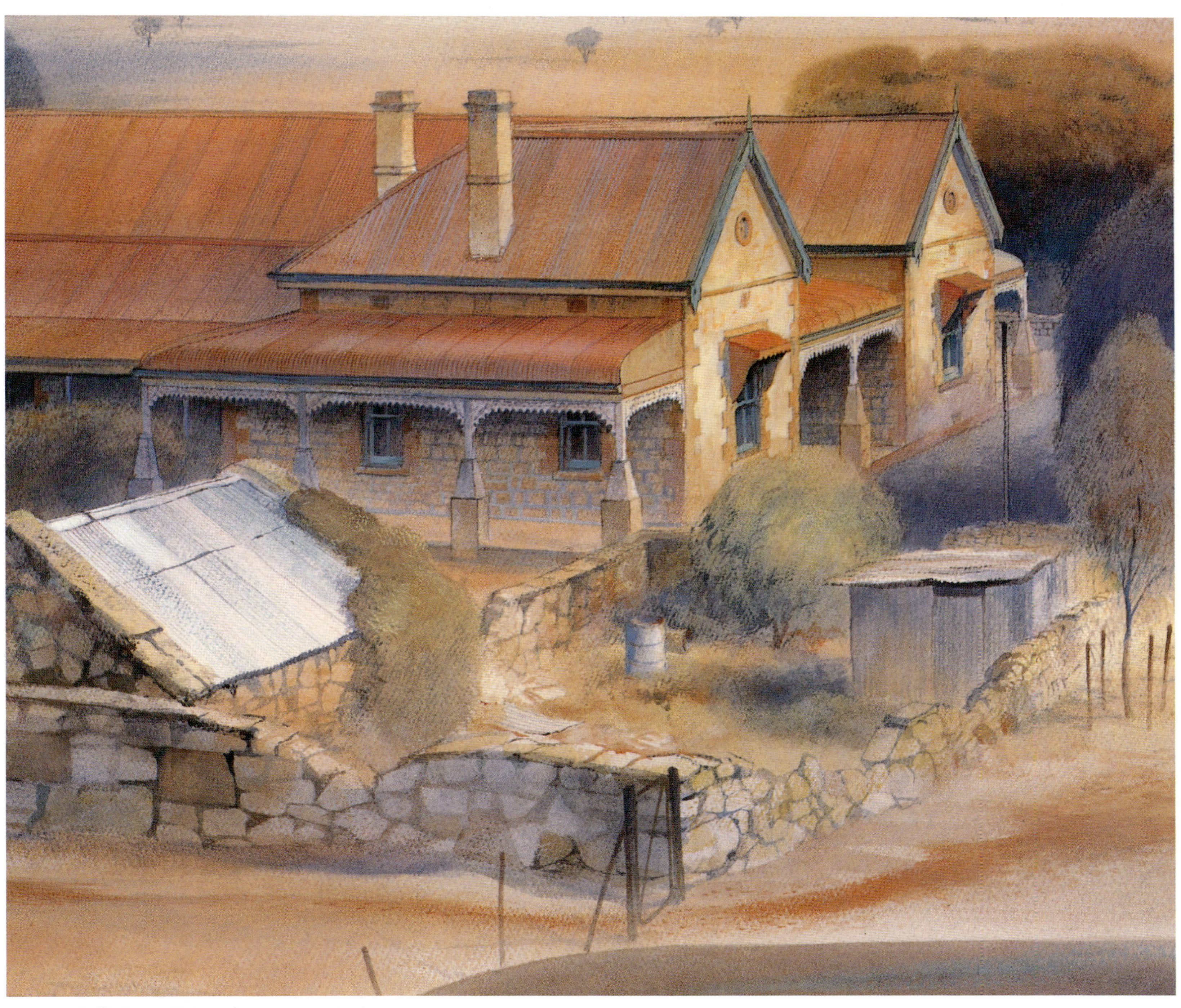

Detail of *Balladonia Triptych* Centre Panel (Plate 46)

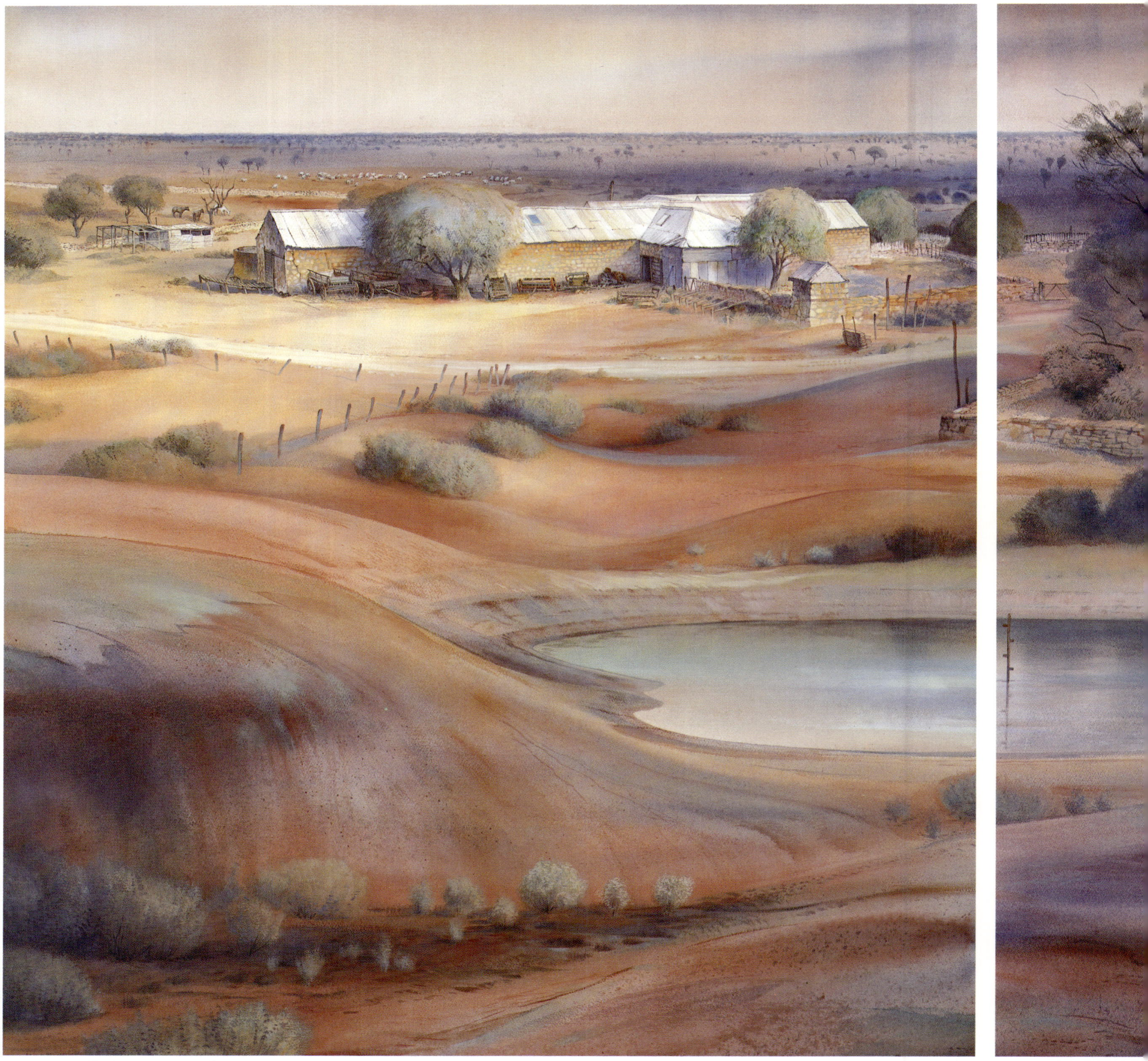

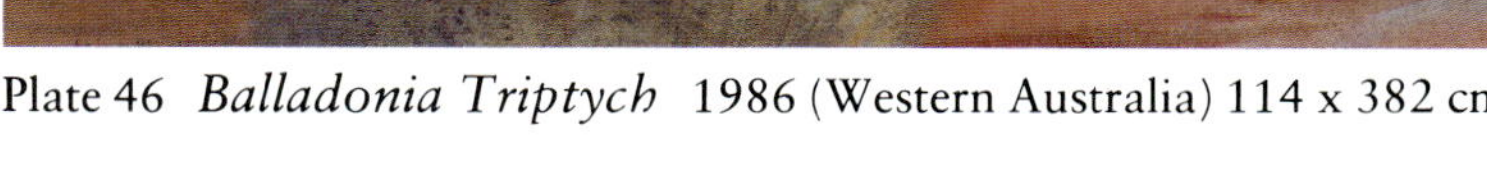

Plate 46 *Balladonia Triptych* 1986 (Western Australia) 114 x 382 cm

Left panel: *The Woolshed* watercolour, 114 x 110 cm
Centre panel: *The Homestead* watercolour, 114 x 162 cm
Right panel: *Old Telegraph Station* watercolour, 114 x 110 cm

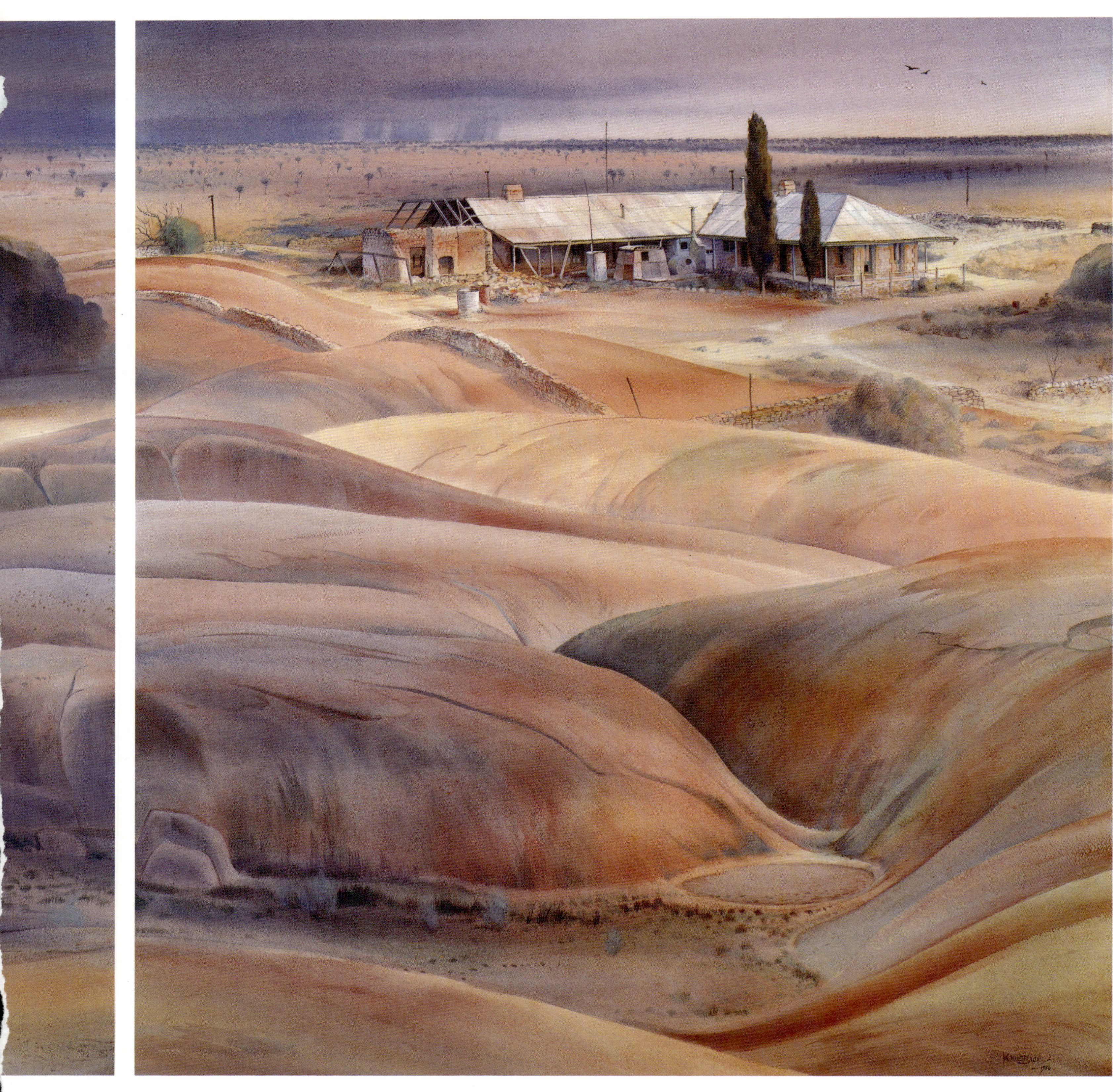

After crossing the Nullarbor Plain and before arriving at the Western Australian town of Norseman, one passes Balladonia Homestead and the old telegraph station nearby. I pulled the Landcruiser up and decided I'd like to ask permission to take photographs. (Time did not permit drawing.) Approaching the homestead along the stony track I was delighted to see a very old woolshed, old stone fences and several other buildings set in granite boulders. It was, to my way of thinking, superb subject matter. Barking dogs came out to meet me as I stepped from the car. The owner appeared on the verandah and was very friendly and readily gave me permission to take som pictures. In about an hour I had wandered all over the place — around the woolshed, the fine old telegraph station and up and down huge domes of granite. I took many photographs and from these I was able to compose the triptych.

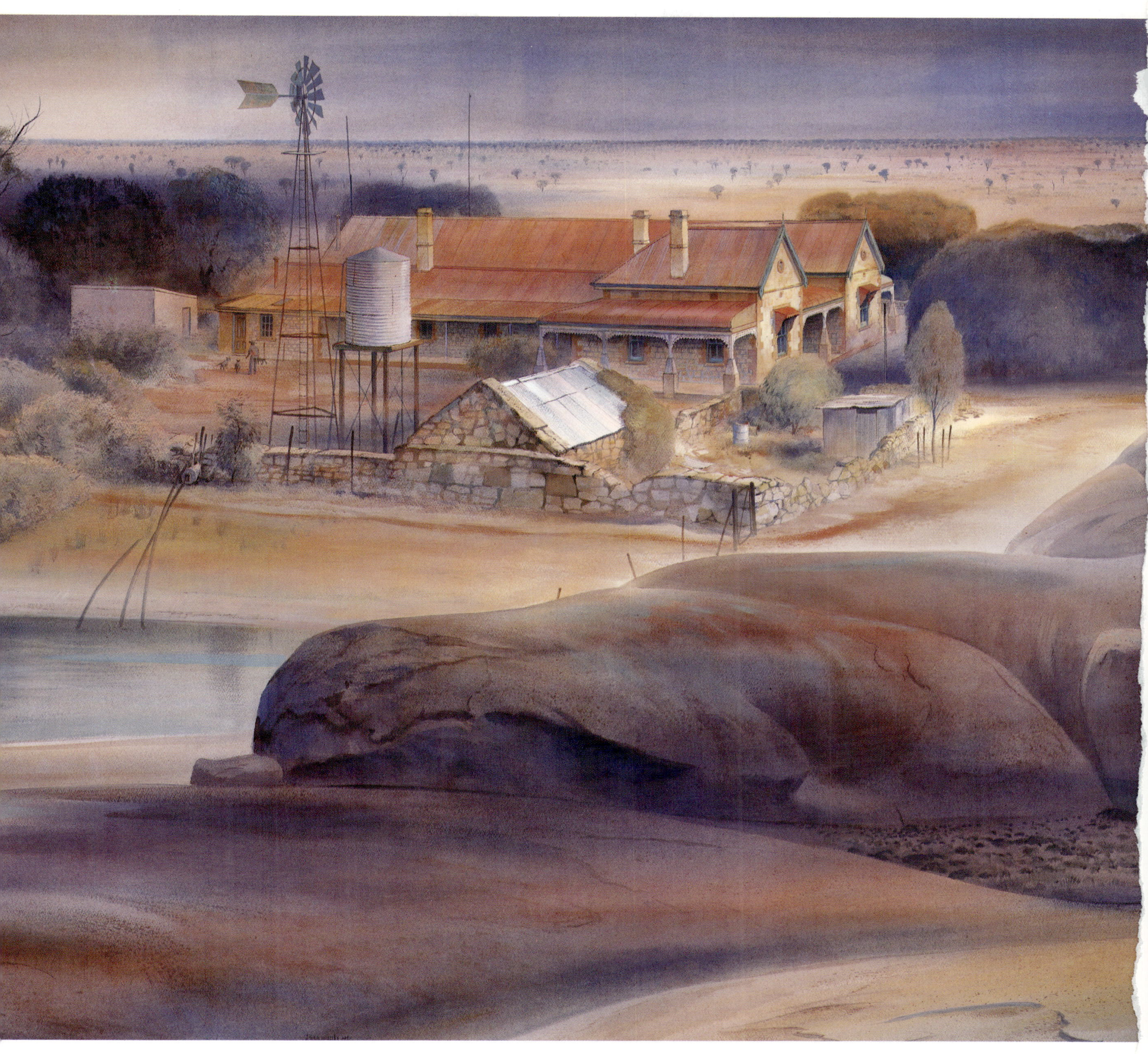

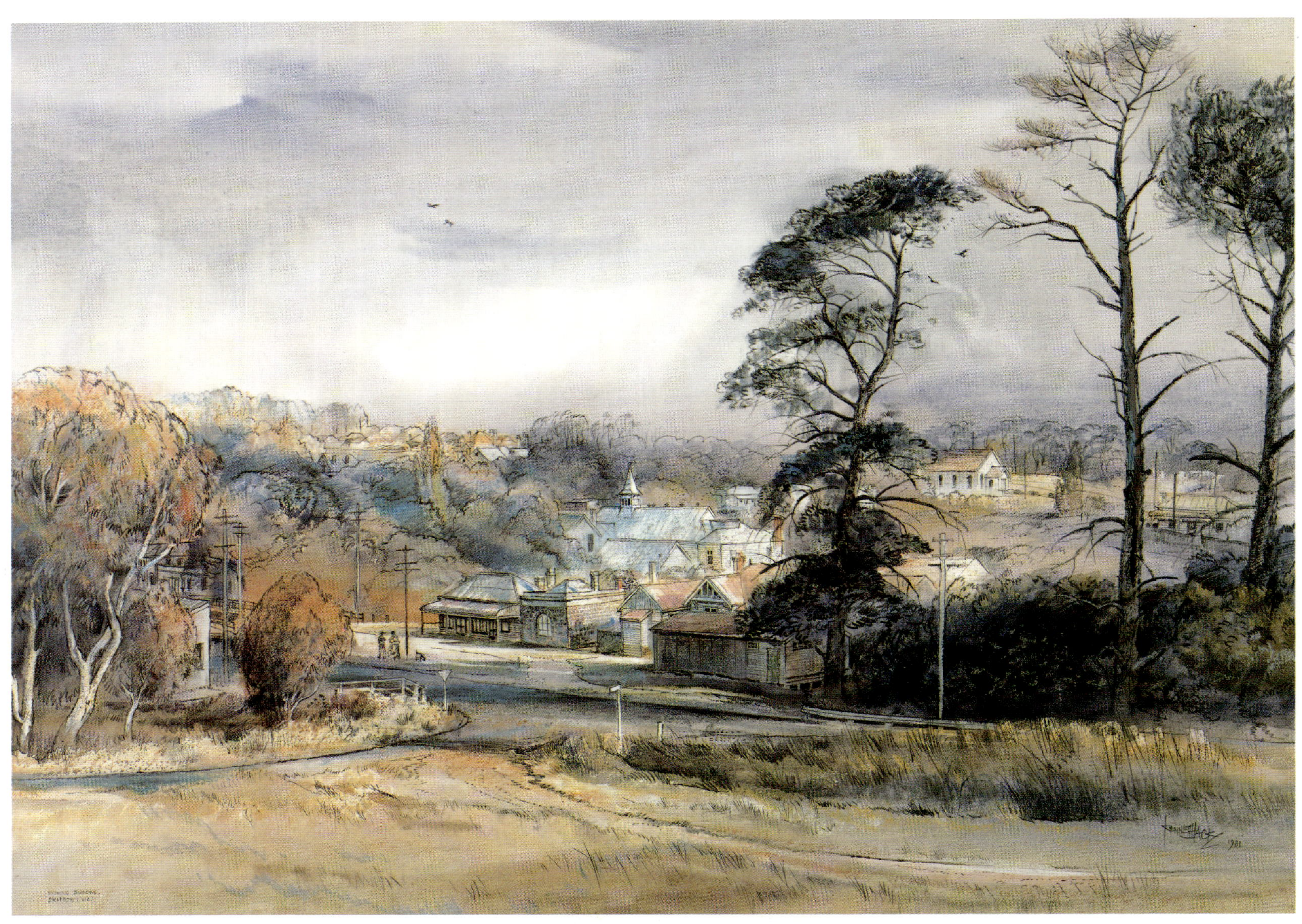

Plate 47 *Evening Shadows, Skipton* 1981 (Victoria) pencil, oil pastel and watercolour, 51 × 71 cm

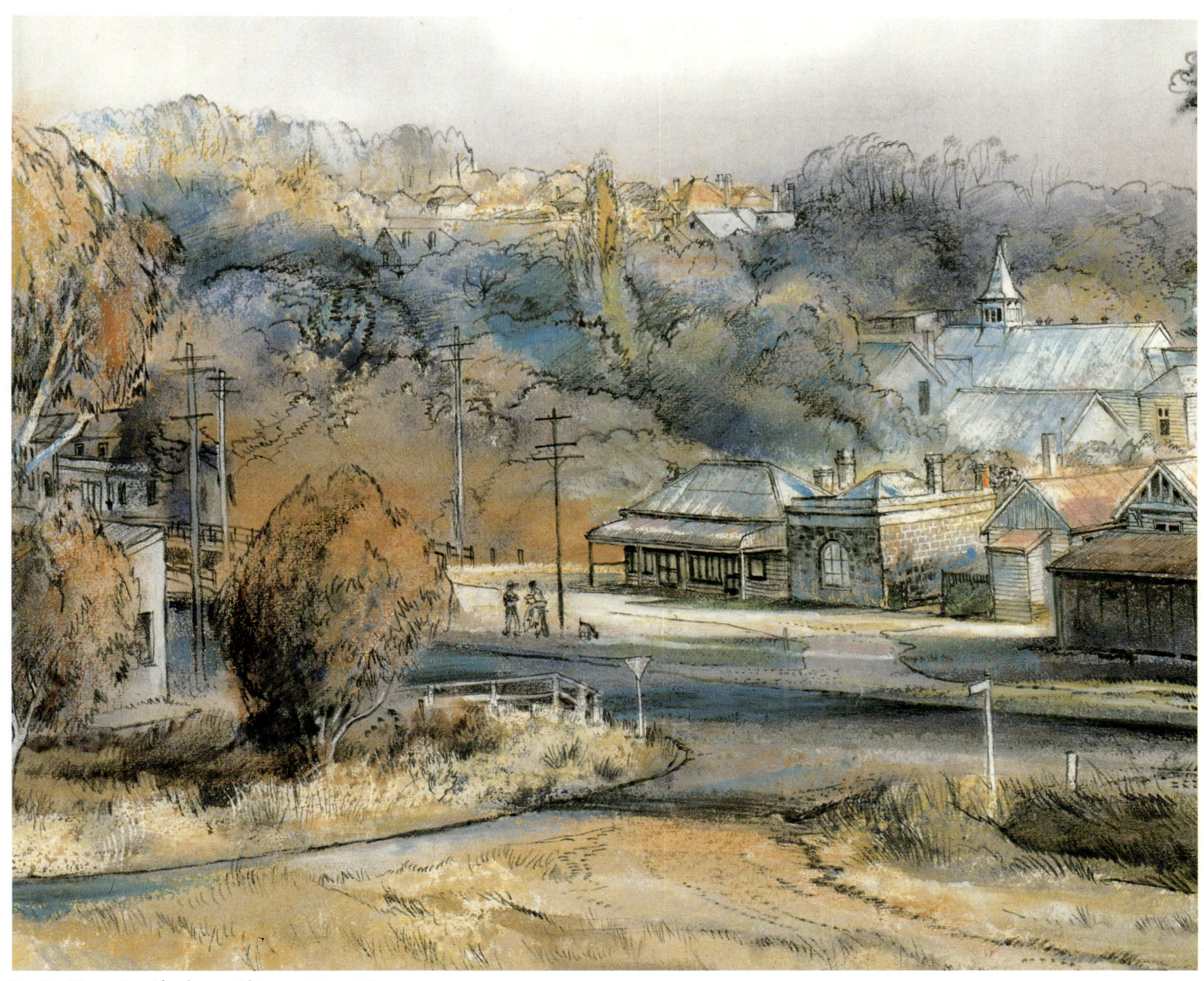

Detail of *Evening Shadows, Skipton* (Plate 47)

When Lloyd Rees was going to have an exhibition in London in 1973 and was planning the trip to England and France, it seemed to Kenneth Jack to be a good opportunity to go as well. He had already achieved a measure of success. He had had a large retrospective exhibition organised by David Dridan for John Martin's Gallery in Adelaide for the 1970 Adelaide Festival as part of a series of retrospectives also devoted to Drysdale, Dobell, Streeton and Heysen. Then in 1972 a small volume on his work was published by Collins in conjunction with Australian Artist Editions. The introduction was written by Douglas Dundas, who had been introduced to his work by Sydney Ure Smith. Dundas had gone to Adelaide to see the retrospective and then joined Jack on a long trip to the Flinders Ranges and Broken Hill.

Jack's trip to England in 1973 was his first time abroad. It was only short but was very important to him. Besides the opening of Lloyd Rees's London exhibition, he was able to see all the museums and galleries he had long dreamed of visiting. Seeing the paintings of his favourite artists, Turner and Rembrandt, who are both very well represented in London, was an unforgettable experience. So too was seeing the exceptional watercolours by Bonington in the Wallace Collection. He also made a pilgrimage to the great English cathedrals.

After their return to Australia the Jacks were invited by Lloyd Rees to stay at his holiday house in Gerringong, a place which is totally identified with Rees, who has painted there for more than forty years. Here Jack was able to do some fine work in the lovely undulating hills of the region. He made a number of drawings using the quill pen which is one of his favourite media. He showed Rees how to cut a quill and left him several for his own use. He was privileged to watch Rees working on the series of cathedrals of France he had brought back from his recent trip. Jack watched him painstakingly dotting the red and blue stained glass windows in watercolour to get the desired effect. It occurred to him that the same effect might be achieved with a fraction of the time and effort but he was uncertain whether he should offer an alternative method to such a master.[17]

The method consisted of using a brilliant red oil pastel to dot the reds and then washing over it with ultramarine watercolour which settled into the untouched spaces giving the required result more effectively and quickly. Rees was most taken with this, and seeing how easy it was, said 'I'll have to watch this!'

> . . . I certainly filled the day of your departure with work and transformed for good in the main (I hope) about five of those Chartres interiors — working with the oil pastels. The medium seemed so suited to the purpose that I feel almost frightened of such quick results! I am very grateful for your gift Ken.

This introduction to oil pastels provided Rees with a medium which he has put to good use ever since and proved vital to his work when his eyesight deteriorated.

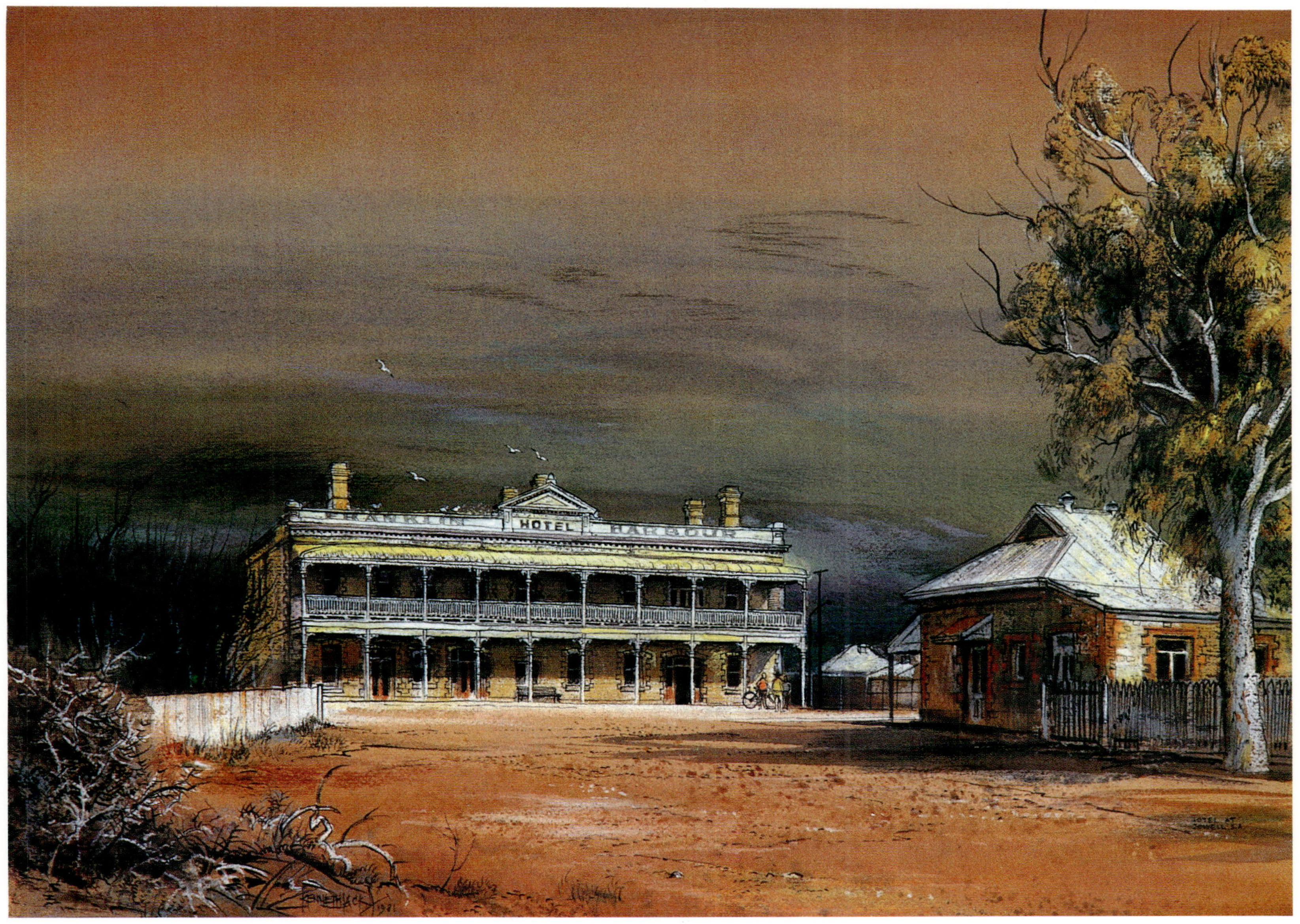

Plate 48 *Hotel at Cowell* 1981 (South Australia) pencil, oil pastel and watercolour, 35 × 48 cm

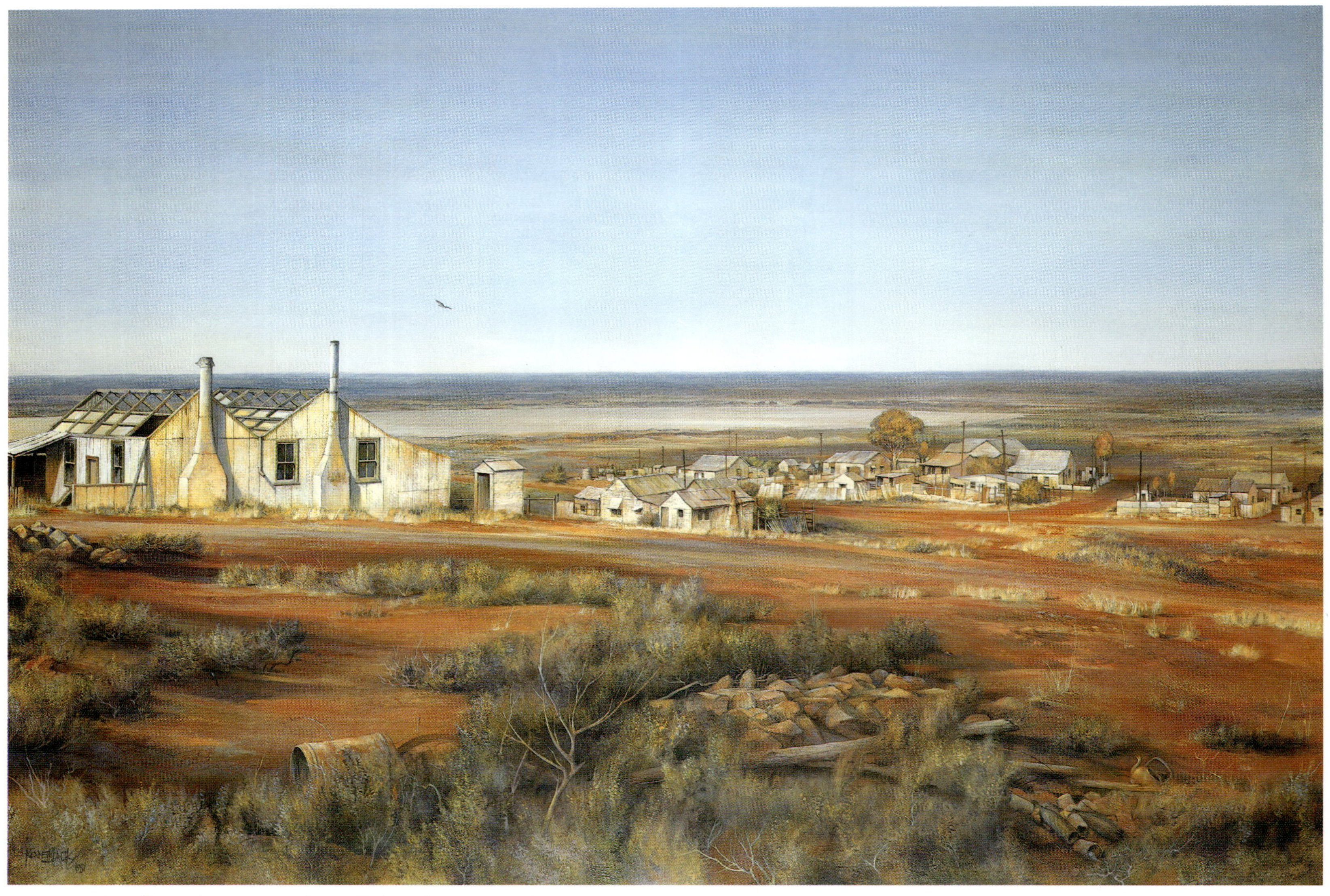

Plate 49 *Gwalia* 1981 (Western Australia) acrylic, 122 × 183 cm

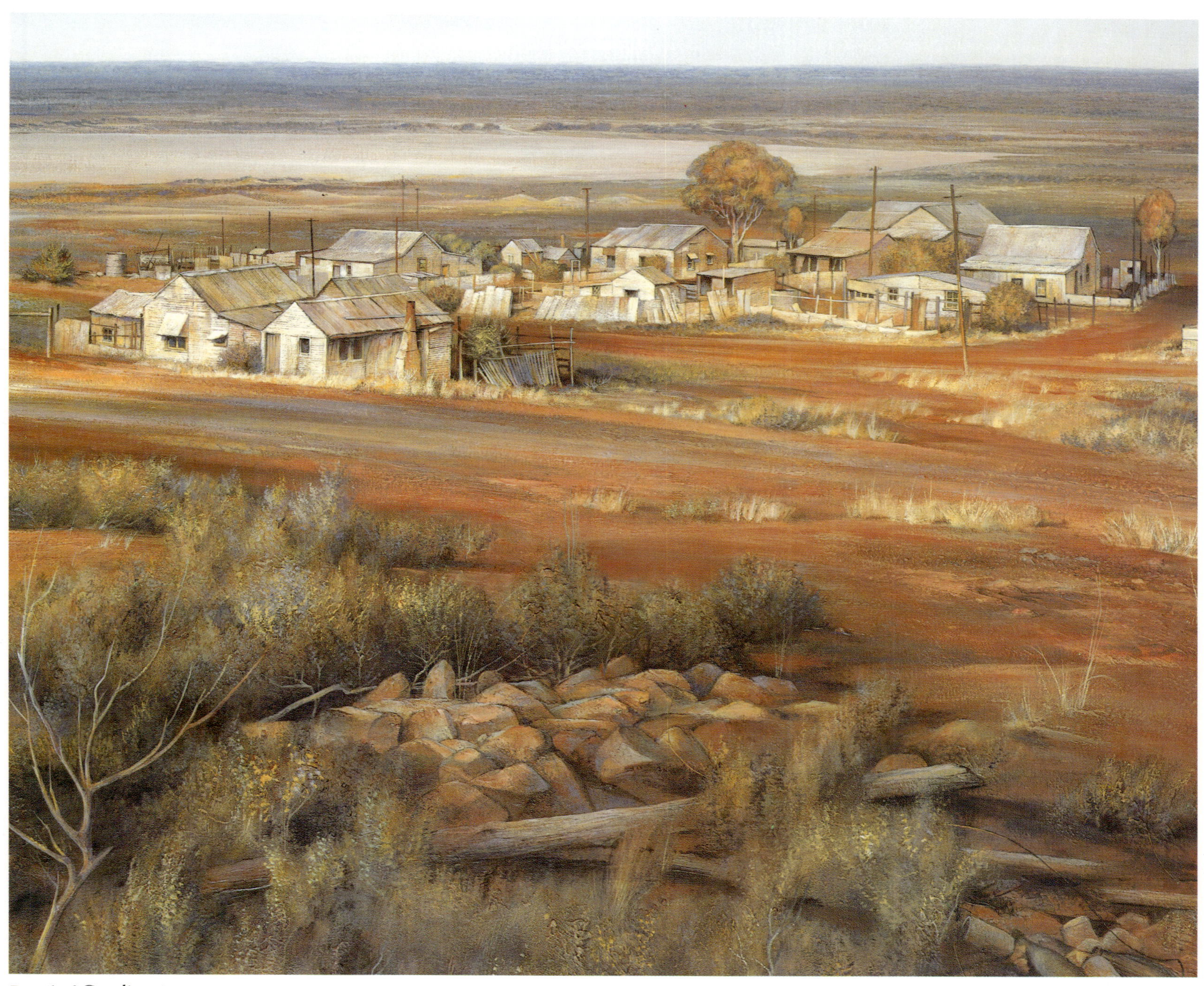

Detail of *Gwalia* (Plate 49)

Although he had many exhibitions in other states, Kenneth Jack did not have a one-man exhibition in Melbourne until 1974, several years after his retrospective in Adelaide. He had a long association with Australian Galleries in Melbourne, which sold his work, but he was reluctant to have an exhibition, possibly because he felt uneasy about the kind of reception he would receive from the critics. In the event, the exhibition was a great success. Lloyd Rees wrote the introduction to the catalogue and by this time Jack was quite sure of his direction. He had realised what his unique mission as a painter was to be and he embarked on a project to paint all the nooks and corners of the outback. He identified with the 'band of new explorers for oil and minerals in their four-wheel-drive vehicles going to ever more inaccessible places. In my case it is to see and experience places at first hand — places which in quite a number of cases have hardly been tracked by the artists. And this searching and knowing of the shape of things belongs to the twentieth century in just the same way as "hard-edge", "colour field" or "abstract-expressionism".'[18]

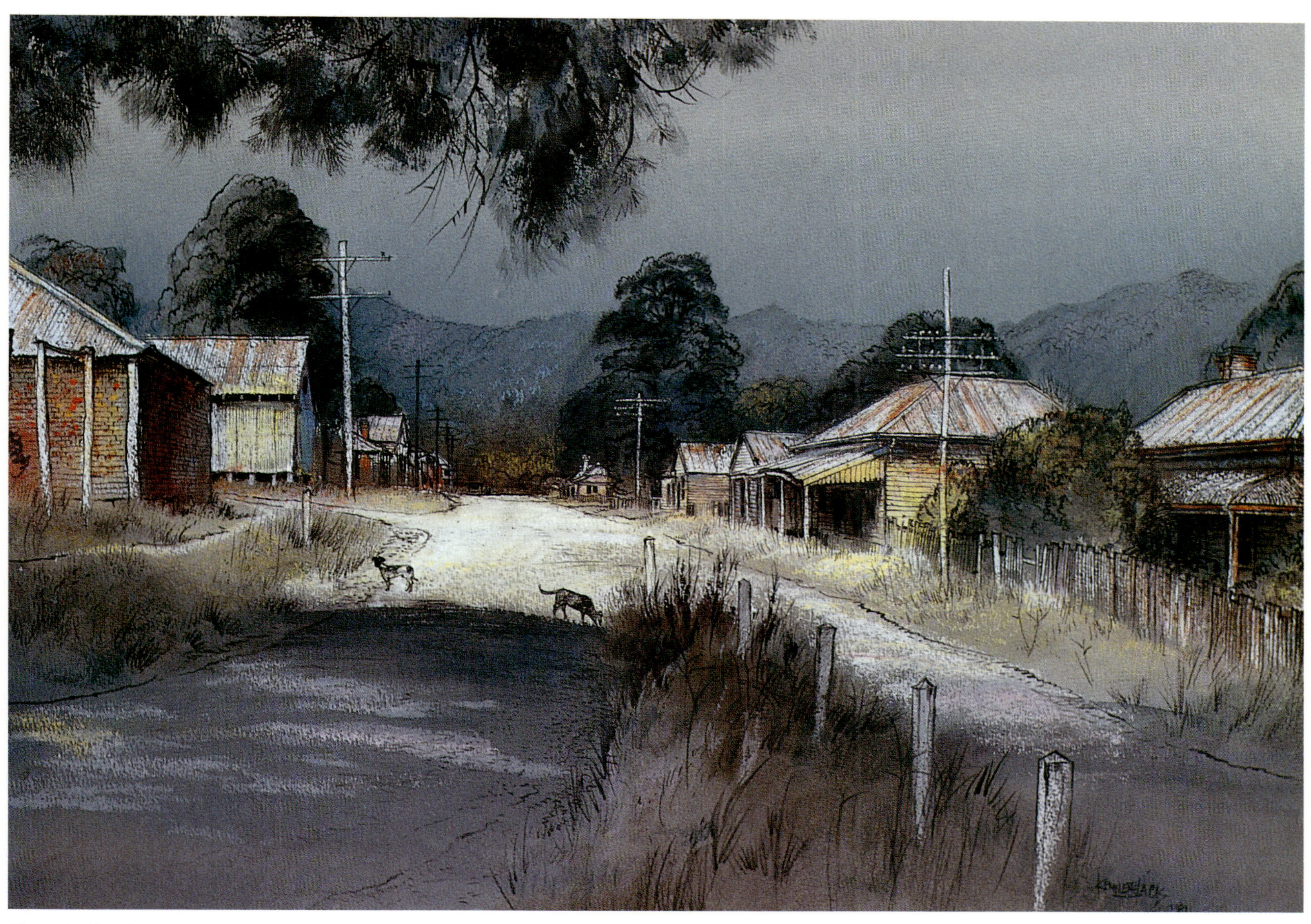

Plate 50 *Jamieson* 1981 (Victoria) pencil, oil pastel and watercolour, 32 × 46 cm

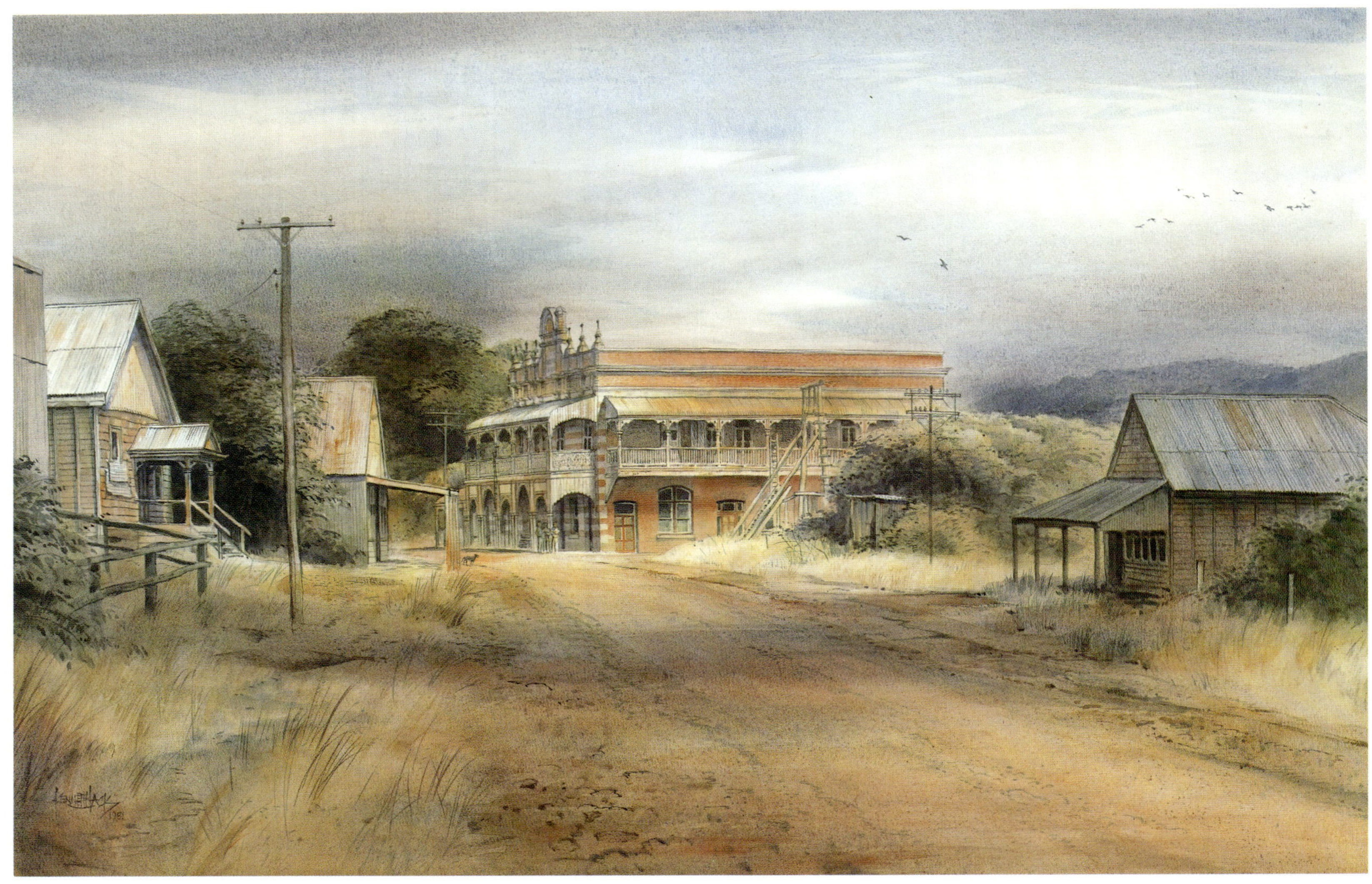

Plate 51 *Imperial Hotel, Ravenswood* 1981 (Queensland) watercolour, 47 × 72 cm

*Ravenswood has been able to preserve much of its
old gold mining history because it is situated well off
the main highway between Townsville and Charters
Towers. This is fortunate because one of the
treasures is the very ornate and rather eccentrically
designed Imperial Hotel with its verandah up to the
second floor and its decorative parapet. It still
retains its batwing doors into the bar. In contrast the
hall and the shop on the left are of simple design.*

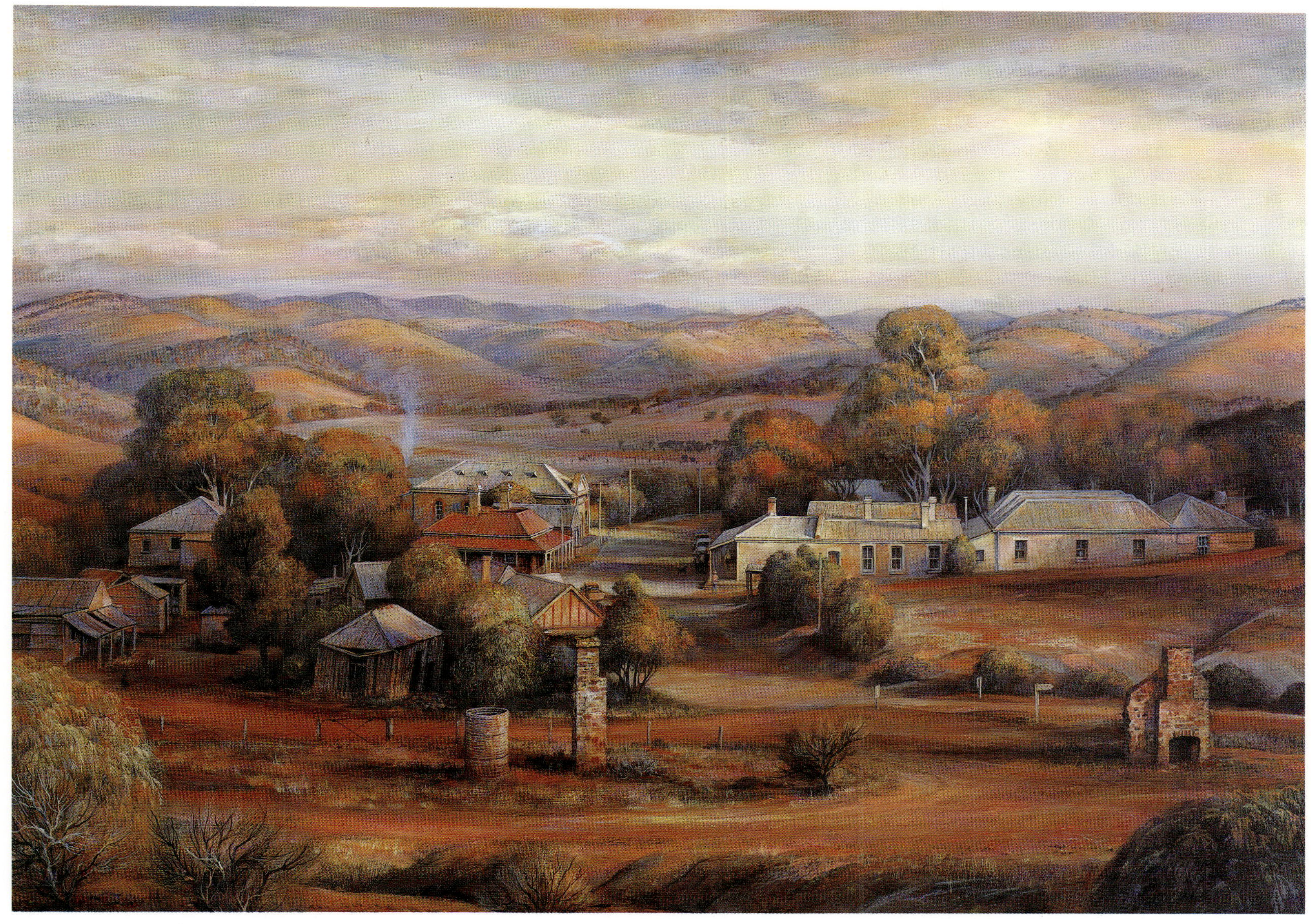

Plate 52 *Evening Shadows, Blinman* 1982 (South Australia) acrylic, 64 × 91 cm

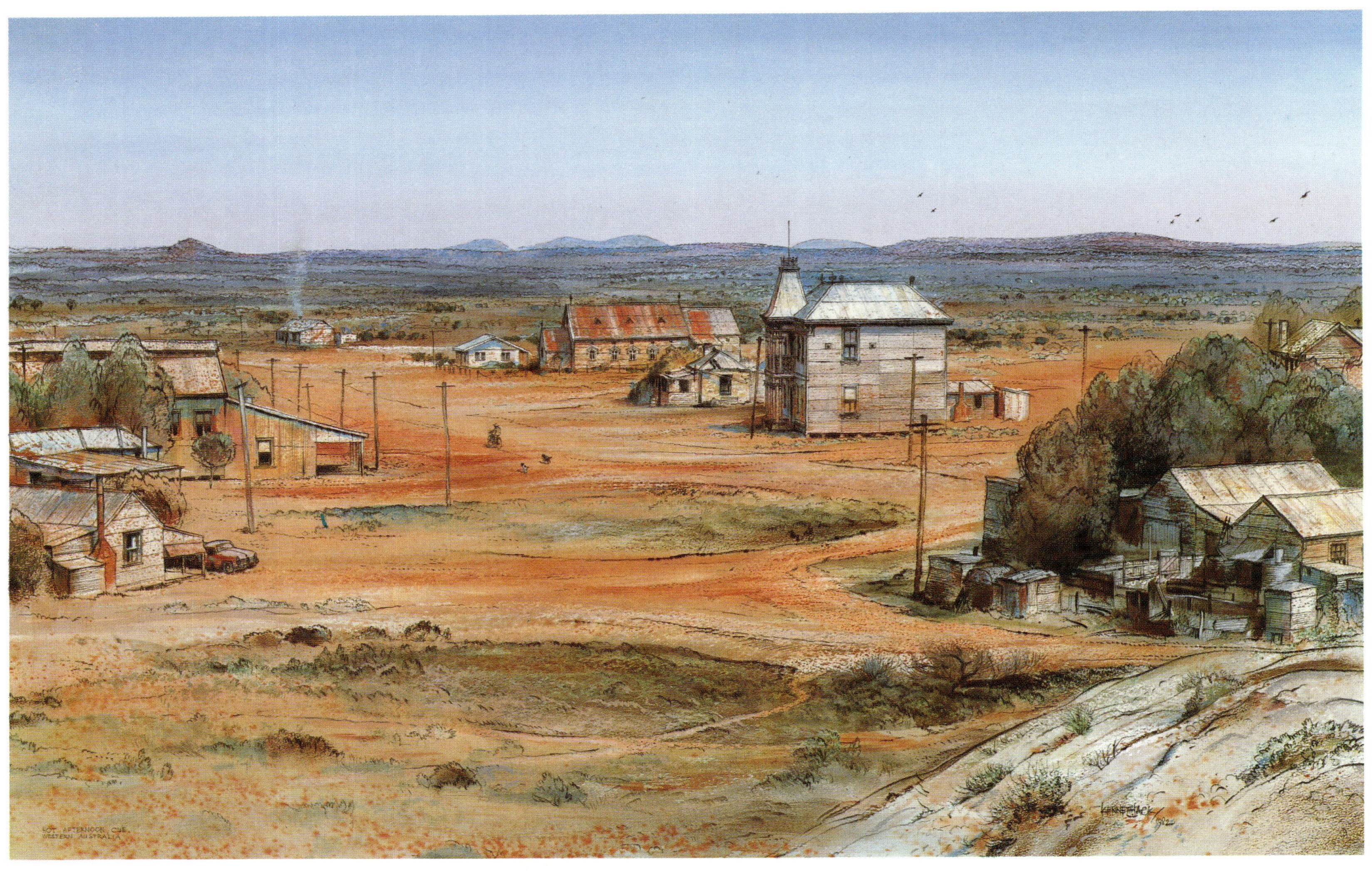

Plate 53 *Hot Afternoon, Cue* 1982 (Western Australia) pencil, oil pastel and watercolour, 50 × 79 cm

KENNETH JACK'S AUSTRALIA

It was not only his early experiences on excursions or holidays with his parents which helped to form Jack's idea of the special character of the Australian countryside. A specific experience is often the door through which we pass to understanding, or at least which leads us to it. In children, whose minds are still unmoulded and open to influence, images seen during the crucial childhood years can play a major role in the future development of the man. In the case of Kenneth Jack it was not the reproduction of a painting of some Thames barges by the British artist Charles Pears which hung in their house that influenced him, but the photographs he saw in some magazines his father brought home; *Table Talk* and *Home*. The work of one particular photographer, Harold Cazneaux, was to sink deep. Besides photographing cities, he photographed the landscape and farms of inland New South Wales. The young Kenneth Jack was fascinated by these places, the beautiful trees, ramshackle farms, sheds and fences and the way in which the photographer imposed his own stamp on them. These images encouraged him to look for such subjects when he went to the country.[19]

Jack may have liked to draw great cathedrals and Renaissance buildings, but the nearest to such things he could find in Australia were buildings like Flinders Street Station, which he drew at the age of fifteen for his school magazine. Town hall clocks and church spires attracted the young artist's attention and his future development follows in a logical progression apart from the encounter with semi-abstraction during his concern with printmaking, when he belonged to the group of contemporary artists who were responsible for the revival of the art after many years of neglect.

We see what we look for and conversely we don't see what we don't know, in spite of the many misconceptions which exist as to what and how an artist draws. He draws what is in his head rather than what is outside him; paradoxically, all art has been based on art. Wölfflin pointed out a long time ago that: 'It is a dilettantist notion that an artist could ever take up his stand before nature without any preconceived ideas. But what he has taken over is a concept of representation, and how this concept goes on working in him, is much more important than anything he has taken from direct observation.'[20]

The idea of Australia which we find in Kenneth Jack's work developed from his various early experiences, as we have seen, nourished by the work of such artists as Donald Friend and Drysdale, who came into prominence after the war. Paintings such as Drysdale's *Sofala* (1947), *The Cricketers* (1947) and *West Wyalong* (1949) showed another Australia from the one we find in the work of Streeton, Roberts and Heysen. They did not paint 'the outback', nor ever imagined the continent covered by the surreal sunless sky Drysdale devised to project elements of the timelessness of the continent, but which was based on an actual experience of dust storms during the great drought of 1944. The black sky was an imaginative device to express certain poetical ideas about the land-scape, just as the English painter L. S. Lowry found a means to depict the

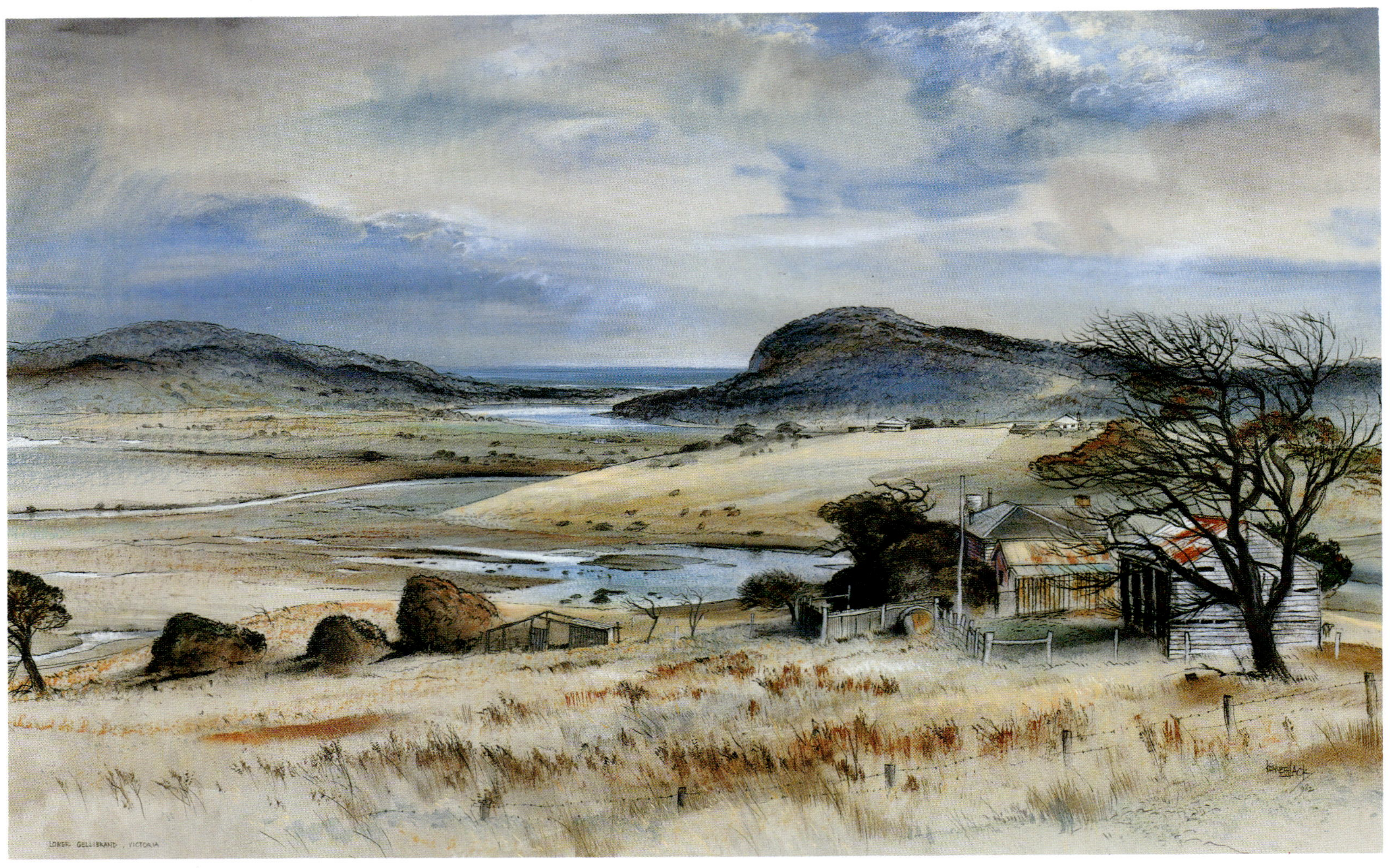

Plate 54 *Lower Gellibrand* 1982 (Victoria) carbon pencil, oil pastel and watercolour, 50 × 79 cm

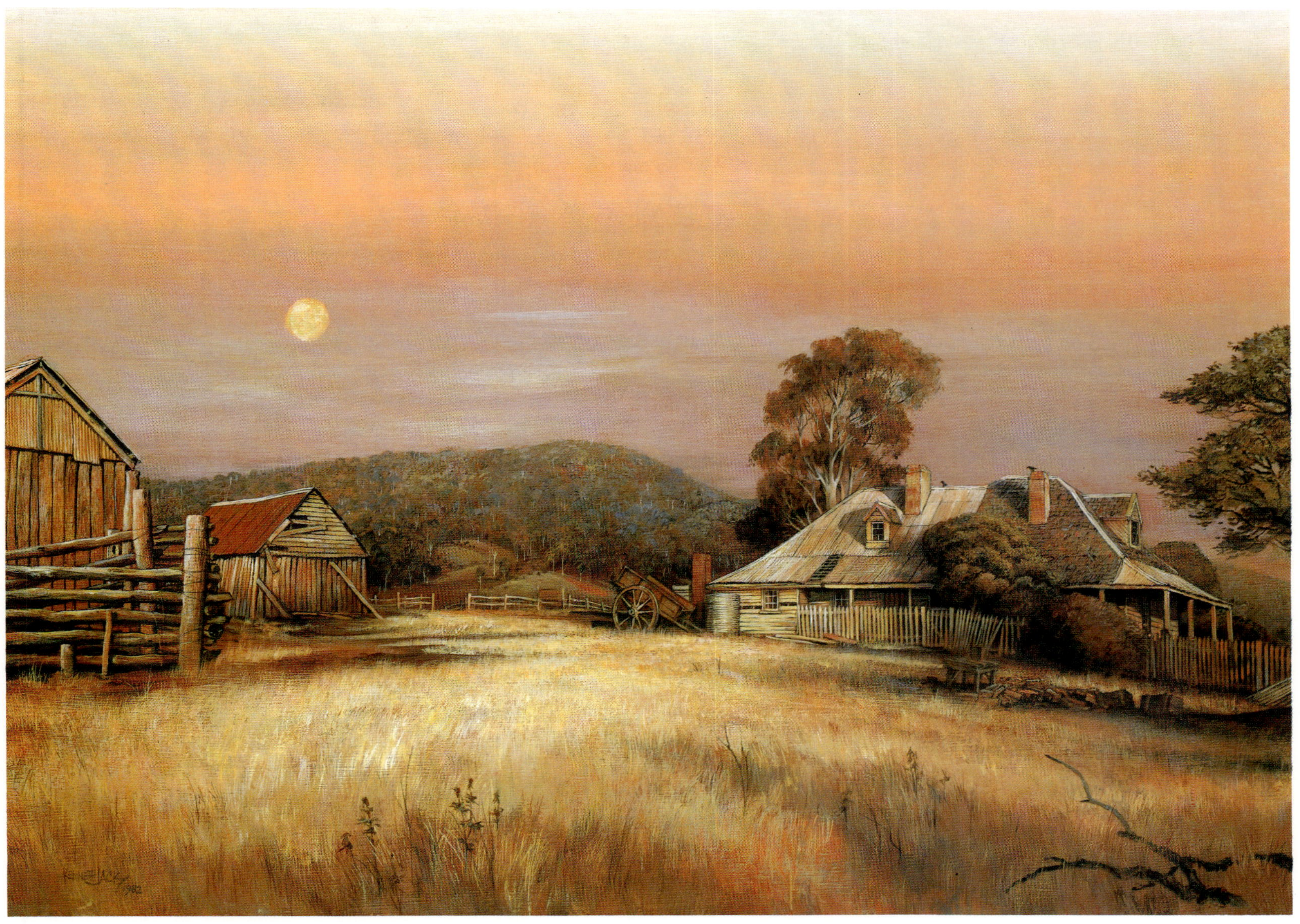

Plate 55 *Moonrise, Dysart* 1982 (Tasmania) acrylic, 40 × 60 cm

grubby, industrial landscape of Salford — as Lord Clark once pointed out — by discovering that the north was not black but white.

Jack took this sunless sky into his work as did many of the painters of the 1950s; at one time they even painted a sky entirely black to create a surreal effect, but gradually Jack's skies have brightened and he has developed his characteristic blond colouring which is quite similar to the late paintings of Tom Roberts.

When he was in his forties, Kenneth Jack realised that deep down his work did not please him. He felt that after so much learning he should be able to do better and his experiences in the outback affected the direction of his work. A new medium helped: 'When acrylic paint came on the market it seemed to make it possible for me to paint in a more realistic manner; it suited my particular temperament as it was quick drying. I could rest my hand while working on any part within minutes of painting and this was an advantage when coming to the details. Oils tended to go muddy but acrylics could be kept clean and rich.'[21]

His best teachers have been persistence and perseverance: 'One of the lessons of experience I've learned is a very simple philosophy indeed, that if one works hard with honesty at his art, something is bound to happen.'[22]

And he is suspicious of anything which comes too easily. If he gets an effect quickly, he will often go over it, deliberately to try for something extra, being

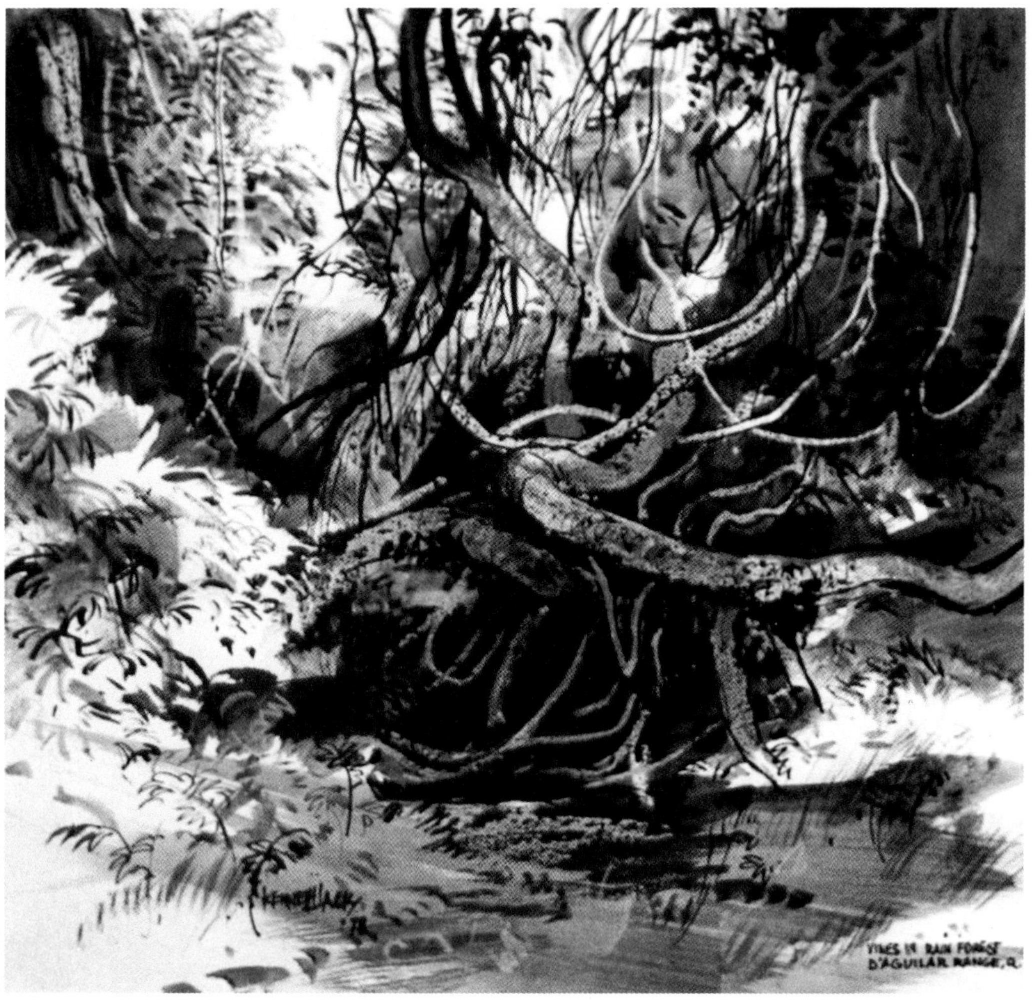

Fig. 23 *Vines in Rain Forest* 1978 (Queensland) quill pen and wash and white crayon, 20 × 20 cm

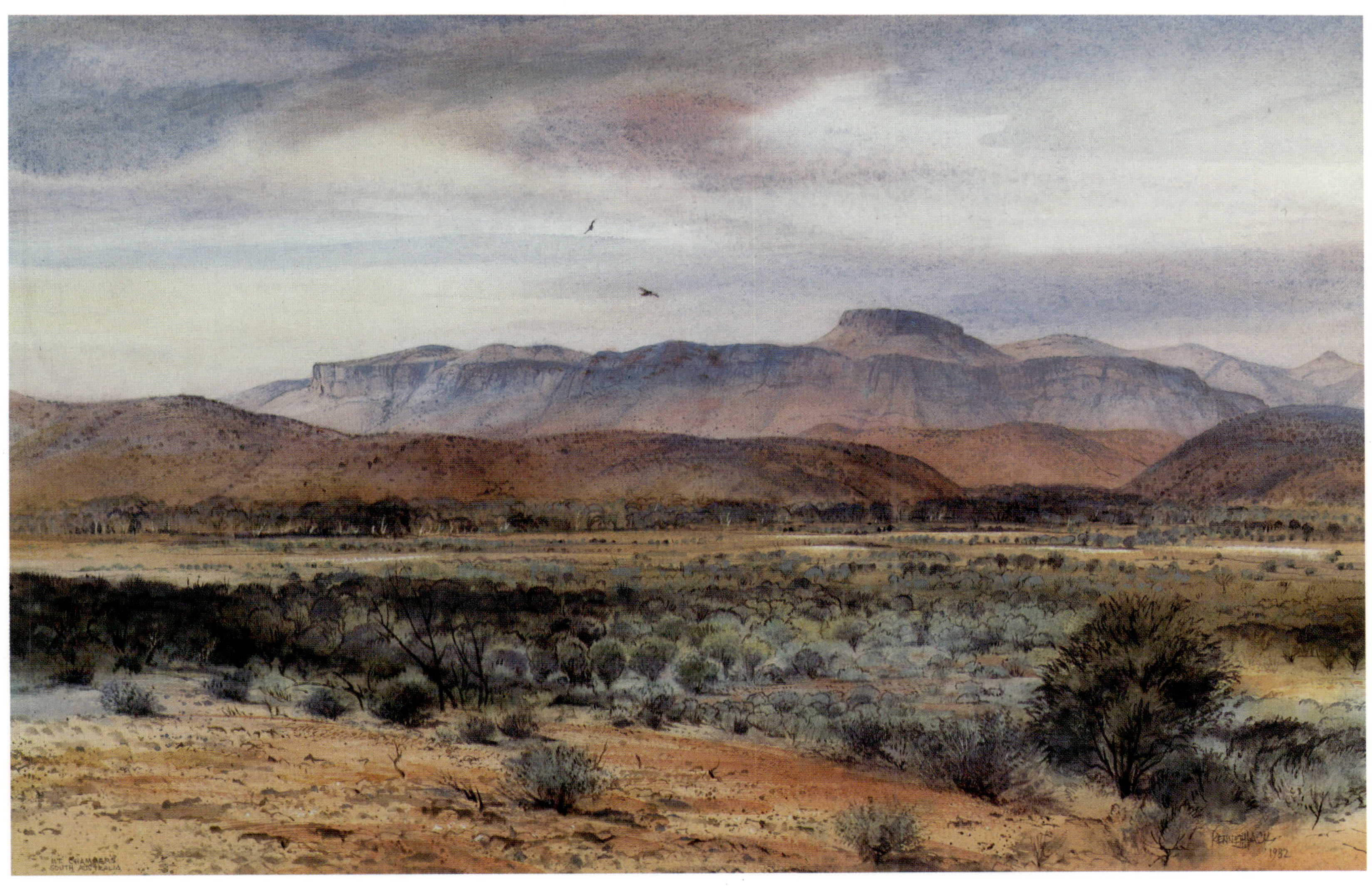

Plate 56 *Mt. Chambers* 1982 (South Australia) watercolour, 31 × 49 cm

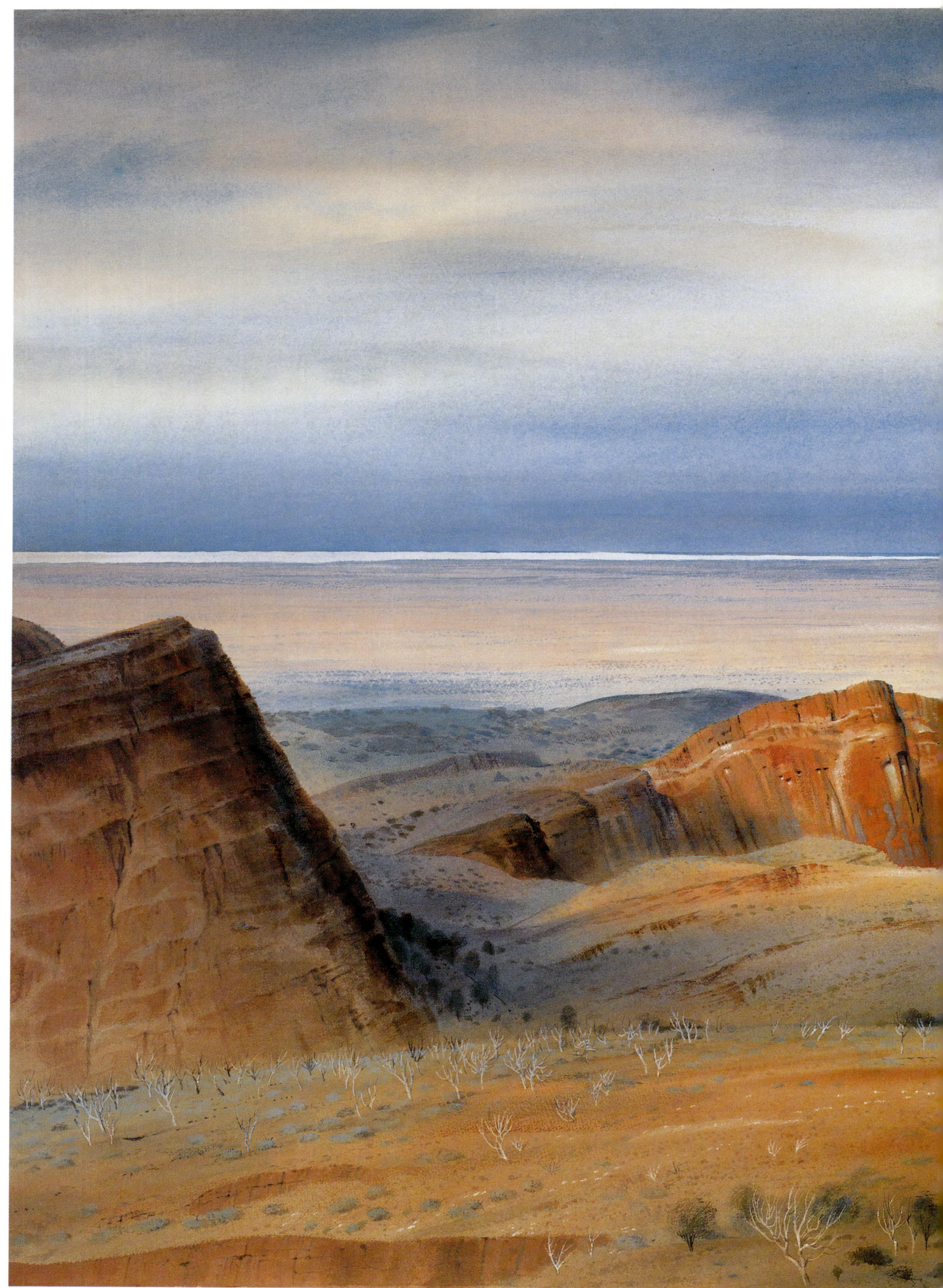

Plate 57 *Eastwards to Lake Frome (Salt)* 1987 (South Australia) watercolour, 101 × 151 cm

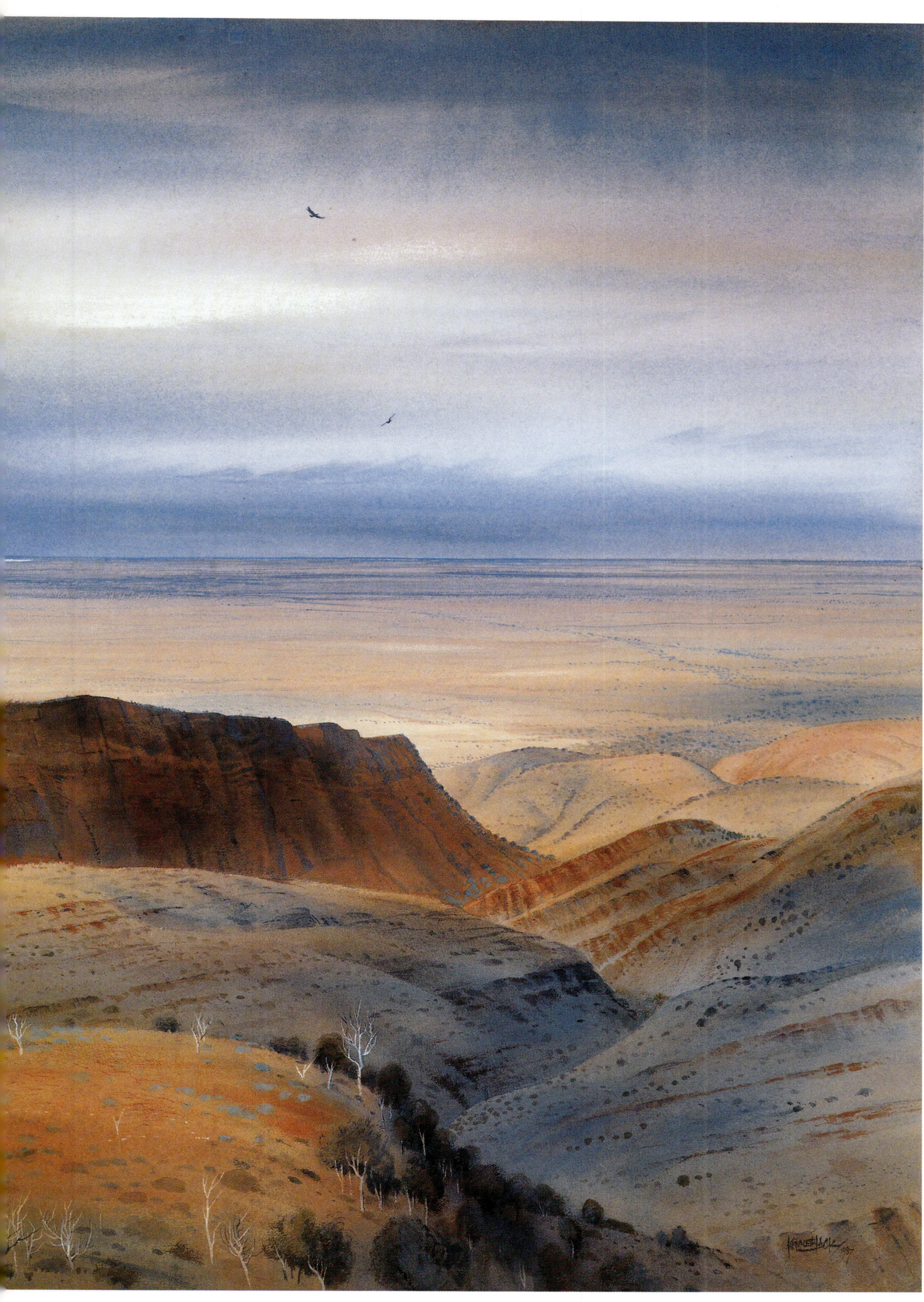

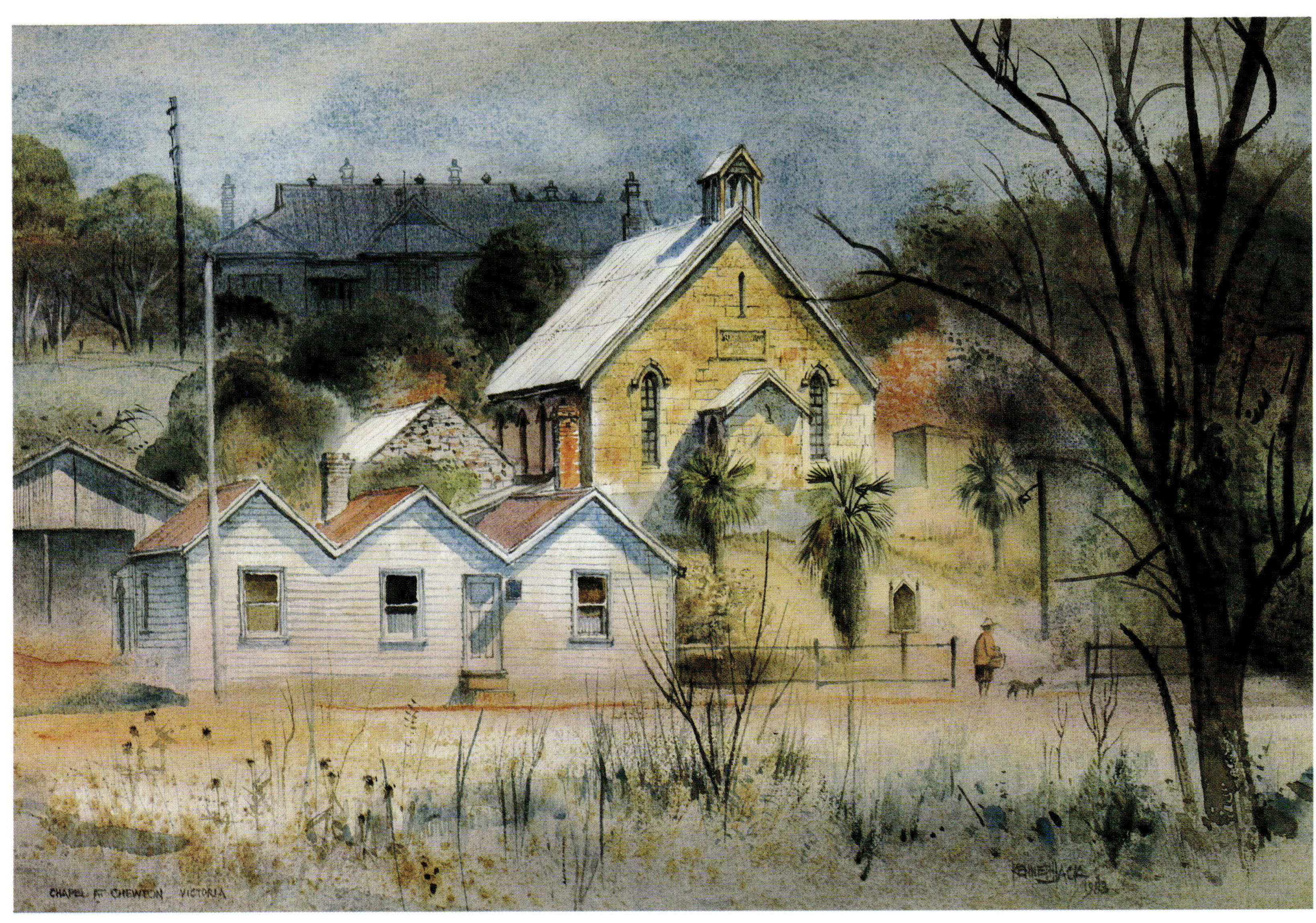

Plate 58 *Chapel at Chewton* 1983 (Victoria) watercolour, 27 × 39 cm

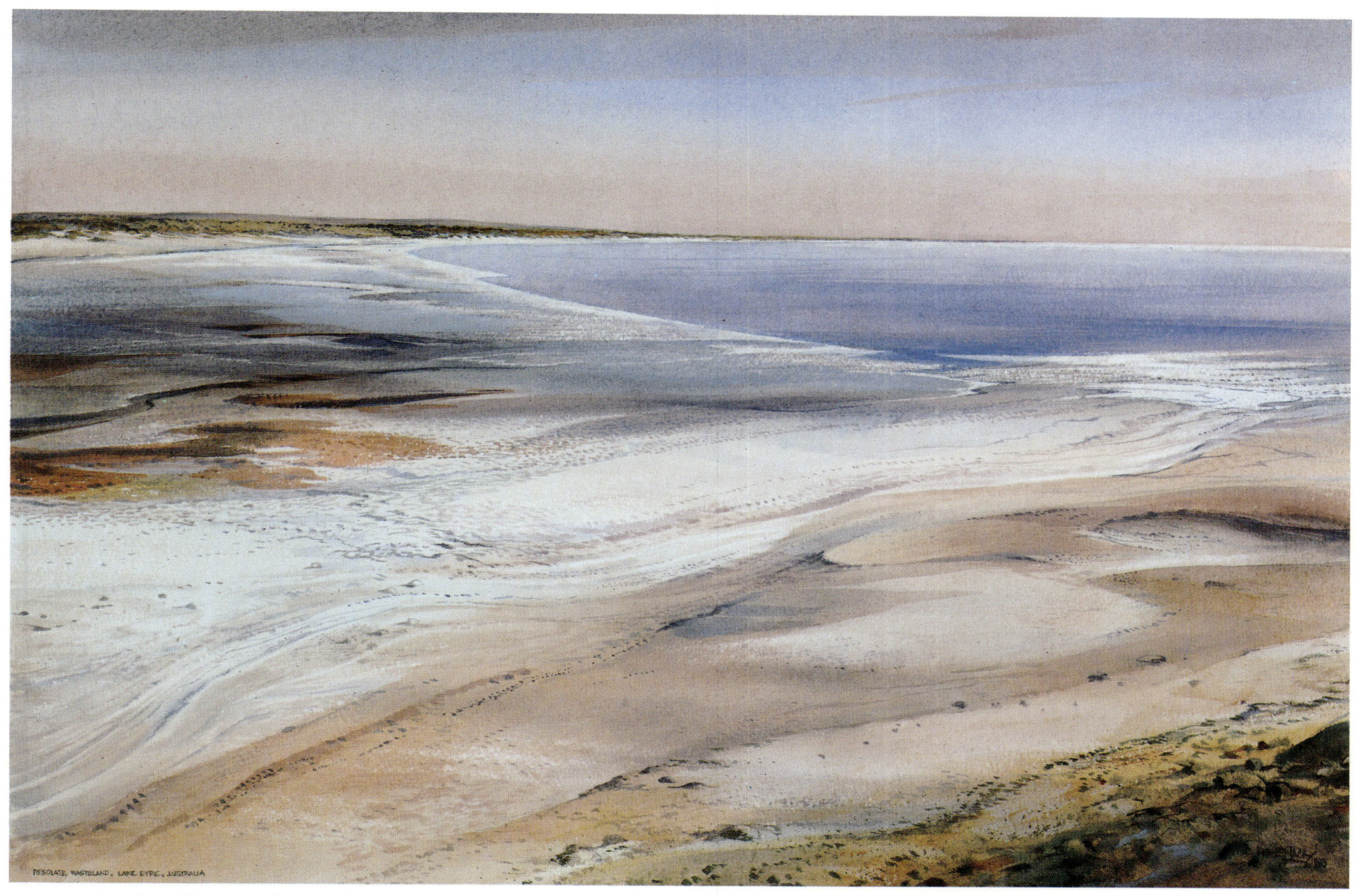

Plate 59 *Desolate Wasteland, Lake Eyre* 1983 (South Australia) watercolour, 36 × 53 cm

Lake Eyre is a place I have visited a number of times for its many picturesque scenes: the marvellous colours of the sky as the sun rises and the first rays hit the ripples on the sand dunes around the lake's edges; the sun setting over the lake; the fantastic clarity of the stars of the Milky Way at night.

To my way of thinking Lake Eyre, a vast inland salt lake below sea level, is really a drainage point for several of the world's oldest rivers (the Frome, the Neales, the Finke and others), and is one of the most impressive sights in Australia. This particular painting is an attempt to convey some of the sense of desolation one experiences so far out there in the vast inland.

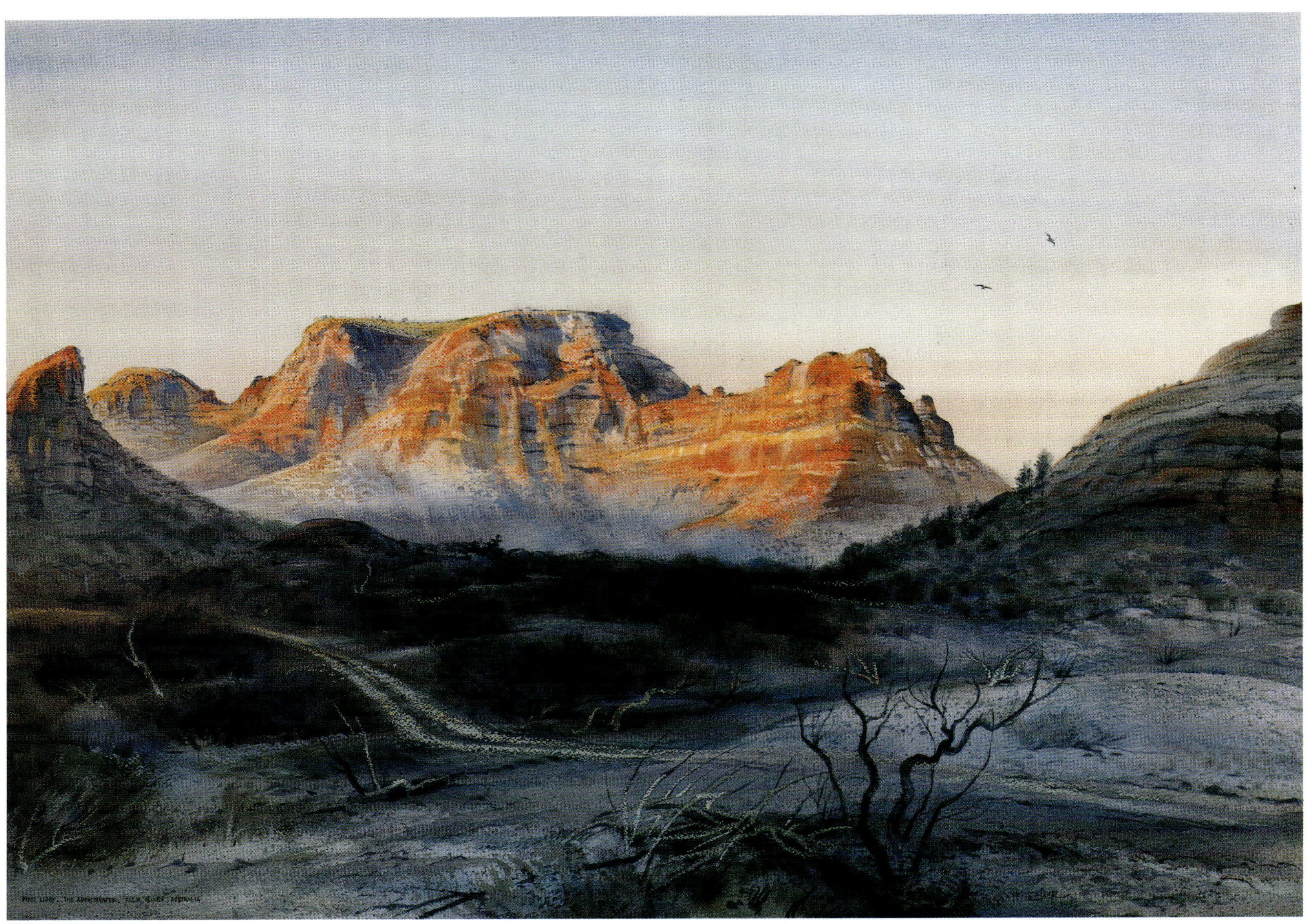

Plate 60 *First Light, the Amphitheatre, Palm Valley* 1983 (Northern Territory) watercolour and oil pastel, 50 × 71 cm

very cautious of the slick and quick. In his student days he was warned by John Rowell about cheap effects by artists whom he called 'the look and put' school.

The realistic nature of his work has drawn Kenneth Jack more toward some of the great artists of the past than toward many of his contemporaries. He always loved Rembrandt, but his idol during the last twenty years has been Turner. Both these artists have a preference for the warm, yellowish colour which is also noticeable in Jack. He is also very interested in the British watercolour school and particularly in the work of Bonington, Girtin and Cotman. He finds a strong affinity with Cotman's series of etchings *Architectural Antiquities of Norfolk*, 1822, which in feeling are not unlike some of Kenneth Jack's pure pen line drawings. These predilections link him with an important concept in British landscape painting of the eighteenth and nineteenth centuries, the idea of the *picturesque*.

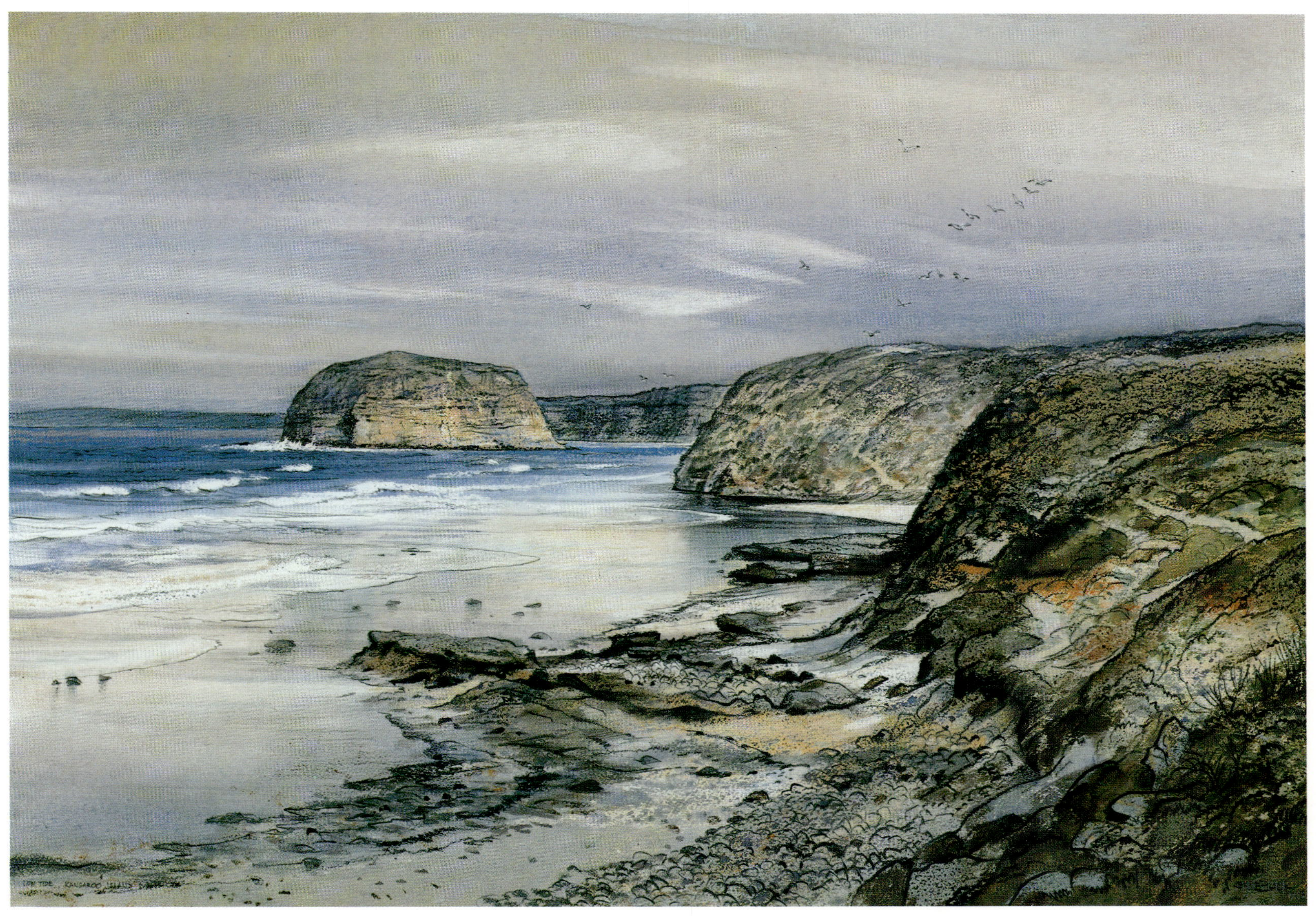

Plate 61 *Low Tide, Kangaroo Island* 1983 (South Australia) pencil, oil pastel and watercolour, 33 × 48.3 cm

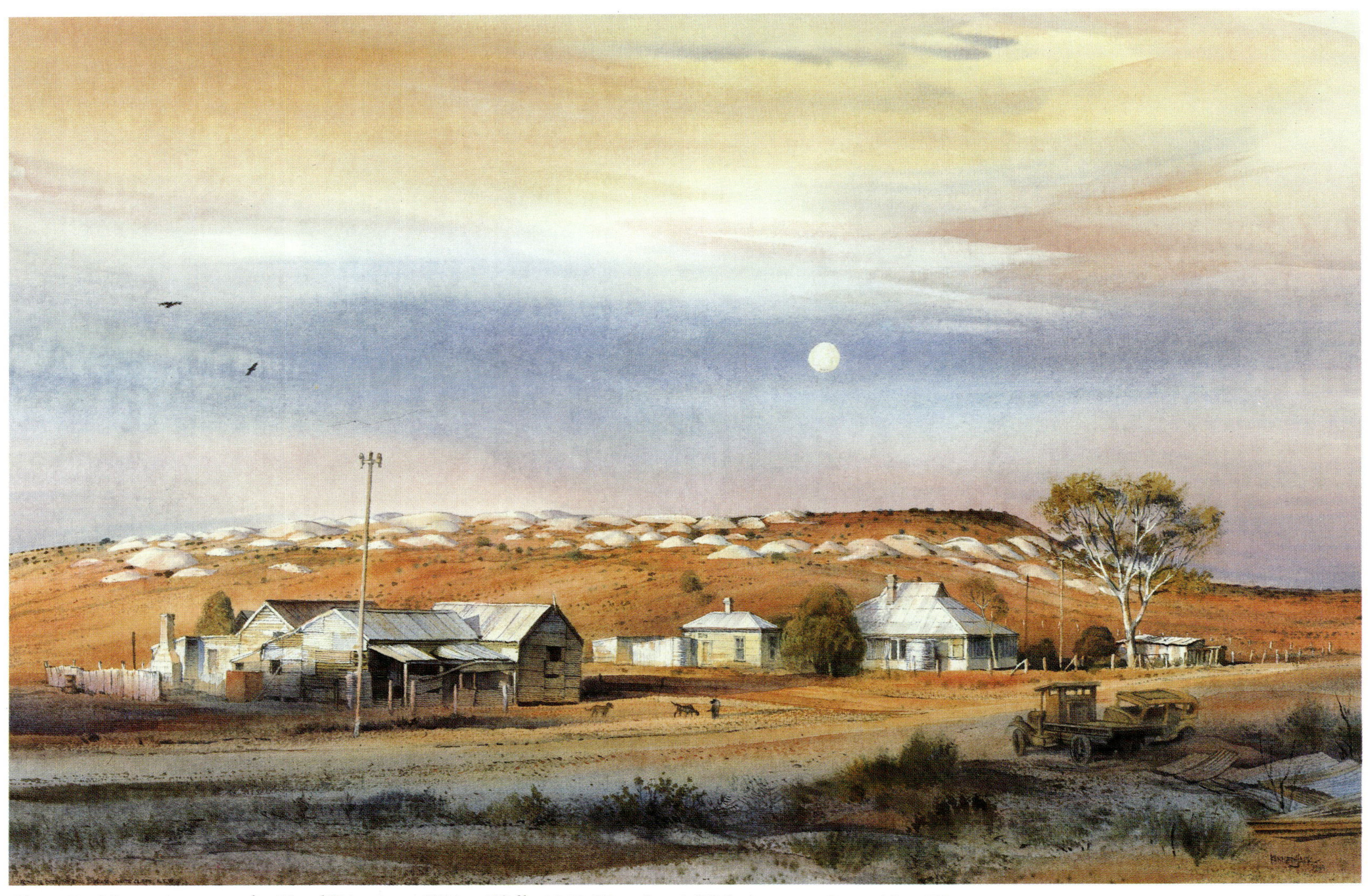

Plate 62 *Moonrise over the Opal Diggings, White Cliffs* 1983 (New South Wales) watercolour, 46 × 72 cm

This is the area in Australia where opals were first discovered, dating back over one hundred years. It is approximately one hundred kilometres north of Wilcannia in the north-west corner of New South Wales. Many of the early buildings have disappeared in recent years, but I was lucky enough to see many like those in the painting still remaining.

Many times I took the family to this strange area to camp, because I had plenty of subjects for drawing while they were happy to scratch around the old diggings with small trowels finding pieces of opal missed by the miners.

The picturesque was a fashionable notion at the time of the first exploration of Australia. William Gilpin, an amateur artist and writer who formulated the criterion of the picturesque,[23] had read with interest the accounts of Cook's voyages. Several standards of what produced picturesque beauty were devised. Uvedale Price, for instance, considered the picturesque to be distinguished by roughness, sudden variations and irregularities.[24] Australia was seen as somewhere exotic and some of the first artists who worked here, like Conrad Martens, John Skinner Prout and George French Angas, consciously saw it through the notion of the picturesque.[25]

Inherent in Kenneth Jack's work is an idea of what is picturesque in the Australia which he paints. The continent may no longer be quite so exotic or 'distant' to his eyes, but the buildings and landscape which attract him have certain things in common.

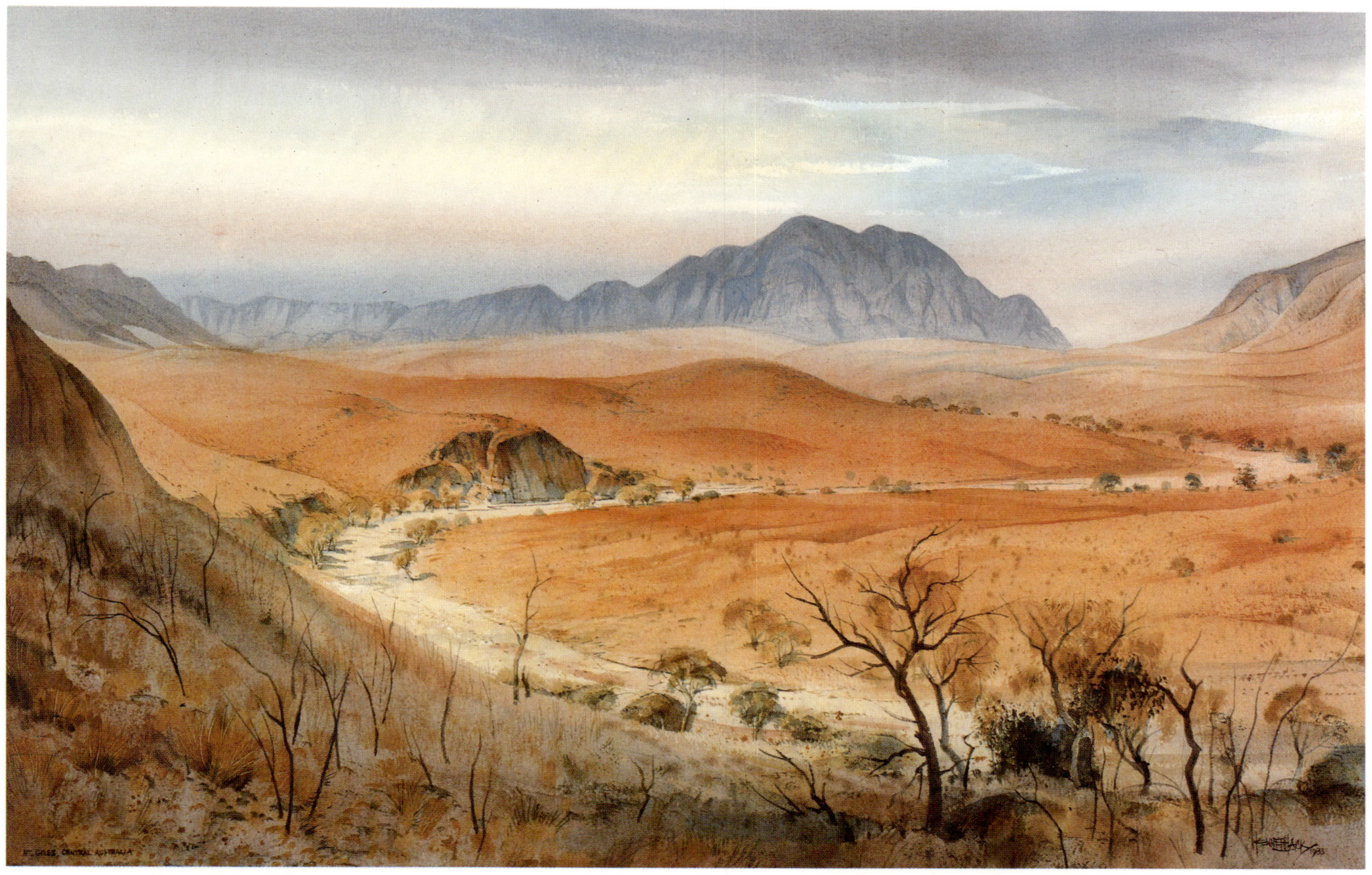

Plate 63 *Mt. Giles, Central Australia* 1983, watercolour, 35 × 55 cm

I found this marvellous subject after walking through the full length of Ormiston Gorge, which in itself is probably the finest gorge in the Macdonnell Ranges. On rounding a bend I could see part of Mt Giles. I climbed to a high position part way up the wall on one side and made a drawing from this rather precarious position. On descending I decided to find out what the full shape of Mt Giles looked like.

The gorge opened out into a large pound, and I climbed a steep slope to the foot of a vertical cliff for a better view. I looked across a dry river bed which snaked its way across it to the superbly beautiful shape of Mt Giles in the background.

By choosing an early afternoon light I was able to show the forms of the ranges but still retain the feeling of a hot day.

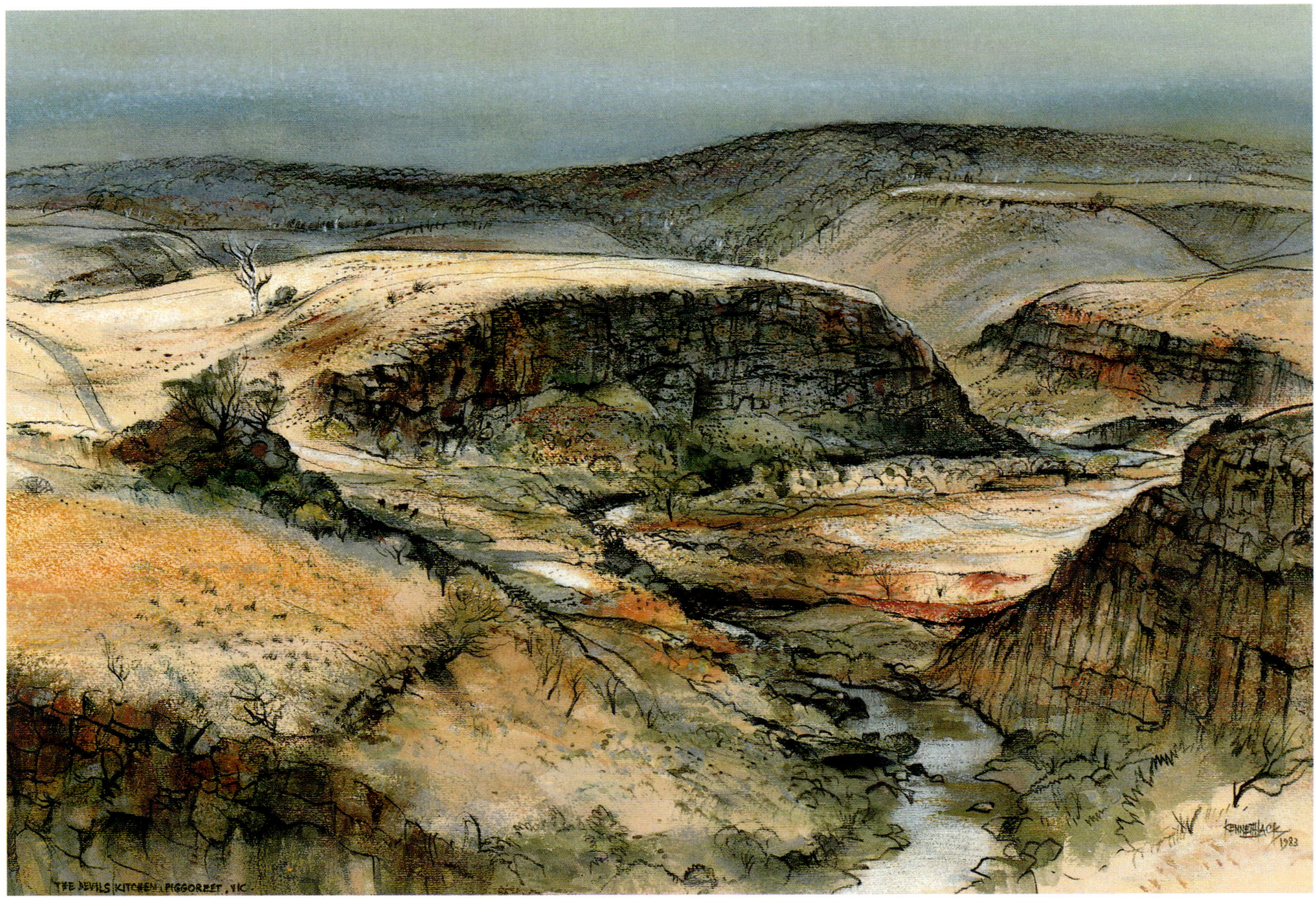

Plate 64 *The Devil's Kitchen, Piggoreet* 1983 (Victoria) pencil, oil pastel and watercolour, 31 × 46 cm

Piggoreet is a few kilometres south of Scarsdale and about thirty kilometres south-west of Ballarat. The name on the map, 'Piggoreet', is intriguing enough to draw the traveller to it, but, when right next to it one also sees 'Woady Yaloak Creek' and 'Devil's Kitchen', it is altogether too much to resist.

I have visited Piggoreet several times. The creek has carved its way through a particularly rugged piece of basalt terrain which looks as though it has all been stirred up in a kitchen pot — it is quite easy to see how the explorer who first saw it gave it its name. The cattle in the bottom of the valley help to give an idea of the scale of this unusual area. I chose oil pastels, watercolour and pencil as I felt this mixture of media could best show the roughness of the textured forms.

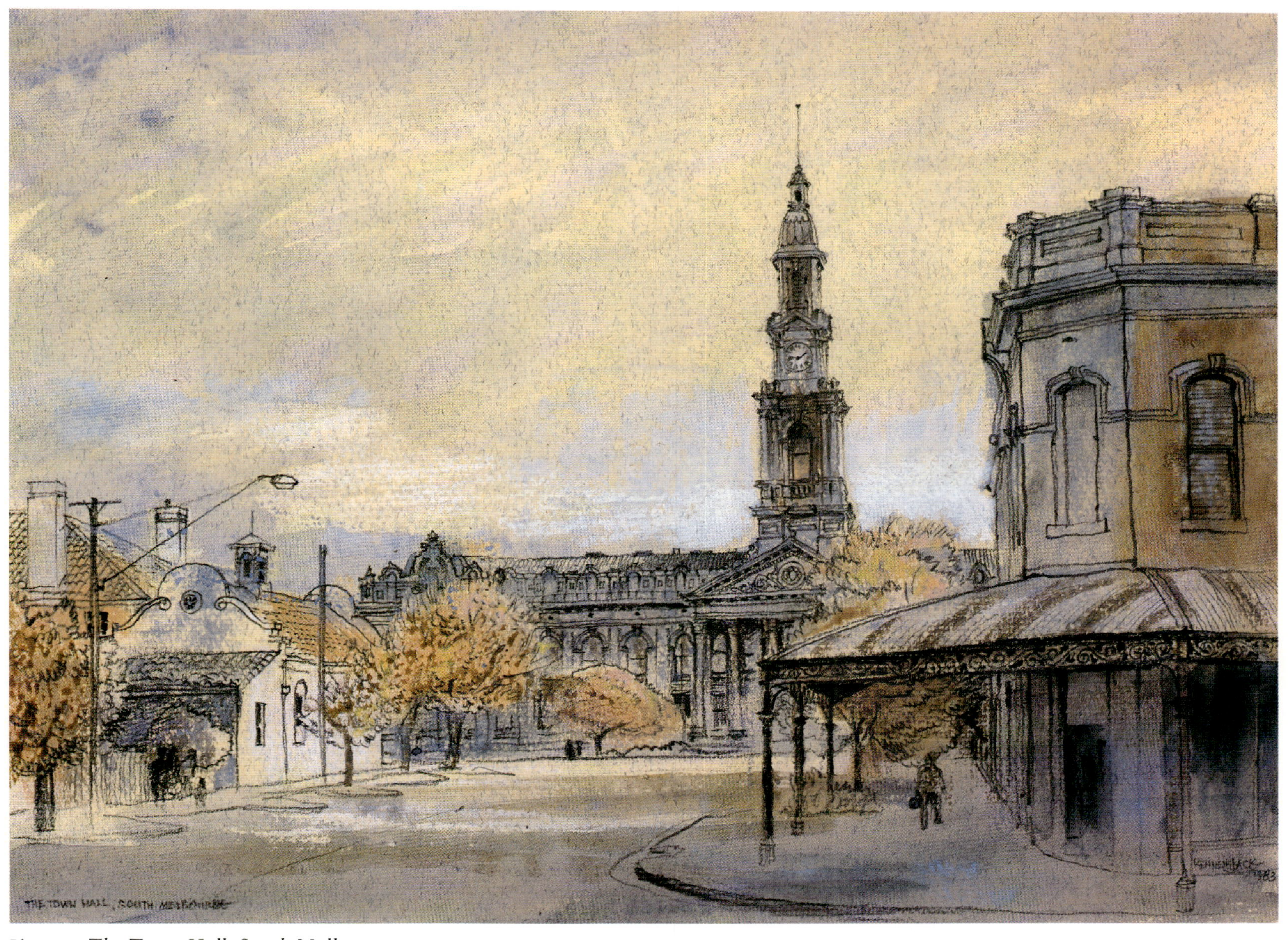

Plate 65 *The Town Hall, South Melbourne* 1983, pencil, aquarelle crayon and watercolour, 21.6 × 30.5 cm

Today, colonial Australia has been transformed into our Arcadia, and the old buildings, barns, ghost towns and deserted mine shafts are remnants of the nineteenth century which produced modern Australia. These relics have become charged with meaning and attract the eyes of poets and painters. In spite of the long denigration of realism in art, they are valid subjects. Their inherent poetry lies in the fact that they are the ruins of another world; they represent a rustic, rural life from which we have distanced ourselves. That world is far more distant and different from ours than appears merely by the years which separate us from it. It may only be fifty or a hundred years, but what is now coming to an end is not a century but a millennium.

Kenneth Jack responded to the imminent destruction of this old Australia and as time has passed he has become more and more motivated to paint as much of it as he can before it disappears. On almost every trip to one of these typical country towns, he has noticed serious deterioration of the buildings. A verandah has been taken down, an old wall has given way and the building will probably have to be pulled down, and many of the characteristic decorations on the old buildings are disappearing, destroyed by time and weather. He has been drawn to paint just those places which seem most at risk and which may not be there the next time he visits the town.

Although many country towns near large cities have been given a new lease of life, the commuters who have taken them over have also modernised them beyond recognition. The facelift often destroys the soul. The further one goes, the more likely one is to find old buildings still retaining their original character. When they have had to be repaired, they have been fixed with materials at hand, in the spirit of the original builders.

The picturesque beauty of the original settlers' cottages and country towns is in great part the result of building the essential with the simple, even though these simple buildings were proudly embellished with filigree wrought iron. Behind the marvellously simple and basic buildings there is the metaphysical element of a dwelling as a shelter for man to protect him from the elements and provide a home for his family.

The nearest things we can find in European art to these colonial buildings and cottages are in the drawings of seventeenth-century Dutch artists, like Rembrandt, Ostade, Van Goyen and many others who felt very strongly for this kind of subject matter. They in turn inspired similar rustic landscapes in English artists like Gainsborough and Crome, through whom the influence has come to us. The special picturesque element of the outback town is not just this metaphor, but the fact that it represents a lost world.

The sensitivity of artists and poets often makes them aware, as by some kind of telepathy, of the impending destruction of some special building or place and directs them to represent it, to witness its existence in their own consciousness and sensitivity so that the idea will continue to exist when the building has been destroyed. Many artists have noticed this phenomenon. Having been attracted to a certain building, they have seen it pulled down almost the very next day. Our world makes its own effort to survive through the clairvoyance of its artists.

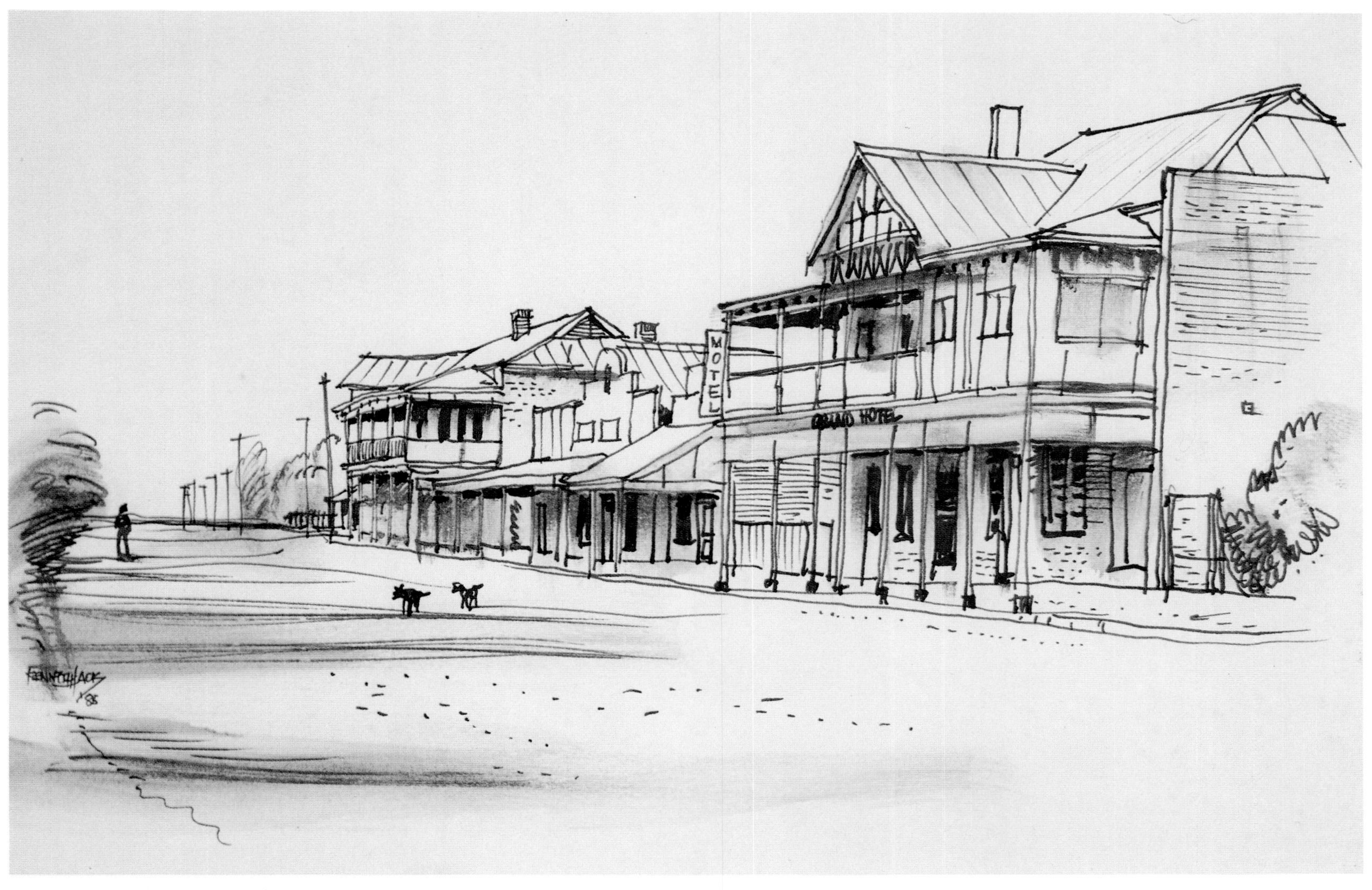

Fig. 24 *Main Street, Mt. Magnet* 1985 (Western Australia) pen, ink and smudge, 13 × 20.5 cm

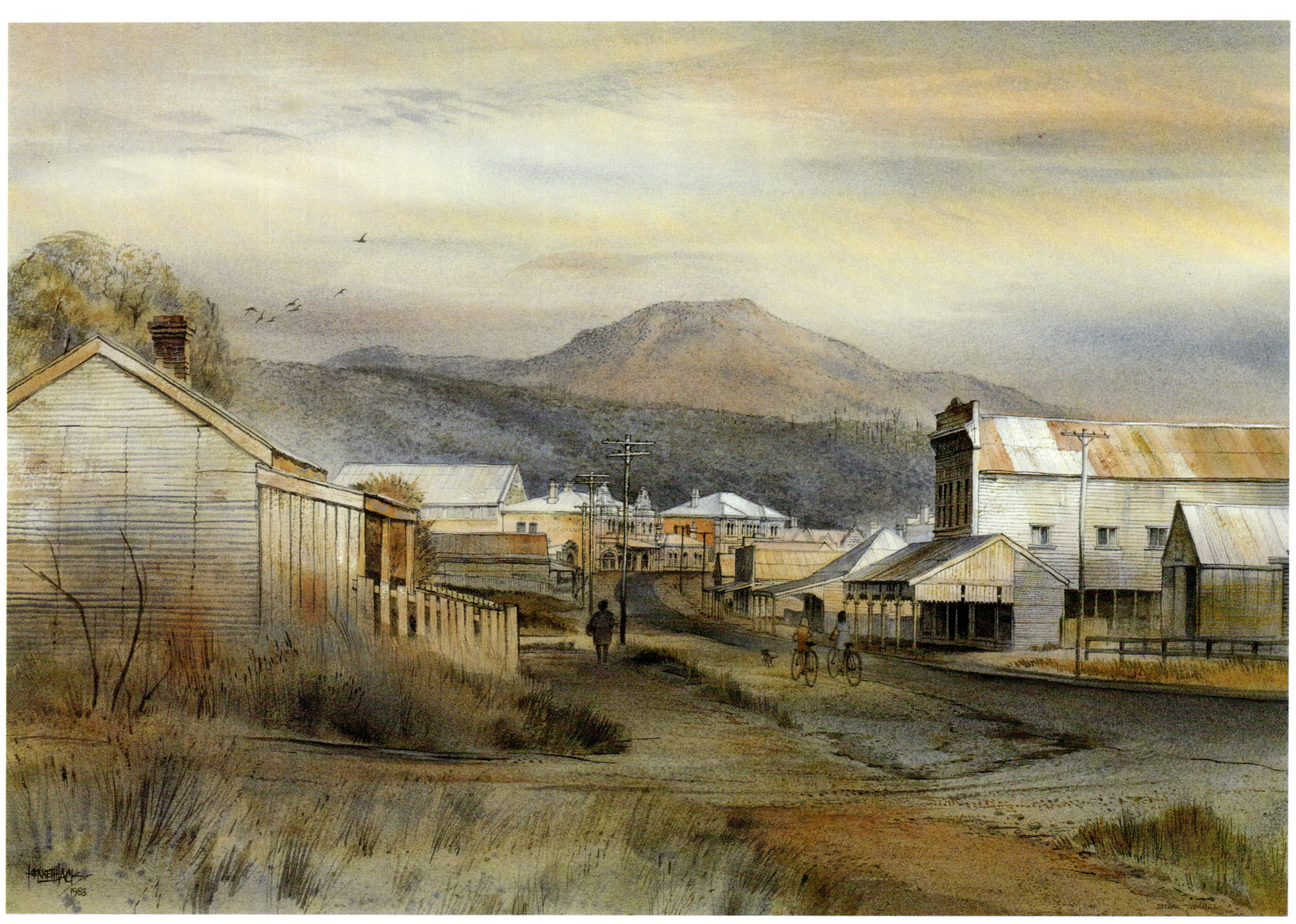

Plate 66 *Zeehan* 1983 (Tasmania) watercolour, 41 × 59 cm

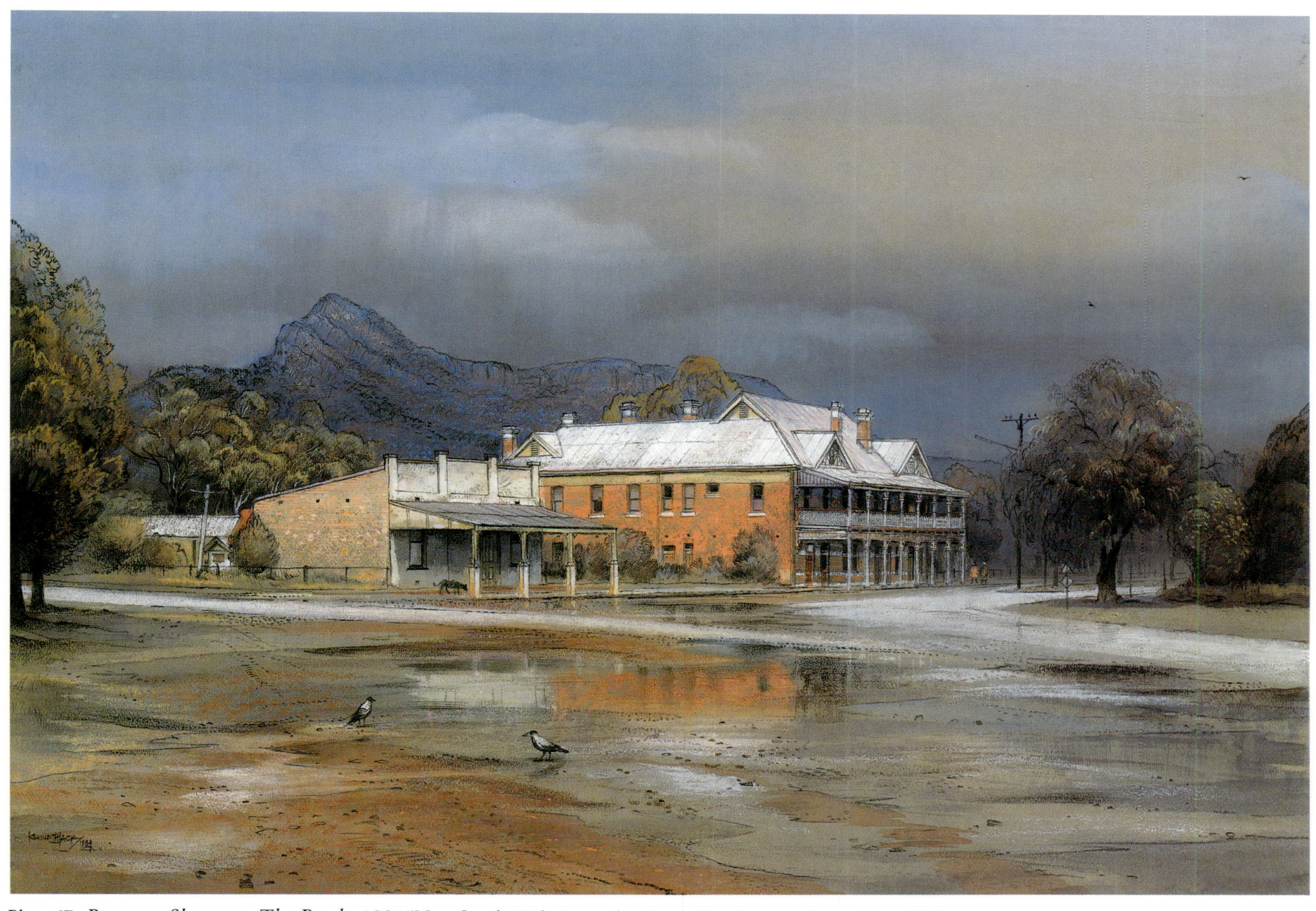

Plate 67 *Between Showers; The Rock* 1984 (New South Wales) pencil, oil pastel and watercolour, 37 × 54.5 cm

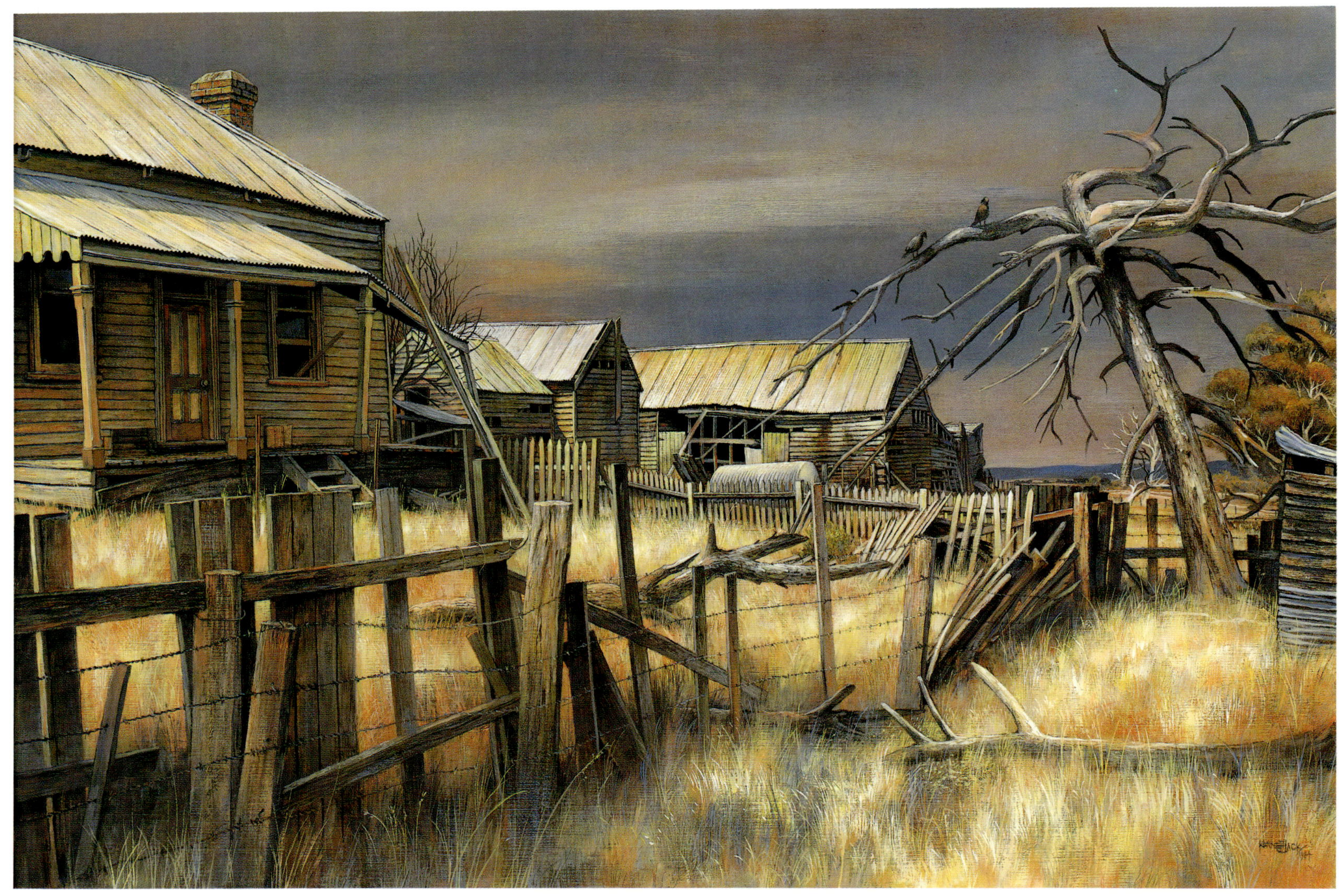

Plate 68 *Ruined Farm, Mt. Blackwood* 1984 (Victoria) acrylic, 51 × 76 cm

*The first time I found this old farm on a back road
it was steadily raining and so I made a drawing of
it from about 75 metres away, outside the front gate
and sitting inside my Landcruiser. Since I wanted to
further explore what looked to me like a particularly
interesting subject, I went back some weeks later and
asked permission from the owners, who had moved
to a newer house nearby. Two whole days were
spent around this farm and its outbuildings as
I found it good to draw from almost any angle.*

*The old, dilapidated buildings make a
wonderfully varied composition of rhythms and
textures in combination with broken fences, long
grass, fallen tree limbs and dead pines. I felt there
was no other way to paint this subject but by an
intense realism and feeling for the forms in space.*

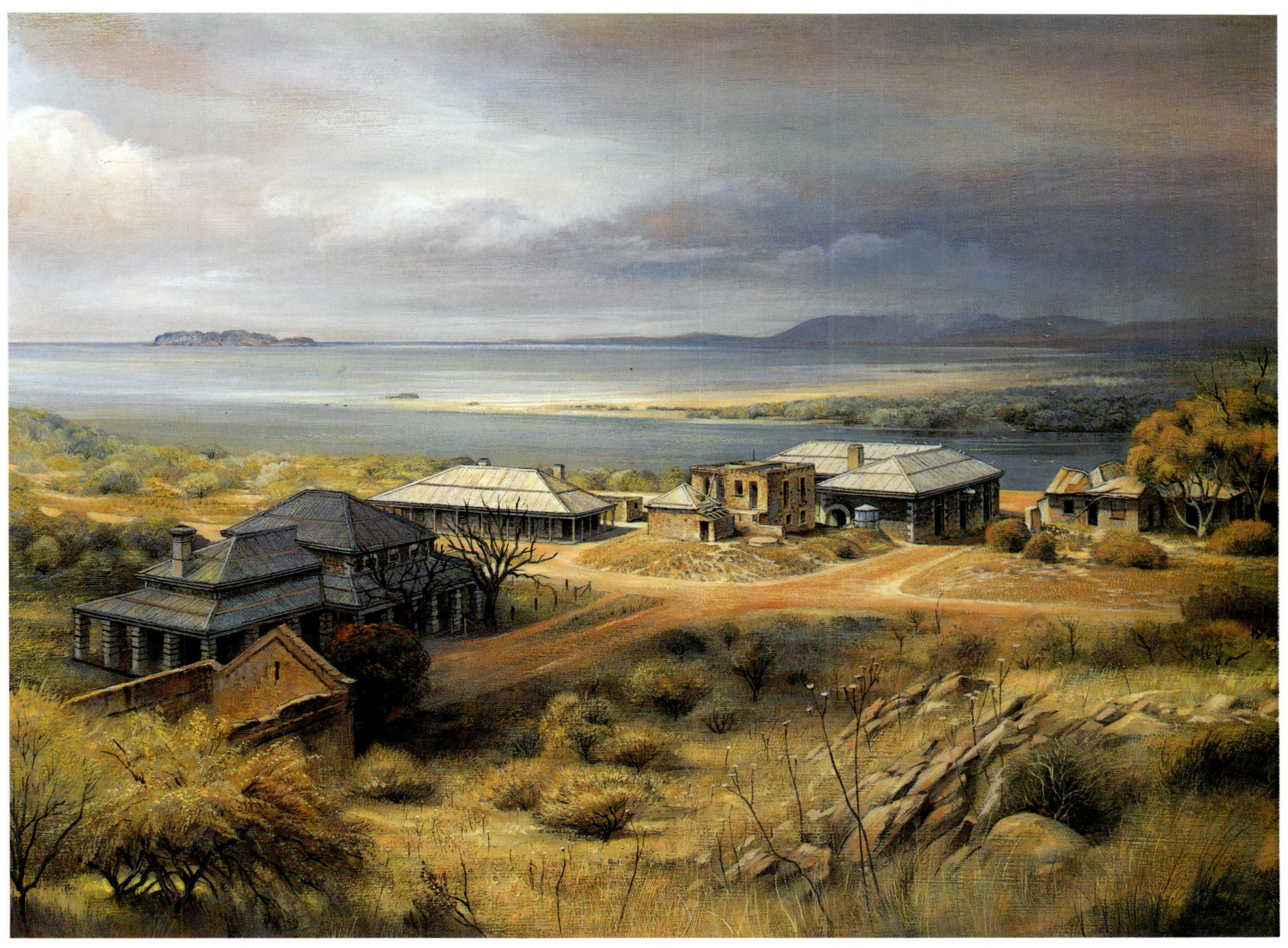

Plate 69 *Abandoned Port, Cossack* 1984 (Western Australia) acrylic, 42 × 57 cm

This old port on the north-west coast of Australia did not have a very long life as it silted up; it was then abandoned and superseded by bigger and more conveniently-placed ports. However, for the artist who is interested in buildings set in landscape, it is a splendid area.

Facing the waterfront is a stone customs house which has arched doorways and windows and a curved corner. In the painting it is centrally placed. To the left is the post office ruin, then the gaol ruin and police building in which the town's only two residents live, an architect and his sculptress wife. They had many projects ahead of them to restore some of the buildings. Possibly the finest building is the court house on the left with its surrounding verandahs and the unusual design of its posts. The ruins of a store are in the left foreground.

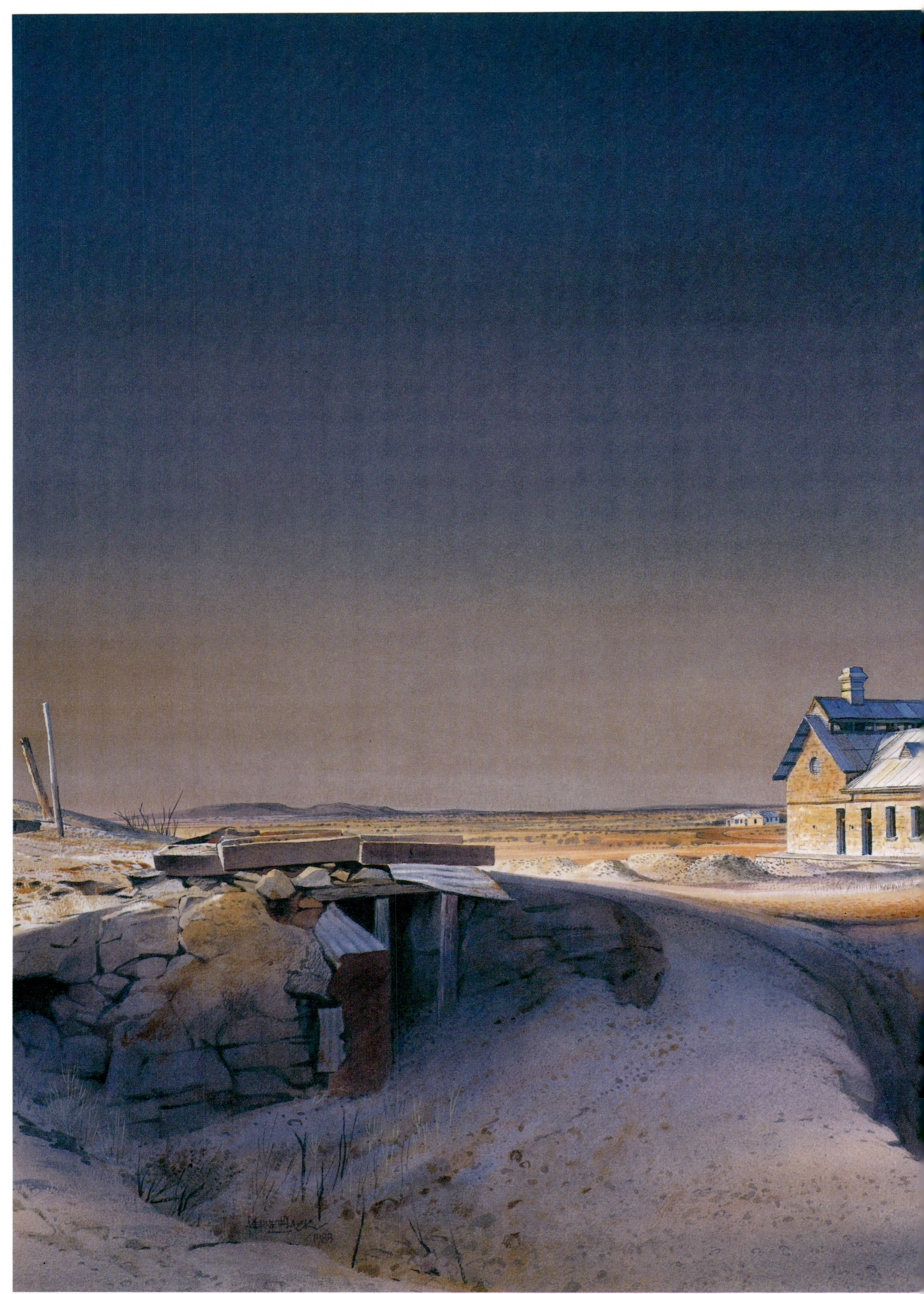

Plate 70 *Abandoned Goldmine Office, Day Dawn* 1988 (Western Australia) watercolour, 70 × 101 cm

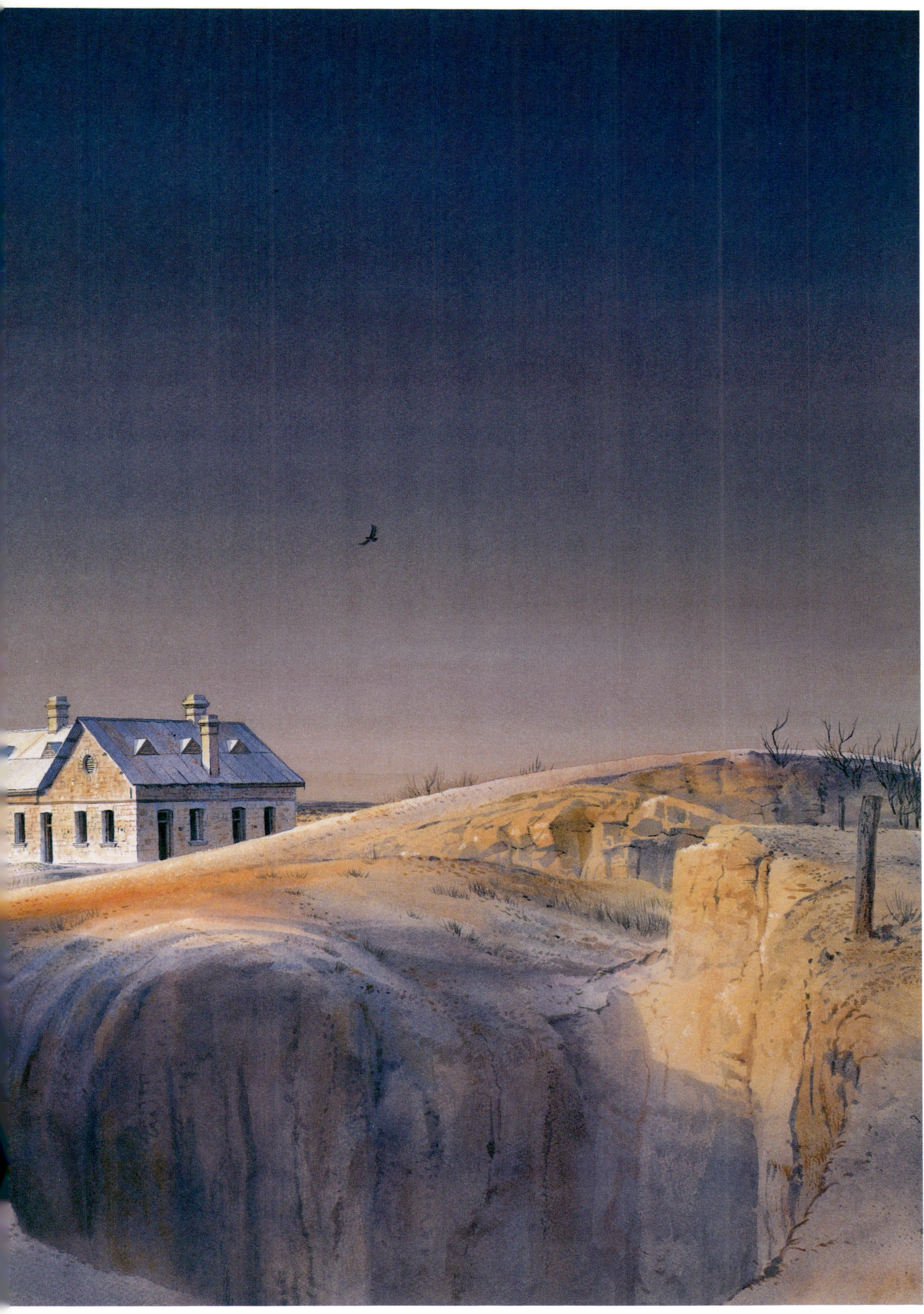

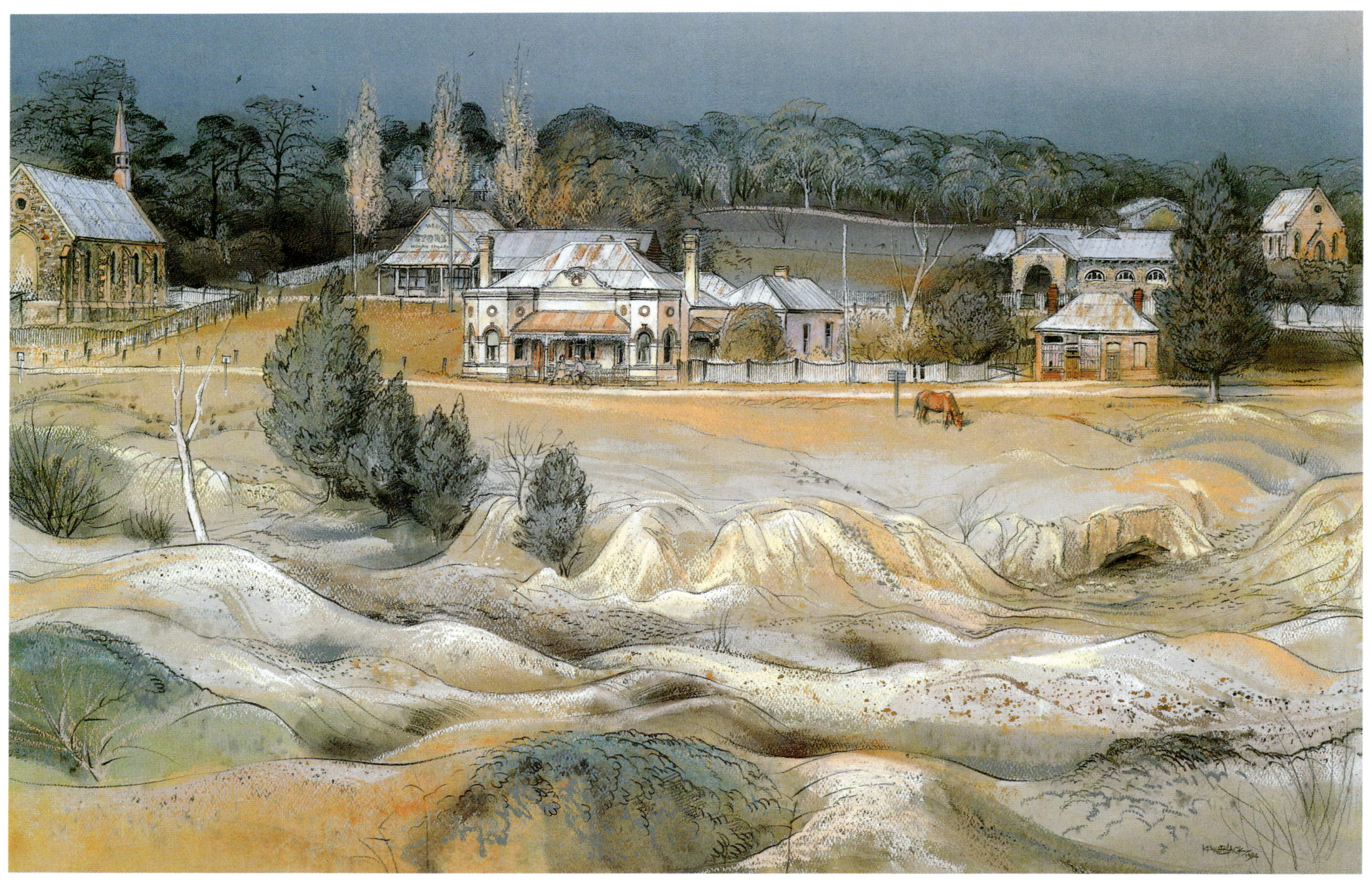

Plate 71 *Across the Diggings, Hill End* 1984 (New South Wales) pencil, oil pastel and watercolour, 50.2 × 78.2 cm

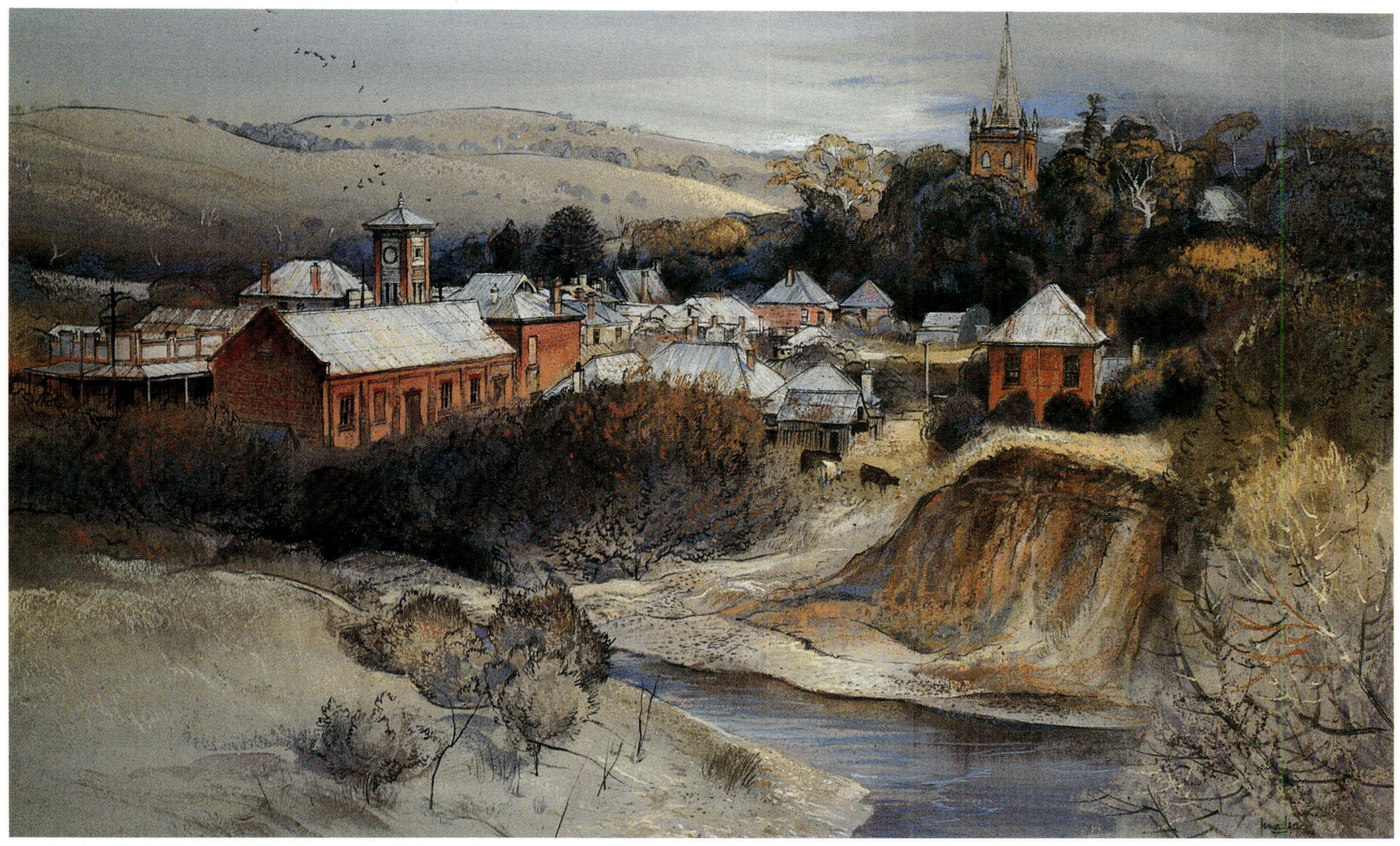

Plate 72 *Carcoar* 1984 (New South Wales) pencil, oil pastel and watercolour, 44 × 73 cm

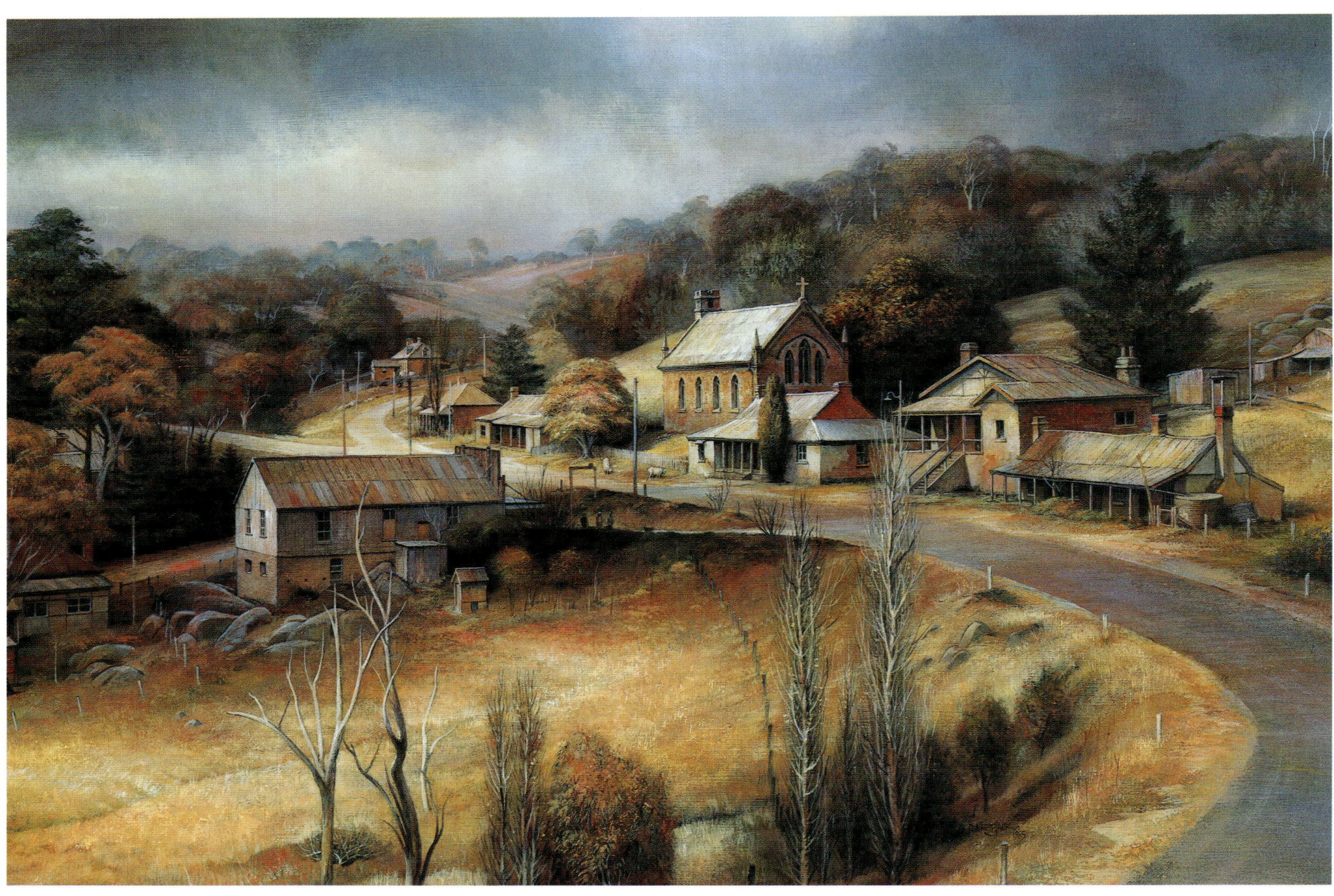

Plate 73 *Hartley* 1984 (New South Wales) acrylic, 61 × 91 cm

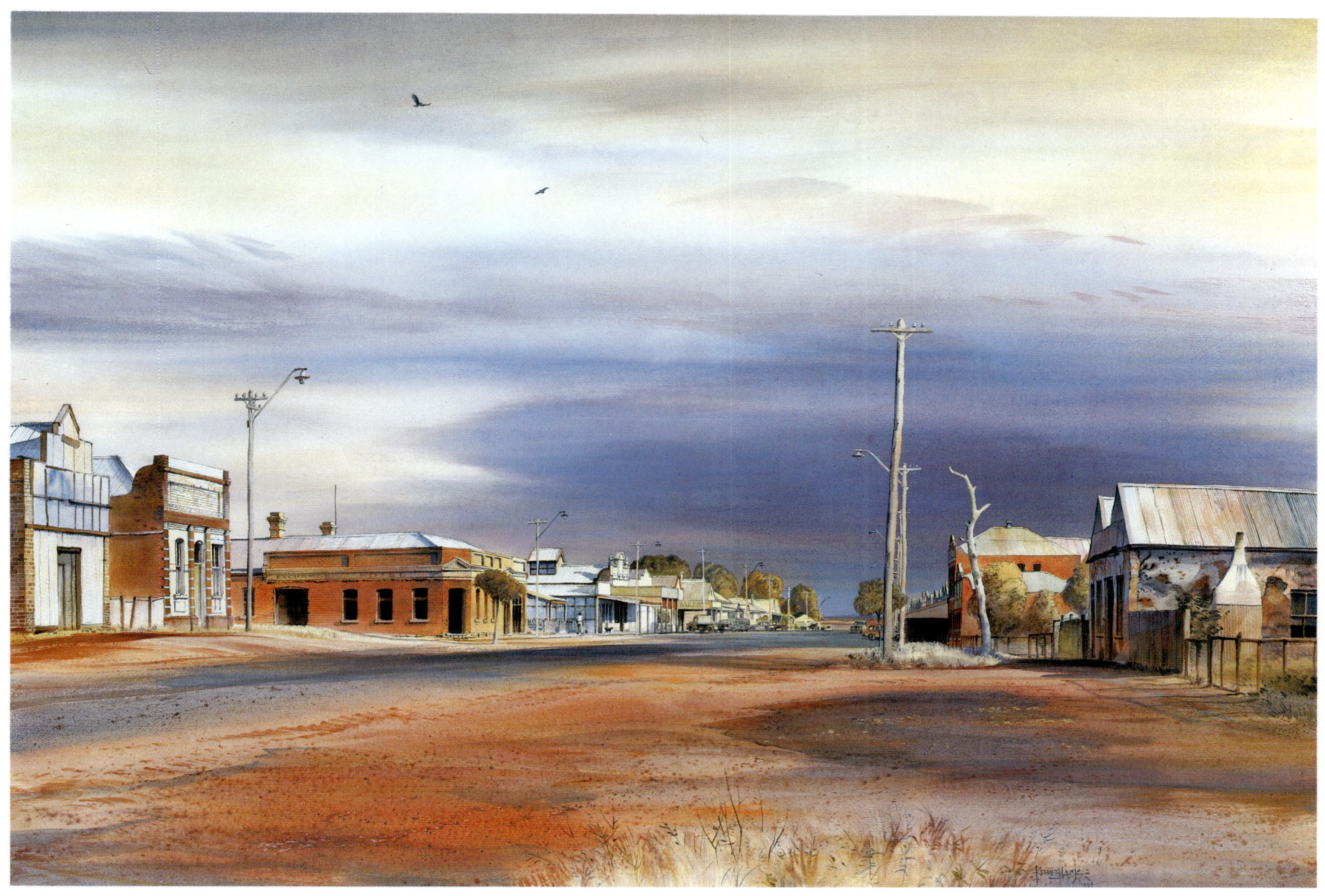

Plate 74 *Leonora* 1984 (Western Australia) watercolour, 69 × 102 cm

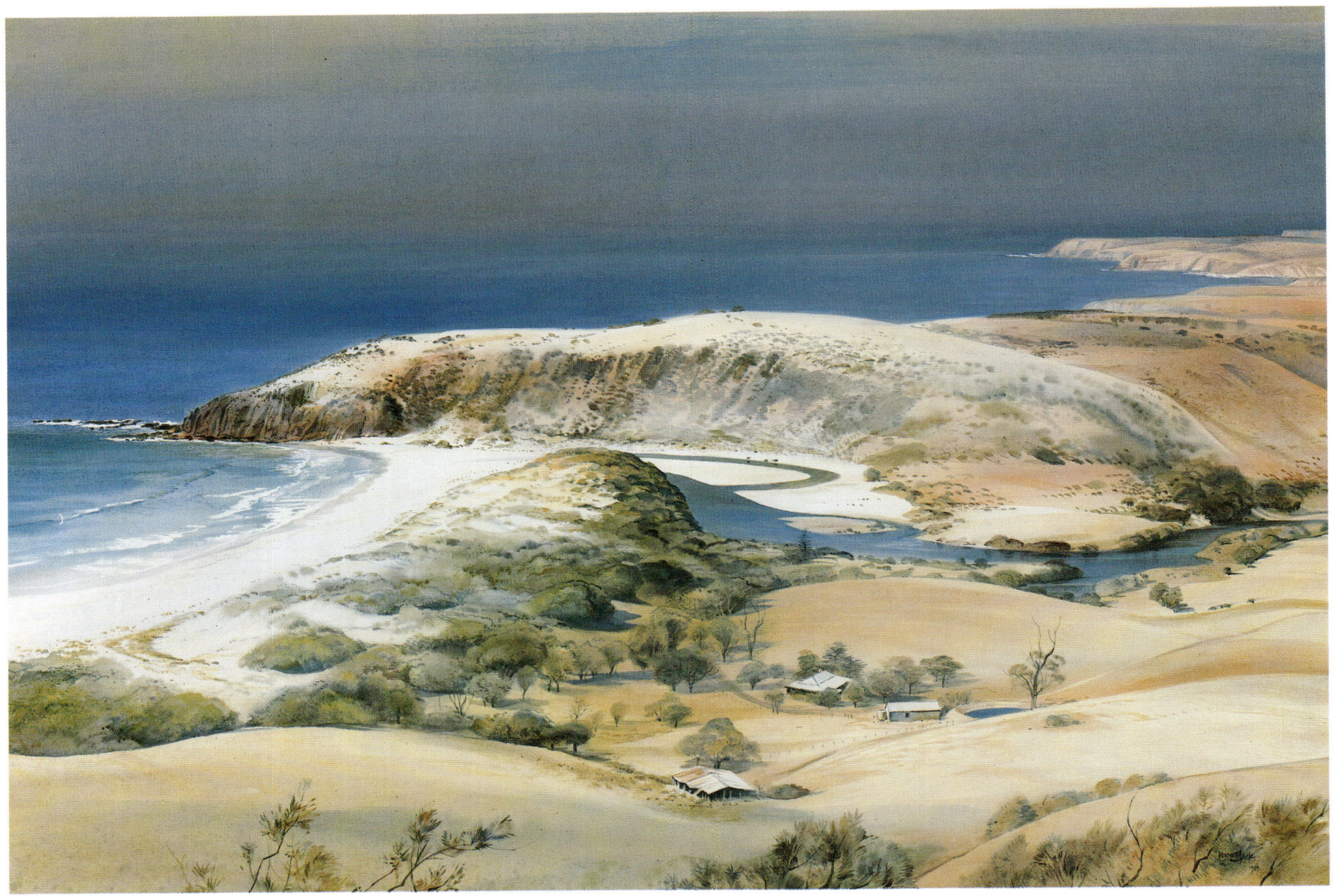

Plate 75 *Middle River, Kangaroo Island* 1984 (South Australia) watercolour, 69 × 102 cm

*Kangaroo Island is the third largest Australian island
situated 110 kilometres south of Adelaide. It is
approximately 140 kilometres long by 50 kilometres
at its widest. One can travel there either by boat or
a short plane flight from Adelaide.*

*We chose the latter and hired a car to motor all
over the island. It is rich in coastal scenery and
affords great subjects for the landscape artist. I can
remember being very excited when we came across
this superb vista in the middle of the north coast.
Below us was a winding stream crossing a sandy
beach next to the projecting headland, itself a very
satisfying rounded shape, jutting out into a
magnificent blue sea.*

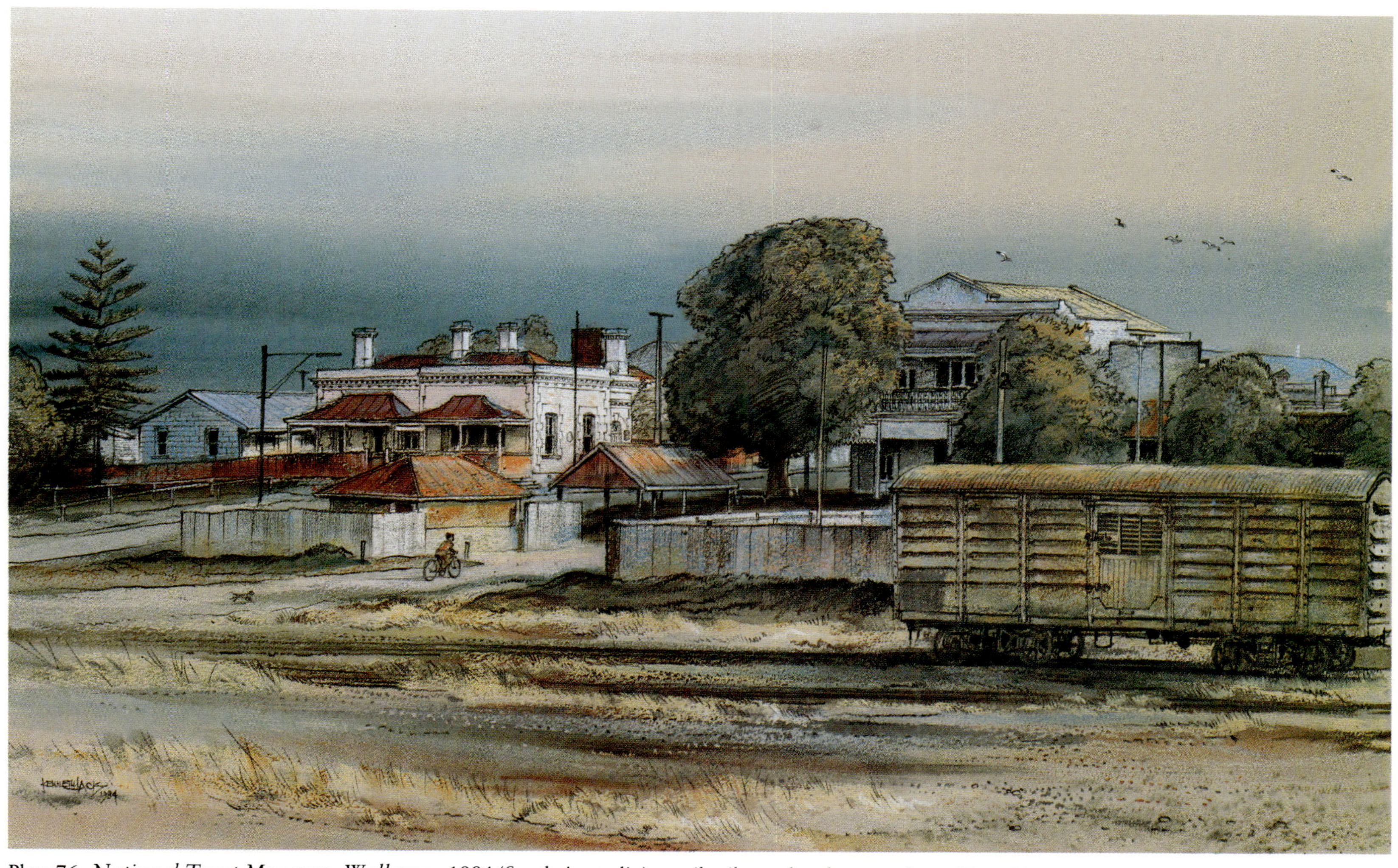

Plate 76 *National Trust Museum, Wallaroo* 1984 (South Australia) pencil, oil pastel and watercolour, 33 × 54 cm

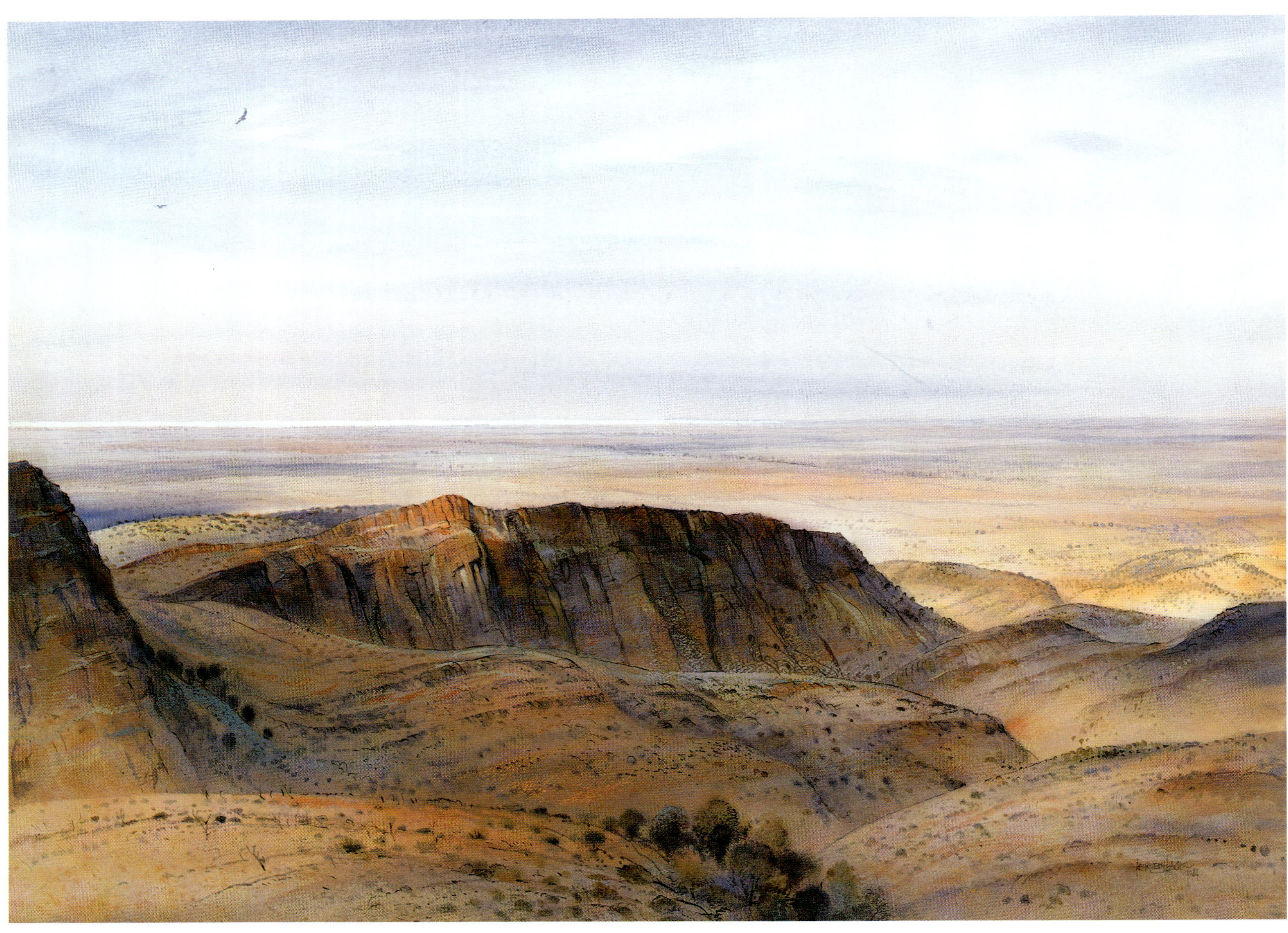

Plate 77   *Towards Lake Frome (Salt)* 1984 (South Australia) watercolour, 51 x 72 cm

The outback towns have been tempered and restructured by the sun and the elements. Nature has begun to claim back its materials and the result conforms well to William Gilpin's theory that the picturesque depends on the accidental qualities of detail found in nature and in simple rustic life: 'Nature is always great in design, but unequal in composition. She is an admirable colorist; and can harmonize her tints with infinite variety and in inimitable beauty.'[26]

The outback has the element of the exotic, but one quality that would not have appealed to Gilpin is its flatness. The monotony of the horizontal line was not deemed to be picturesque.

When explorers and artists first looked on Australia they saw it through the canons of science and art of their time. The world they saw projected onto the continent as the future is the world we look back at now. The two gazes meet in the outback.

This world of fading memories is the world which Kenneth Jack has chronicled with loving care. Drawing after drawing, little by little, over the years the work he has done has fallen into a pattern, and the pattern which has evolved and which each new work is now a conscious effort to reinforce, is the vision of Kenneth Jack as artist. Because he is a realist artist it may not be obvious that what he draws is in fact extracted from a mass of infinite distractions to the eye. The job of distilling a simple drawing of a building or a town is an effort of imagination and of skill.

We may notice 'the outback' if we are crossing a desert and then reach a lonely group of buildings, but we find it hard to *see* an old Victorian town unless we have been given a 'pattern' with which to interpret the data which enters our eyes. We all have absorbed such patterns which have preconditioned what we see. Once we have seen drawings of old Victorian country buildings we find it much easier to single out the significant in our travels. Artists provide us with such guides. The drawing is an idea lifted from the material world and placed in the realm of thought and perception. It is not unlike the looking at a starry sky. Until a pattern has been pointed out and a constellation given a name, we see only a confusion of stars.

It might be useful briefly to compare Kenneth Jack's Australia with Andrew Wyeth's U.S.A. Though there are some obvious similarities there is also a radical difference. Some of Wyeth's most persistent themes such as farm buildings set in a bare countryside may resemble certain works by Kenneth Jack but what is different is the world implied by each. Andrew Wyeth has tried to hold on to a lost world while Kenneth Jack has painted the remains of an Australian past. Americans have tended to see Wyeth as an artist who has supposedly painted an anti-materialist image of their country. Not only is this something of a delusion, but there is also something sinister and unhealthy about Wyeth's world.[27]

Wyeth has painted only a small region of middle America and the few people who figure in his paintings one might well term misfits. There is no accord between them and the world as it is and they appear as outcasts and marginal dwellers. Behind the technically brilliant, symbolic super-realism, there is an atmosphere which is a typically recurring element in American art and literature. It is a self-pitying melancholy which we can find in O. Henry, Steinbeck, Sherwood Anderson, Tennessee Williams, Hopper and others. This could well

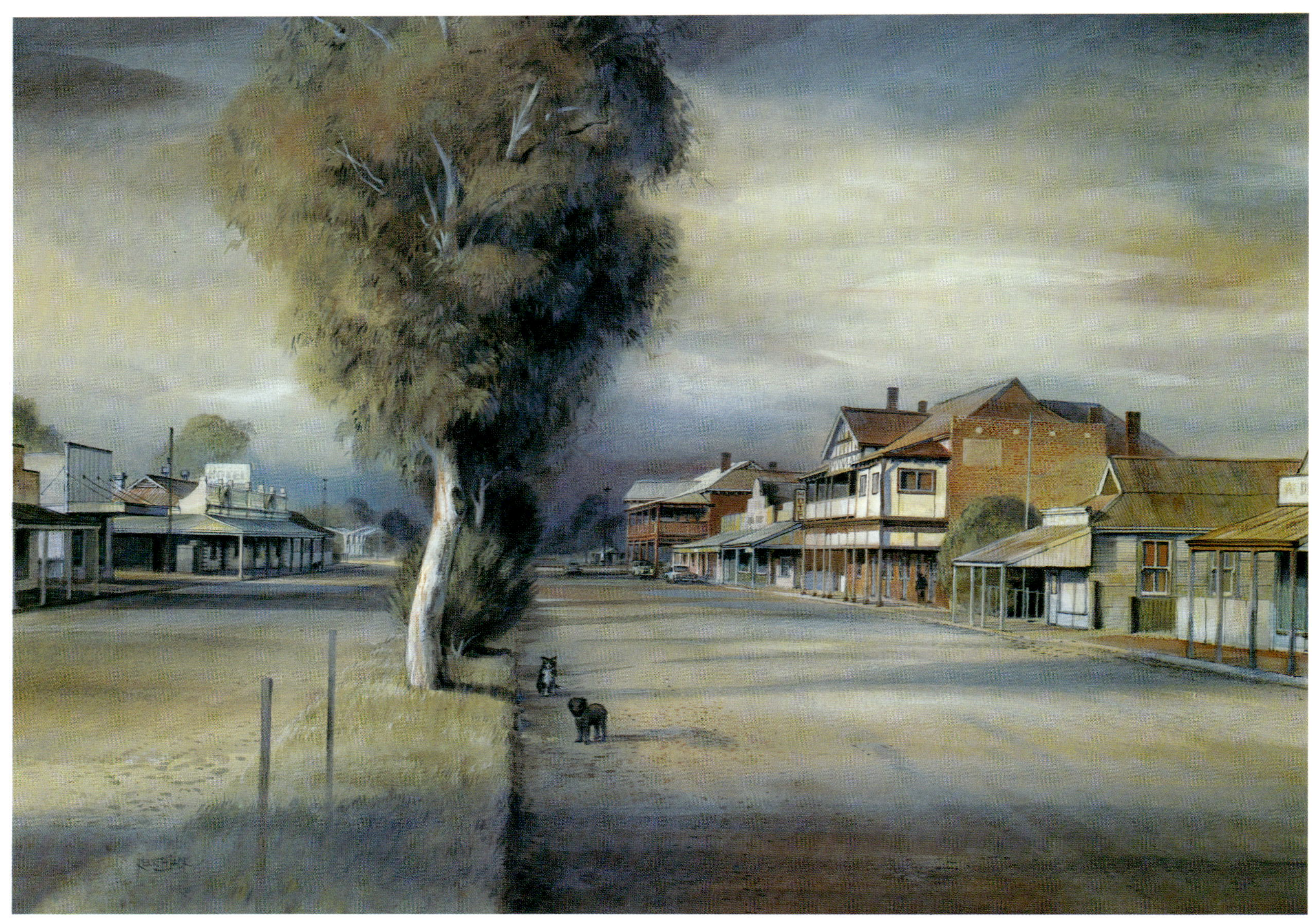

Plate 78 *Main Street, Mt. Magnet* 1985 (Western Australia) gouache, 50 × 71 cm

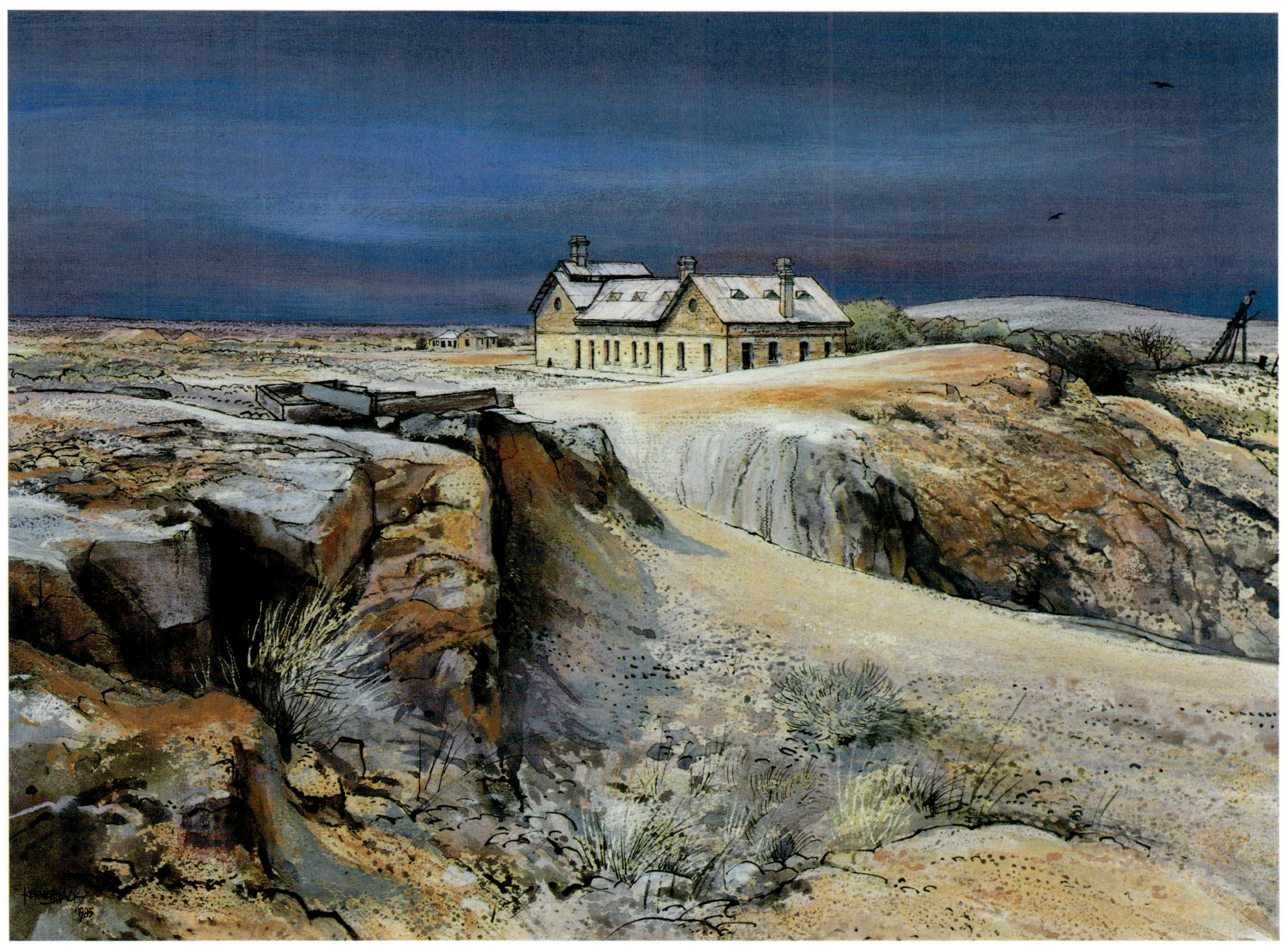

Plate 79 *Mine Building, Day Dawn* 1985 (Western Australia) pencil, oil pastel and watercolour, 35.5 × 48 cm

be an attitude inherited from the pilgrim fathers, a puritanical inability to grasp and enjoy the pleasures of this world or to face the present; only the ability to grieve over its passing. It is a need to suffer rather than to face life, to watch rather than participate and to confront life only after it has been defused by time.

Wyeth stalks the world with binoculars and microscope. He adds detail to detail in an effort to achieve his intention 'to get to the bottom of reality'. But as the process is neither analytical nor metaphysical he complicates rather than simplifies. The creative act of an artist like Drysdale achieves its impact by eliminating inessential detail to bring out the metaphysical elements; in his case, the timeless qualities and unreal character of a place. Wyeth's method produces frenzied journalism; the other poetry.

Kenneth Jack, in spite of similarities with Wyeth, belongs to the Drysdale tradition. He is not unhappy in his down-to-earth and healthy world. He is an explorer who records the effects of time on a bygone Australia for which he has strong feelings. As the world which preceded ours, it is our past and is therefore important. It is the epic record of a continent and a nation and it is a heroic story of effort and determination. But what he paints is also our world overlapping the past; it is a comment on our world and our time. The vast continent remains as it always was, engulfed in endless space and heroic grandeur.

Both Wyeth and Hopper worked with a belief that American art should reflect the character of the American people and possibly this is what makes their work appear selfconscious to others. Kenneth Jack has discovered and mastered a way of painting Australia which is his own. He has perfected the way in which he can represent the architecture and run-down buildings of the typical Australian country town. And he has devised a poetic conception of atmosphere and light in which he submerges these 'typical' places so that they become part of his world. But because he does it all so well, he can change and adapt his subject matter and angle of vision so that anyone who sees the final result never thinks he is anything but photographically accurate. Yet the licence which he takes is considerable, and it is exactly poetic licence, because he believes it is the picture which must dictate the conditions of composition and design so that everything looks plausible. If he takes liberties with the facts, he also believes that in order to paint a subject one needs to see it, to walk about it, to be immersed in its space and feel it. Only then can one begin to draw it.

There are certain country towns which Jack loves and has gone back to constantly for decades, watching them pass into history. Talbot in Victoria is one of them.

He knows the town well and has seen it change. He has grieved over the deterioration of some of the buildings while trees have grown so tall that they obliterate a view he once painted and of course the Town Hall no longer has the little tower on it, although not all the buildings are deteriorating or being pulled down. Some are being restored by residents. Over a period of more than thirty years he has made many drawings, an oil painting and an acrylic painting, mixed media paintings, two lithographs and a colour linocut, a print of which was purchased by the Victoria and Albert Museum in London in 1958.

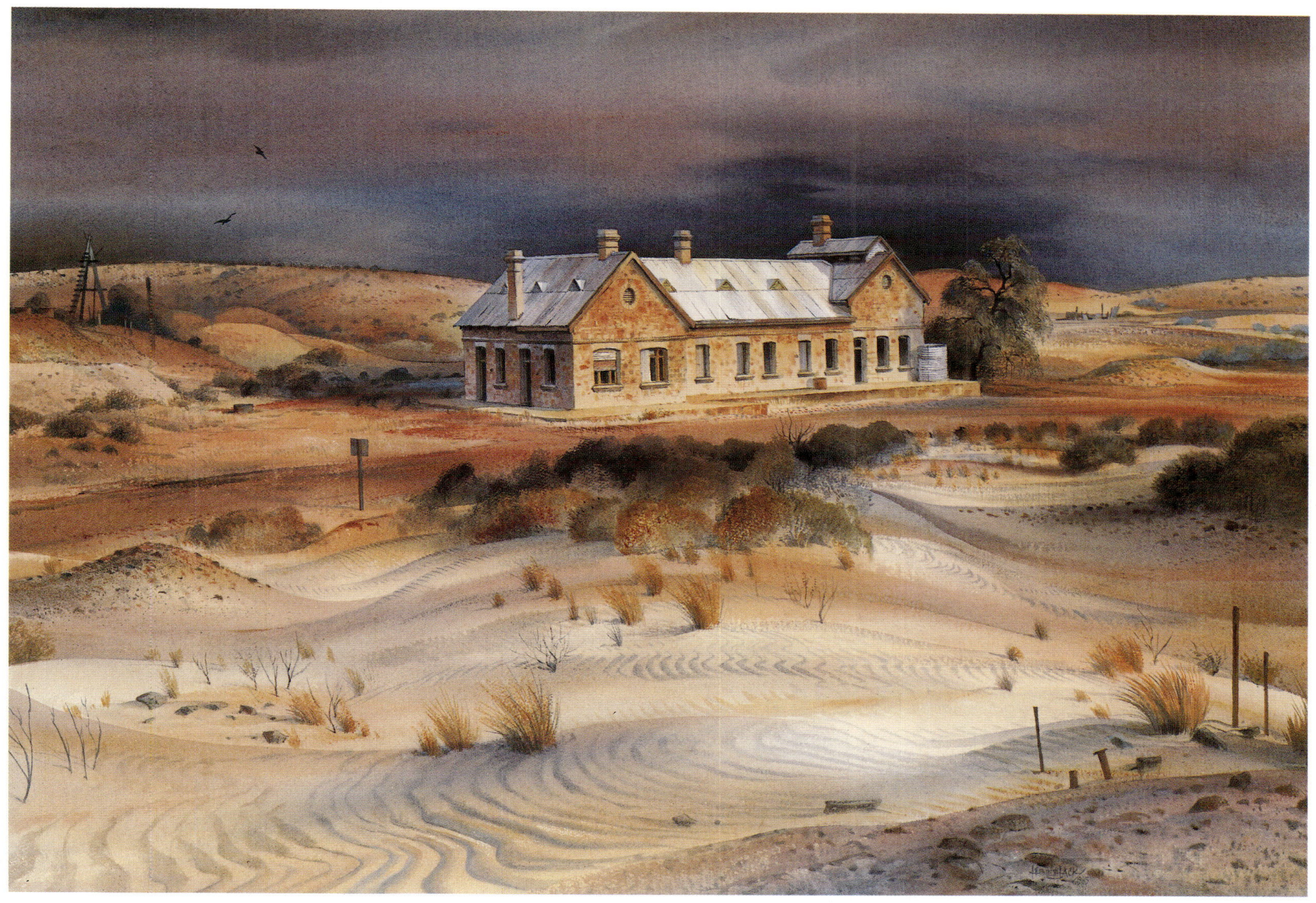

Plate 80 *Mine Building, Day Dawn II* 1985 (Western Australia) watercolour, 70 × 101 cm

This fine old building stands on a saltbush plain near the edge of the Day Dawn Mine, which is a few kilometres south of Cue in central Western Australia. The only other remains of this once very busy mining area are broken bits and pieces of mine buildings, miners' cottages and the ruined post office. This particular building, which has lost its verandah, has a very large chimney in the spacious and lofty-ceilinged room on the right side. It was in this room that the gold was melted down and made into ingots.

The great appeal to me in painting this composition was the way the surrounding landscape of road shape, sand drifts, bushes and mine remains contrasted with the strong, geometrical shapes of the building.

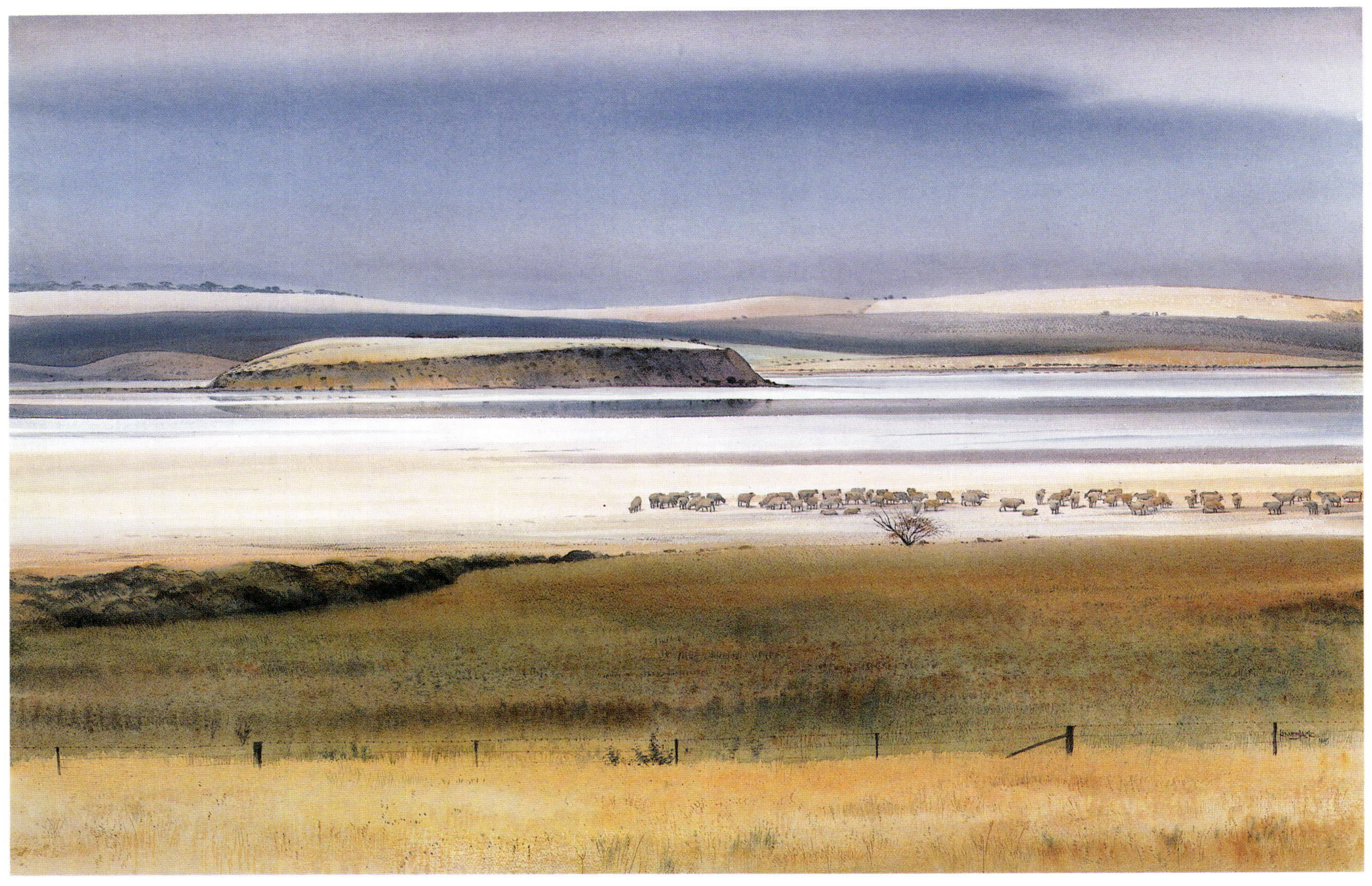

Plate 81 *Sheep on a Salt Lake, Lake Bumbunga* 1985 (South Australia) watercolour, 77 × 119.3 cm

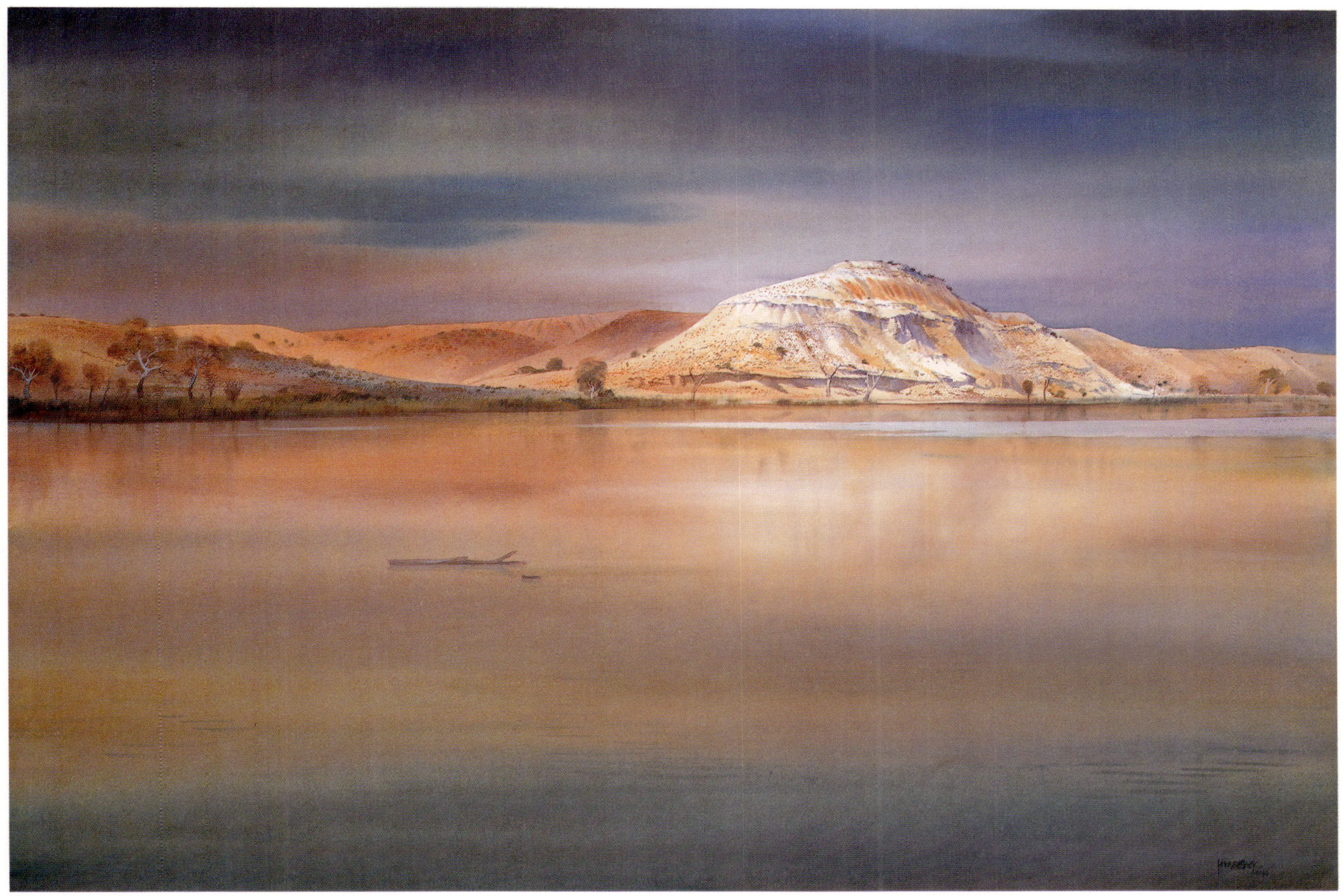

Plate 82 *Gal Gal Reach, Lower Murray* 1986, watercolour, 101 × 152 cm

This large watercolour is based on my experience of cruising along the Murray with some American friends who had invited my wife and me to share their hired houseboat for a couple of days.

Being the passenger, able to draw as we travelled along or paint when we pulled in to the shore, meant a really rewarding time for me on the river. The painting was executed in the studio. A few months earlier I had painted a small watercolour as a preliminary study and had exhibited it in London at the Royal Watercolour Society. In this larger one I improved the design and colour. I have tried to capture the magic of this beautiful cliff reflected in the river.

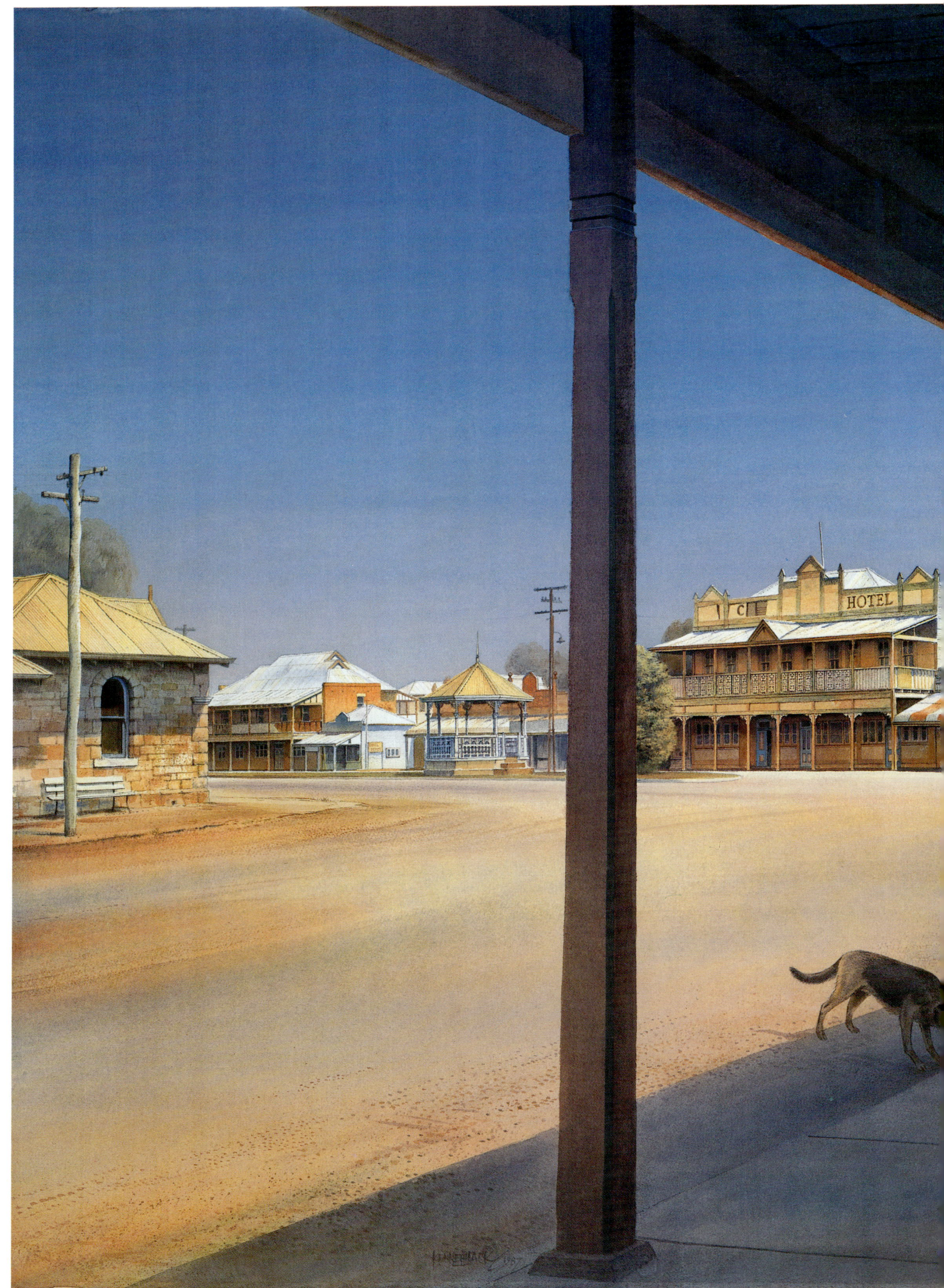

Plate 83 *Midday, Cue* 1987 (Western Australia) watercolour, 101 × 152 cm

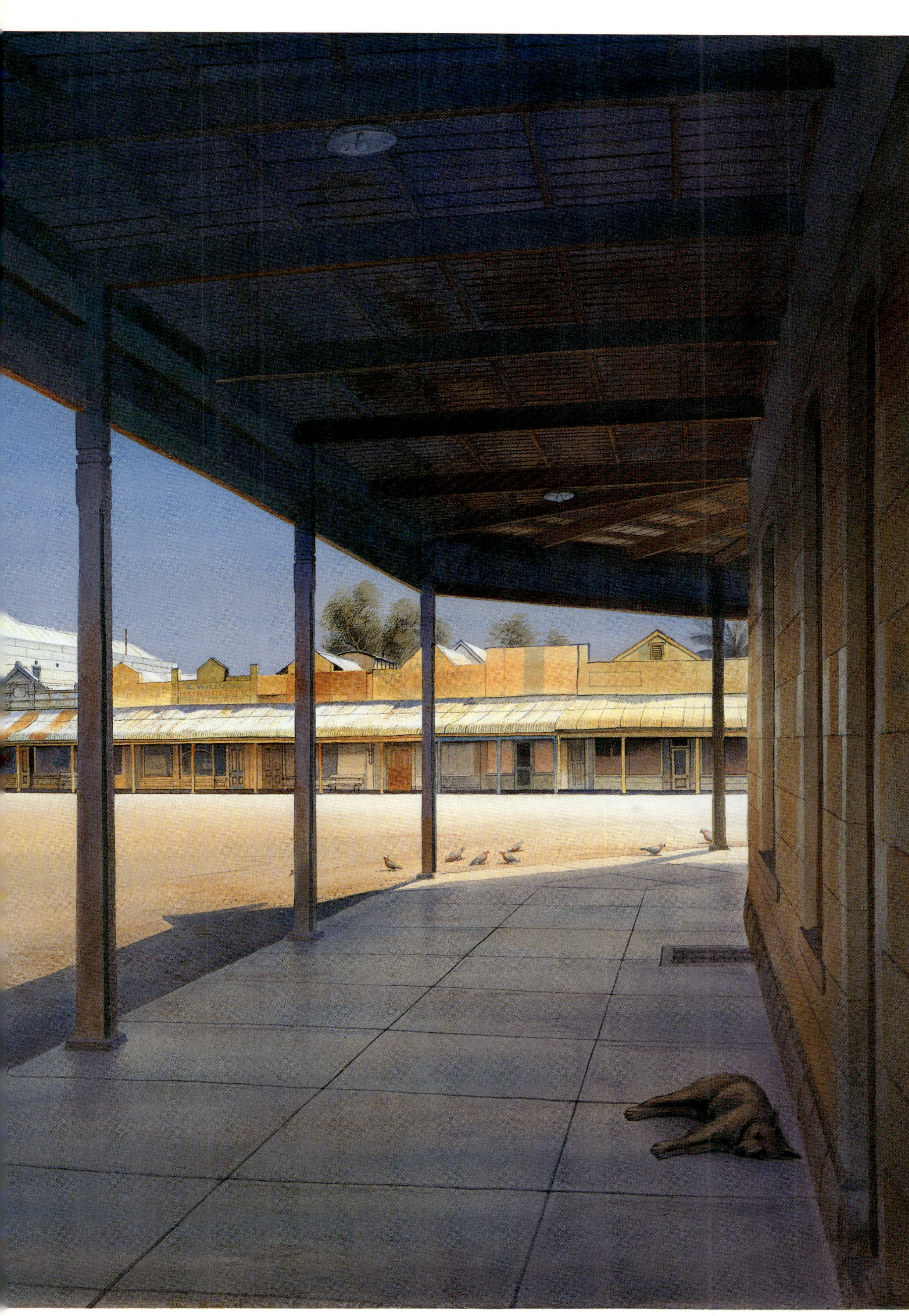

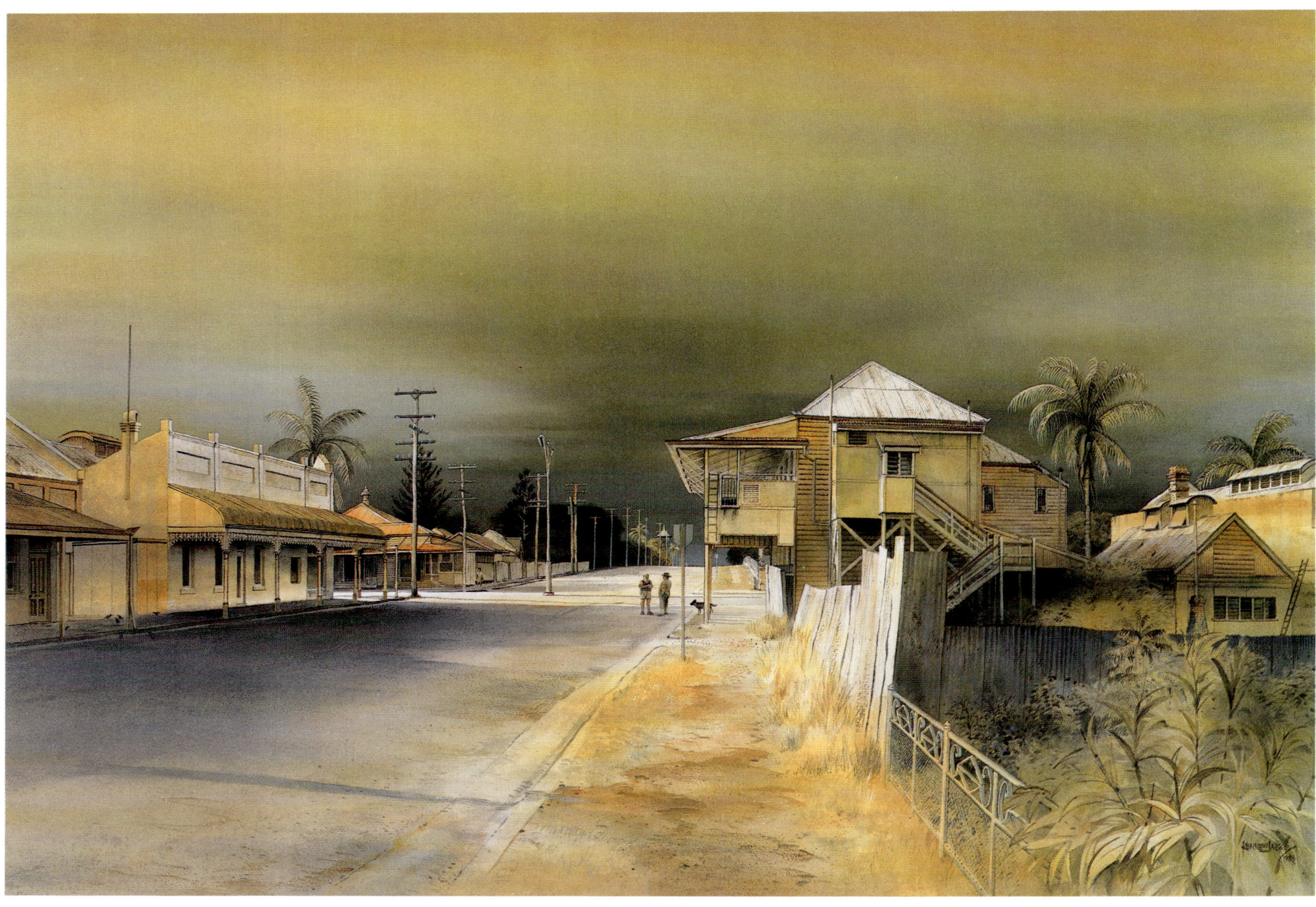

Plate 84 *Northern Gold Mining Town — Charters Towers* 1986 (Queensland) watercolour, 72 × 106 cm

Over the years Kenneth Jack realised that the camera was an important part of his sketching equipment. He finds it a useful tool for gathering information, particularly when there is no time to make a sketch or when a viewpoint is such that one cannot adequately sit there to make a drawing. The camera has proved invaluable in recording information which is too distant and inaccessible for the eye but not for the telephoto lens.

For a long time he restricted his photography to black and white, so that the colour of the photographs would not influence him. Now that colour prints are not very different in price to black-and-white and can be made in an hour, and as he has developed his own colour scheme, he takes colour snapshots which, as he says, actually provide more detail than black and white photographs. But although he may use photographs for reference, he does not like photo-realism. He believes that one should not copy a photograph to make a painting. A camera does not have a mind or a heart and an artist should never be subservient to it. He believes that an artist who wants to work in a realist way will never develop a proper knowledge of forms and space relationships if he uses only photography and fails to constantly draw 'on the motif'.

In the early 1980s the Jacks moved away from the city to a home they had built on a ten-acre block near the foot of the Great Dividing Range. It is an ideal house with a magnificent studio. The space and comfort among other things allowed him to experiment with very large watercolours. Recently he has completed a twelve-foot watercolour (Pl. 19) — a triptych based on one of his favourite ghost towns — Gwalia in Western Australia. It was a challenge and a labour of love in that he has tried to impart to the work all the things he feels in the marvellously charged atmosphere of this legendary place.

Jack has depicted Gwalia during the last light of the day, at that poetic moment when everything is still and magical. The subject is beautifully conceived with strong design and yet in the twilight one can still see the scattered buildings and the mine shaft. Night will soon swallow it into darkness, but for the moment everything appears perfectly still and calm. It is like a dream, balanced gently on the abyss of night and extinction. Everywhere there are signs of human activity, houses where people once lived, the pub where they drank, but now it is all deserted. The great silence suggested by the scene is enhanced by its only sign of life, a few birds gliding over a darkening hill.

This is a fine and sustained work and a marvel of technical achievement, but the technical challenge has been taken up for poetic ends and not merely for itself. The colour is restrained but it has achieved one of the special qualities of watercolour, its luminosity.

Kenneth Jack's philosophy, when it comes to work, is very simple. He knows that artists have highs and troughs and believes that one must keep on working no matter what. He also believes that one should never destroy anything and never give up on a work. By working and reworking a difficult picture one is likely to extend one's knowledge and even discover some new technique. His use of mixed media, which he employs mostly for works made from nature, developed in this way.

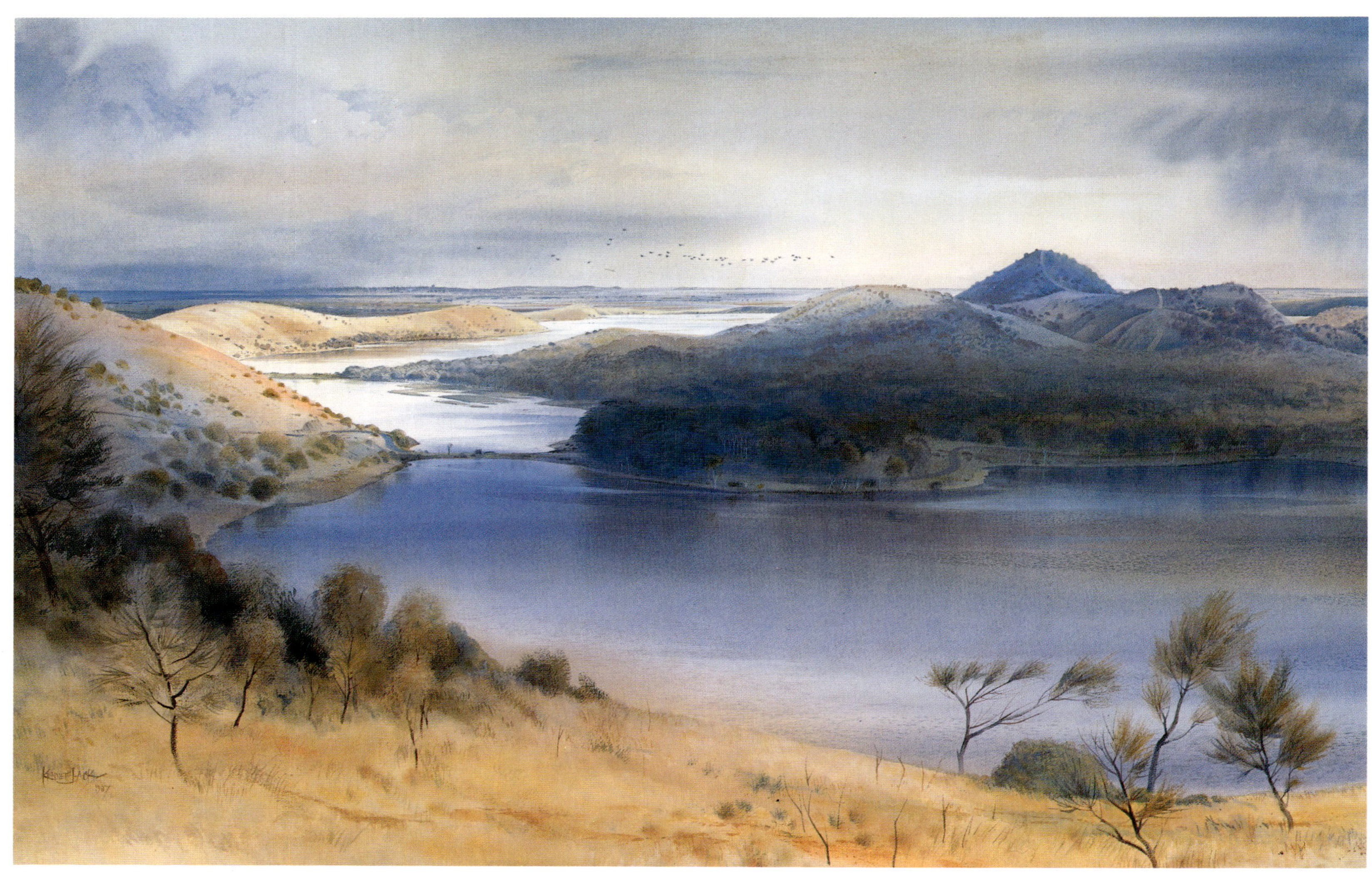

Plate 85   *Tower Hill, Caldera* 1987 (Western Victoria) watercolour, 79 × 122 cm

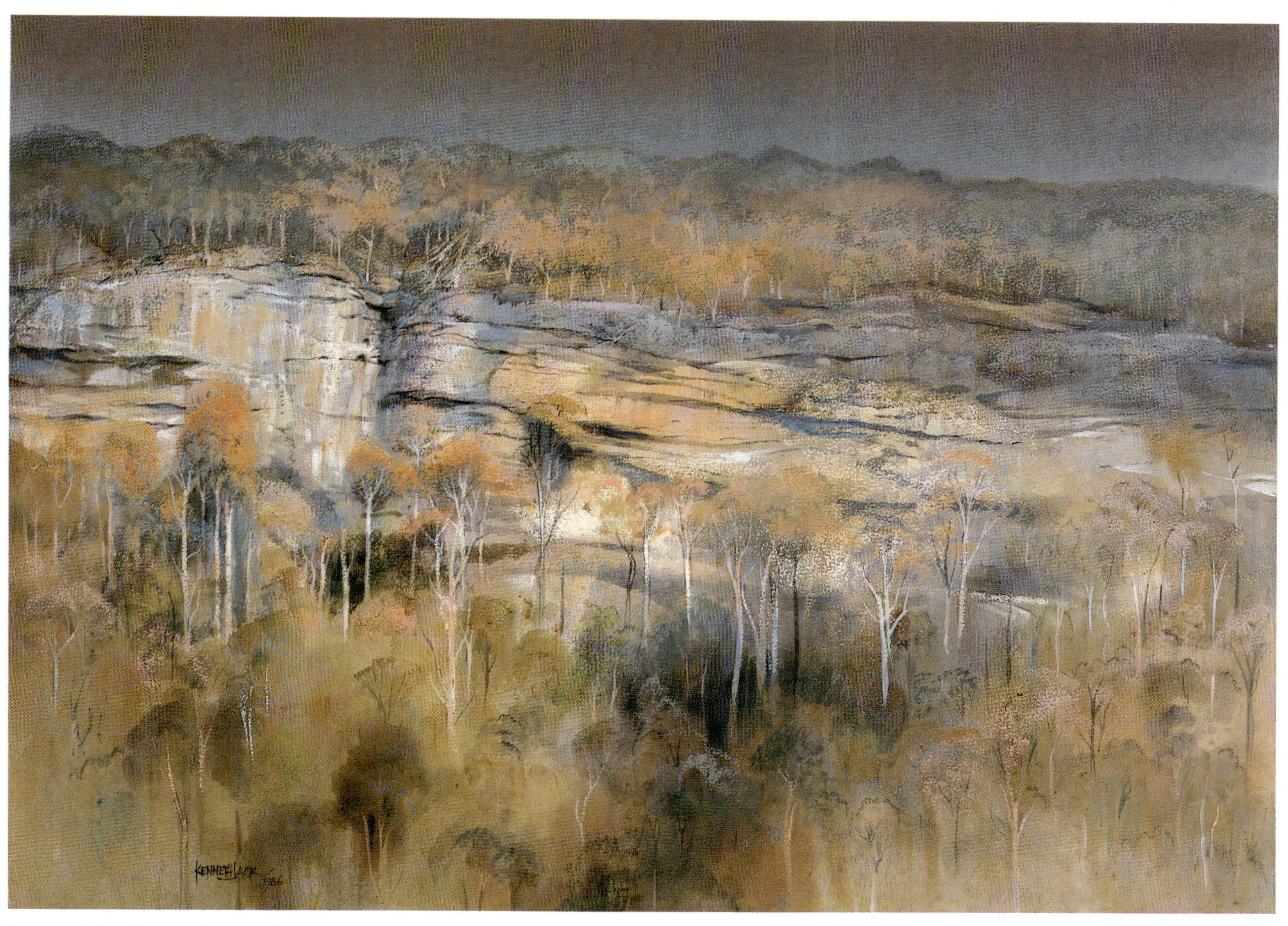

Plate 86   *The Plateau Edge, Lithgow*   1986 (New South Wales) pencil, oil pastel and watercolour, 51 × 72 cm

Writing to Lloyd Rees in 1971 about just such a problem, where endless layers were put one on top of the other to try to get the desired effect on a sky, solicited the following reply:

> The description of your painting problem strikes a warm echo in me I can assure you, as it would appear that our attitudes and methods are very much alike. I too paint over and over not even at times knowing what I want but knowing (I hope) when it comes!
>
> Sometimes I have nightmares over the realisation that at one stage I have it but in a mood of impatience or at least, sometimes, it can be sheer tiredness, I've added ruinous brushstrokes. The visions of the last picture can haunt me. Don't you find it so?
>
> To paint a sky every day for three weeks as you have done is a terribly exacting and exhausting experience. Do you get plagued with the idea that you should *know* what is wanted? The consoling thought to me when in such a situation is that if you *know* then the picture is no longer an adventure — a stepping into the unknown — which all creative art should be.[28]

Watching his father working at home, he inherited from him the use of a piece of paper as a palette. He has never used a conventional palette for mixing watercolours, other than a simple piece of paper. He also still recalls some useful advice given to him by his father: 'Always have your darks well organised.'

Watercolour is the medium which he says suits him best. He finds that it has a special magic: 'That blending of colours together which can be got on a white paper but never to the same degree with oil paint. It is less predictable, more exciting to paint. You don't know, except a vague idea, what the result will be. It takes you along as it develops.'[29]

For Kenneth Jack watercolour has proved the medium with which he can best capture the light, the atmosphere, the sense of magic and the timelessness of those typical country towns which he often depicts just before nightfall. He has brought his own poetry to this already exceptional subject matter.

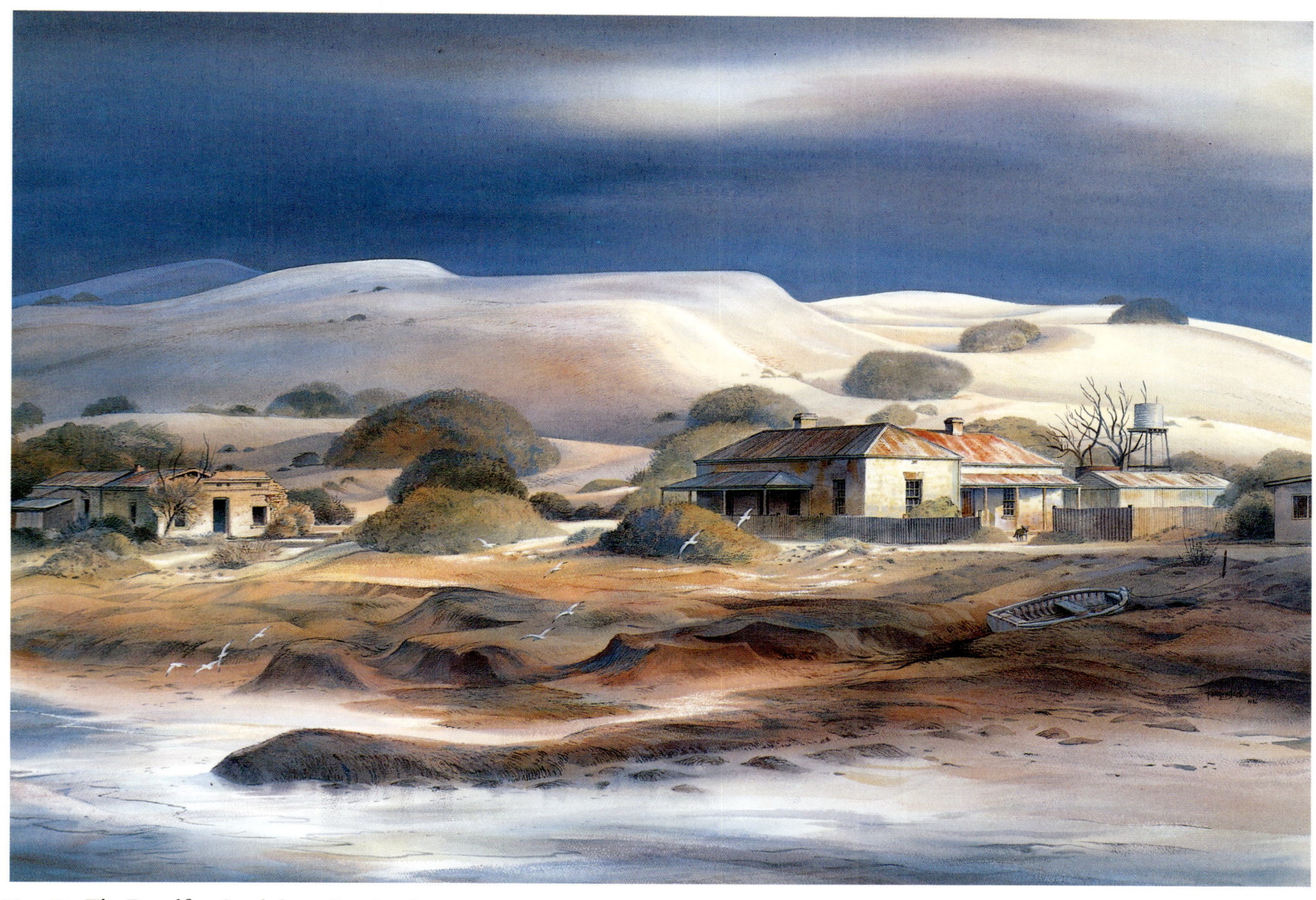

Plate 87 *The Engulfing Sand-dune, Fowlers Bay* 1986 (South Australia) watercolour, 72 × 107 cm

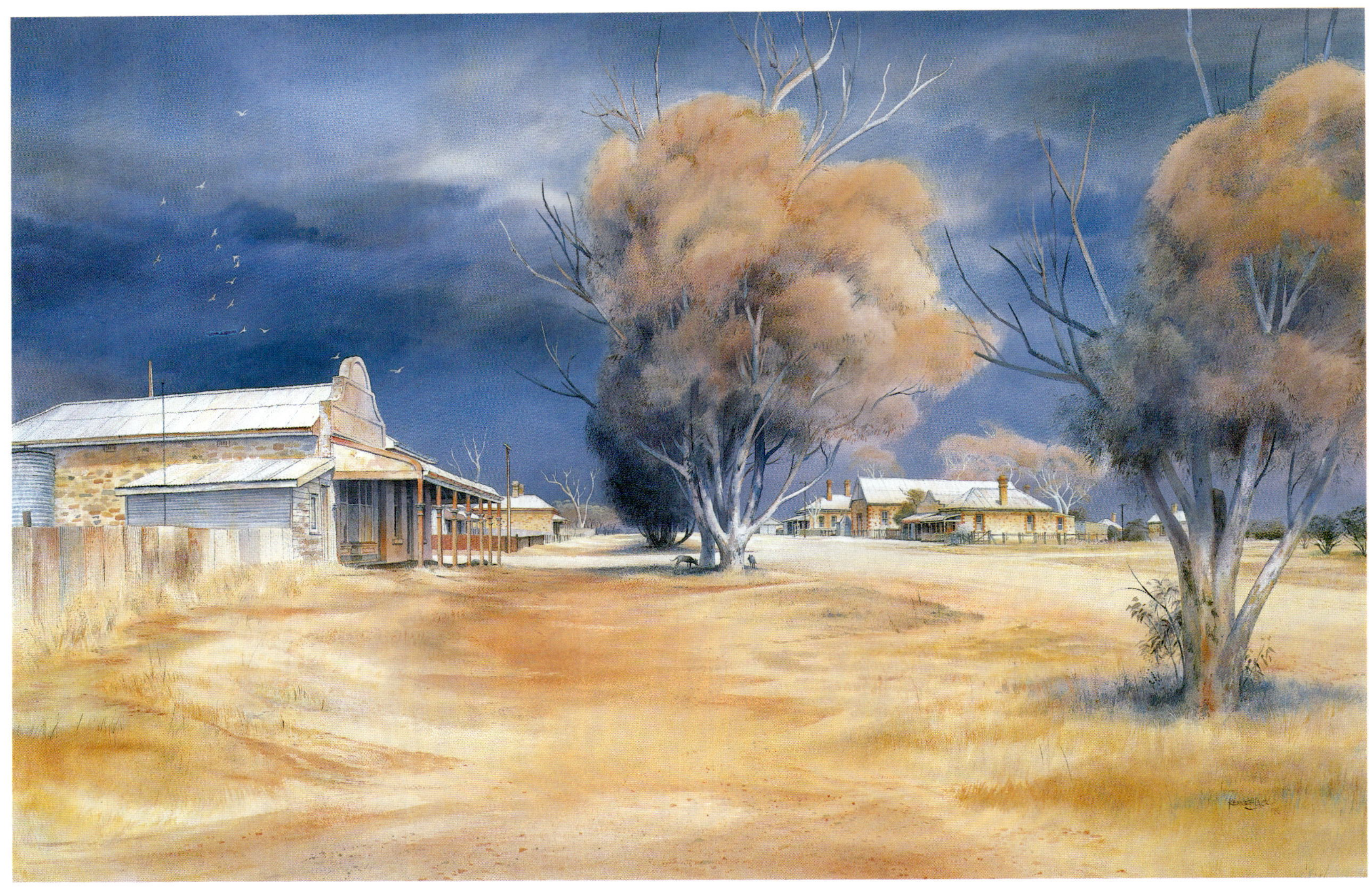

Plate 88 *The Main Street, Whyte-Yarcowie* 1986 (South Australia) watercolour, 101 × 152 cm

The surprising thing about this little town was that for over twenty years I had passed along the main road from Adelaide to the Flinders Ranges and to Broken Hill at the end of the main street, and although Whyte Yarcowie always looked interesting to me, I continued my rush to the north — to Lake Eyre, Arkaroola, Chambers Gorge and beyond. When I finally did take the time to stop it was well worth it.

Whyte Yarcowie is a very small settlement in the northern wheat farming areas of South Australia. It seems typical of many places with a store, post office, hall and one or two other buildings. This appealed so much with the old verandahed buildings set on either side of a very wide street and shaded by thoughtfully-planted large eucalypts.

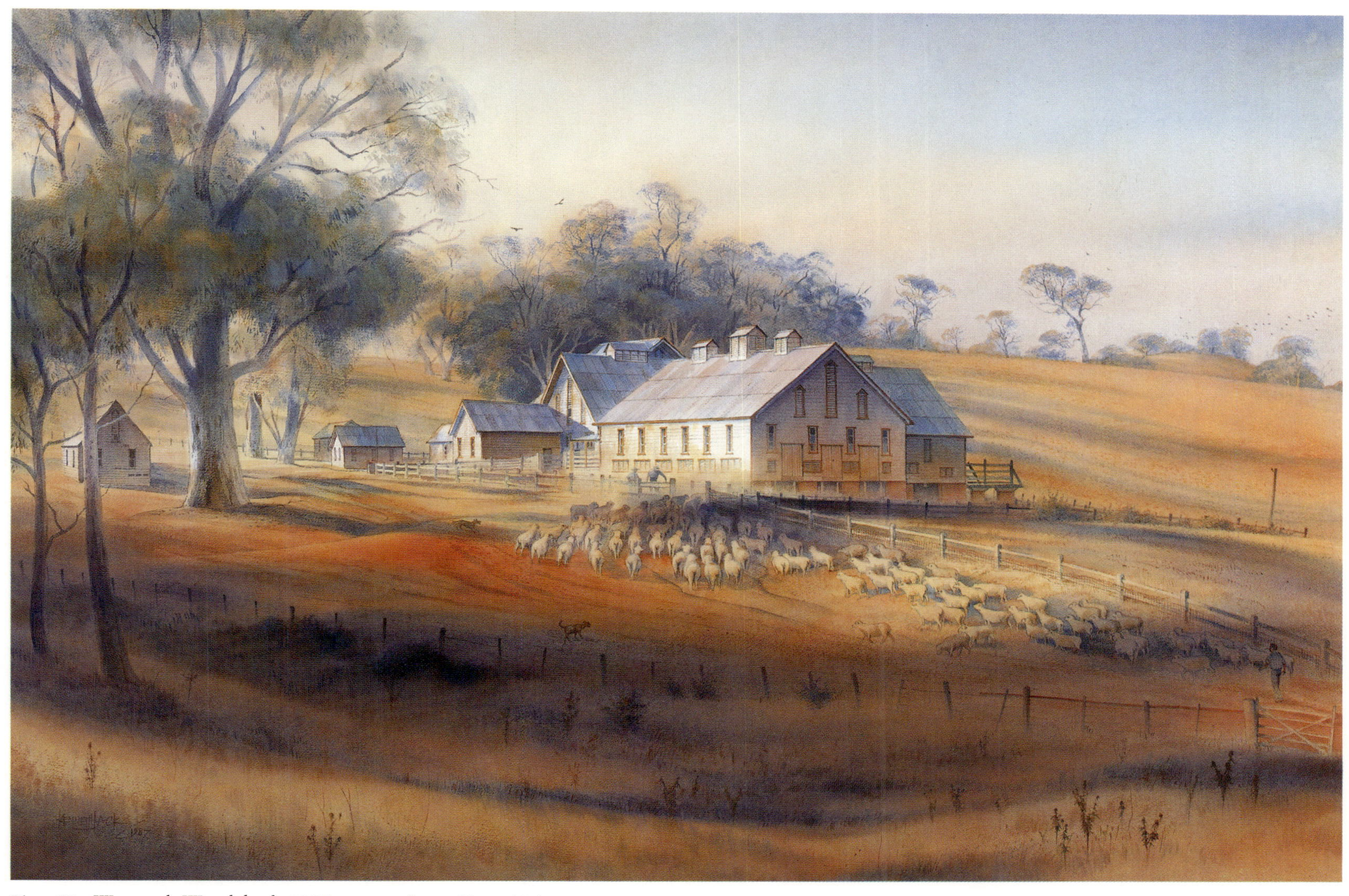

Plate 89 *Warrock Woolshed* 1987, watercolour, 71 × 106 cm

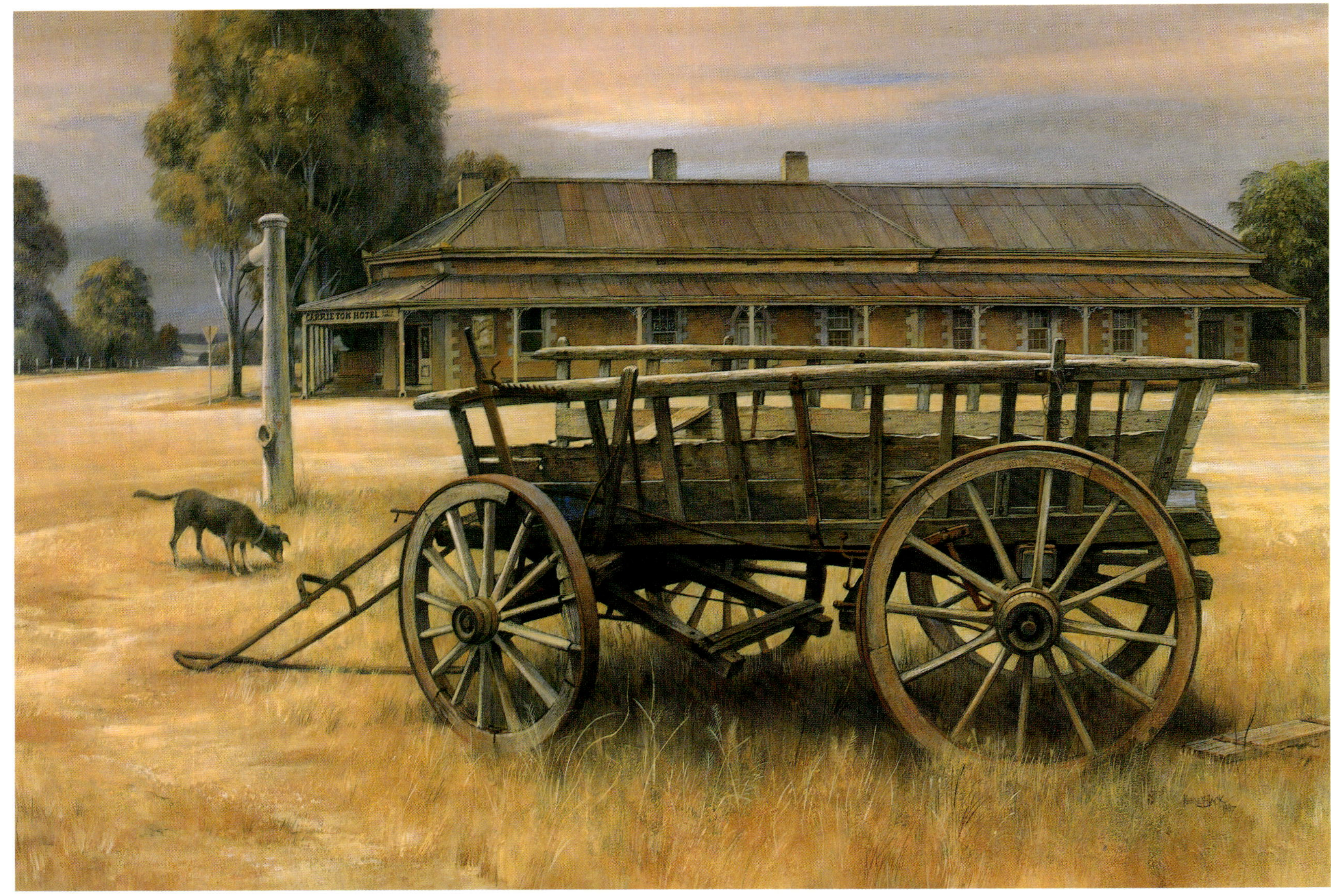

Plate 90   *Wagon at Carrieton* 1987 (South Australia) acrylic, 61 × 91 cm

*This is one of those subjects which appeals so much
to me because of the tactile quality of the old timber
wagon frame and wheels. I wanted to make the
viewer feel he could almost touch the wagon itself as
I was able to do when I first saw it standing on a
main corner in the small, sleepy, inland township of
Carrieton.*

*I tried to convey the effect of the dryness and worn
quality of the timbers; and the old blue paint
washing off over the years. Some of the wheel
timbers have rotted away and left the iron tyre
unsupported. Over the road and behind the wagon
is a typical South Australian, old-style, one-storey
hotel which seemed to form a satisfying background
with its largest shapes parallel and set in opposition
to the wagon.*

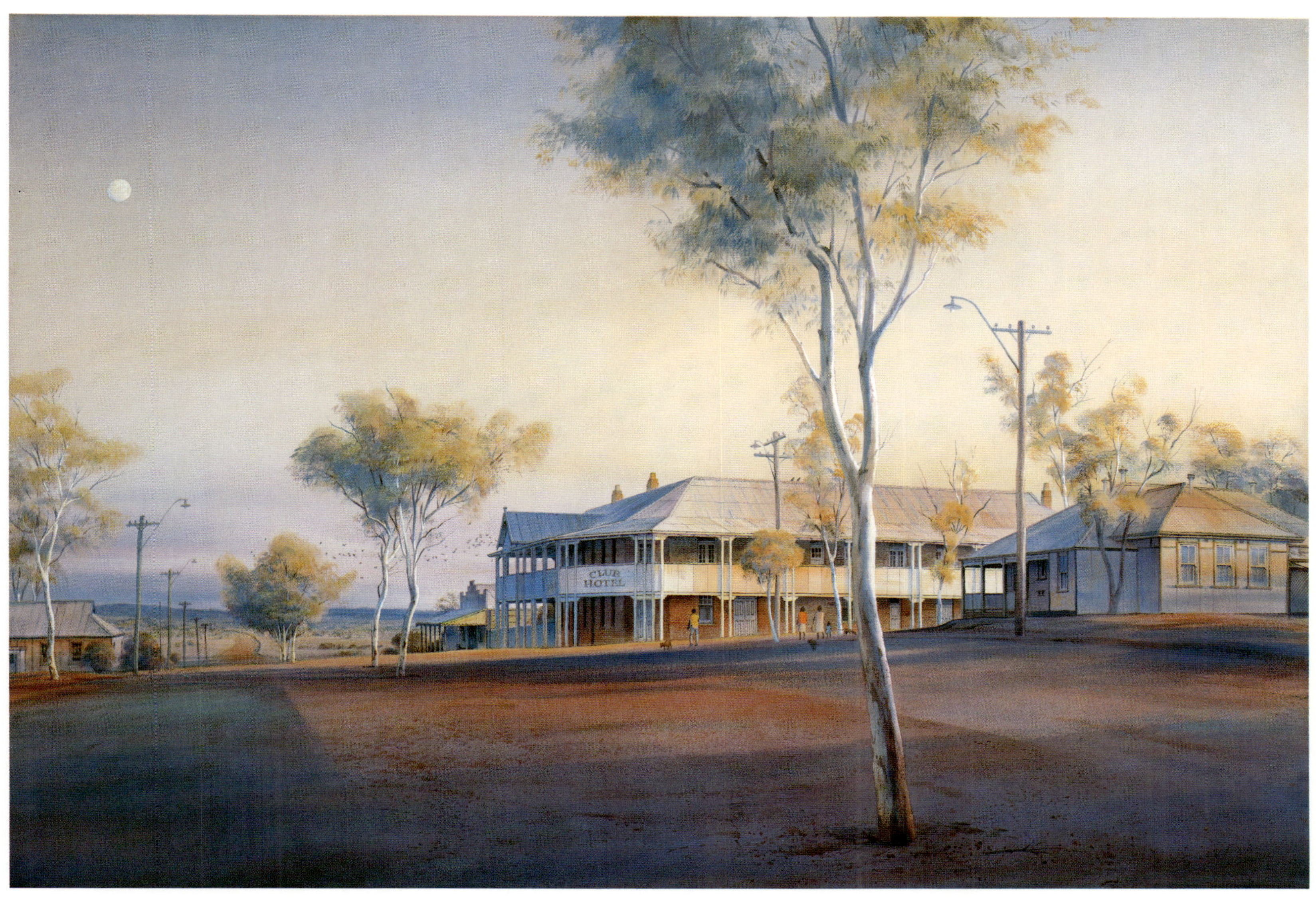

Plate 91   *Wiluna* 1988 (Western Australia) watercolour, 101 × 152 cm

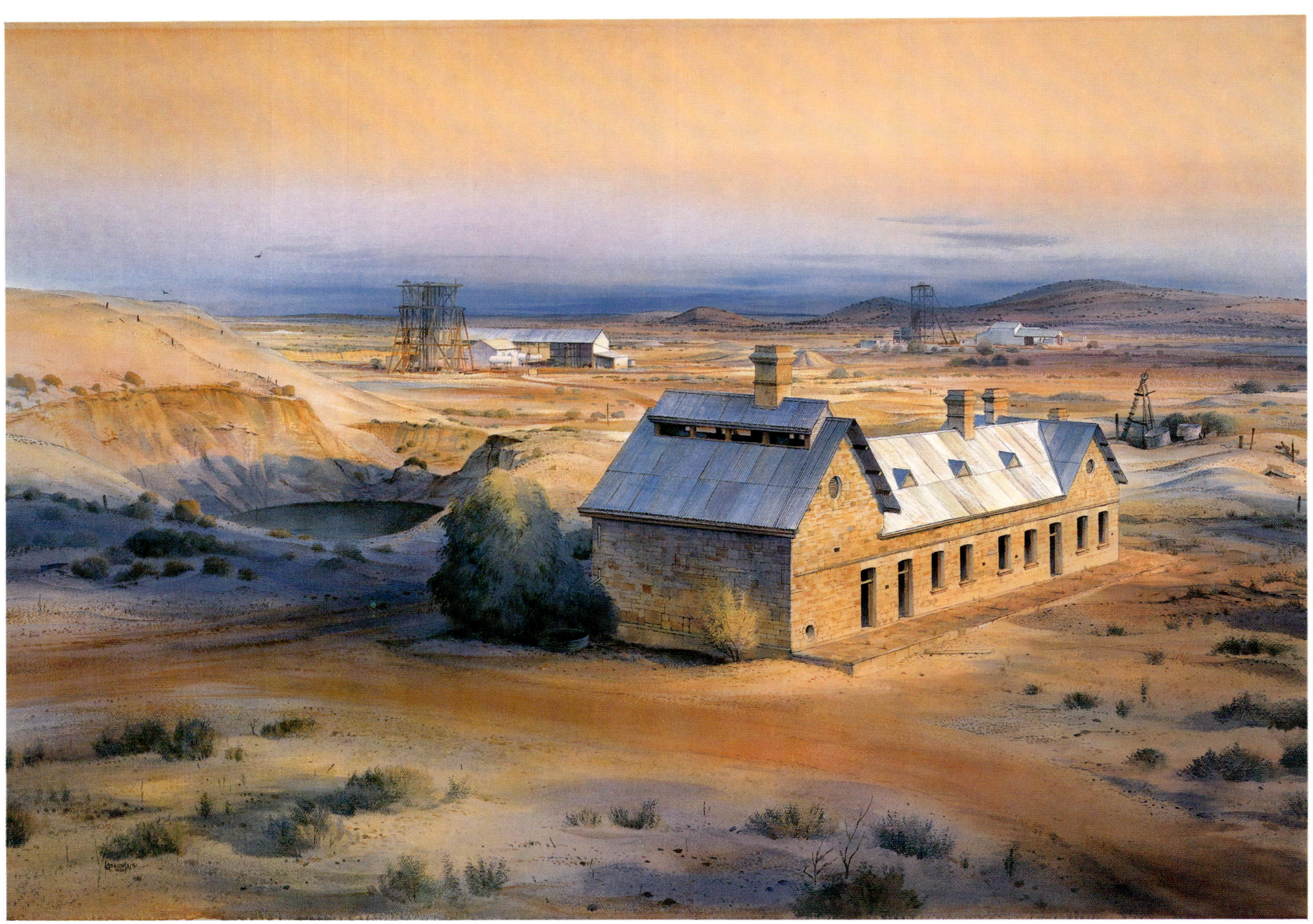

Plate 92 *Day Dawn* 1988 (Western Australia) watercolour, 101 × 152 cm

*In this painting I am looking from the ruin of the
gold-mining office across the old, open-cut mine and
mullock heap to two new mining developments with
their purely functional mine buildings built out of
galvanised iron. I was interested in placing man's
activity in the context of the vast, open and empty
landscape. To achieve this I had to imagine myself
in a birds-eye position because at ground level the
stone building blocks out the distant landscape.*

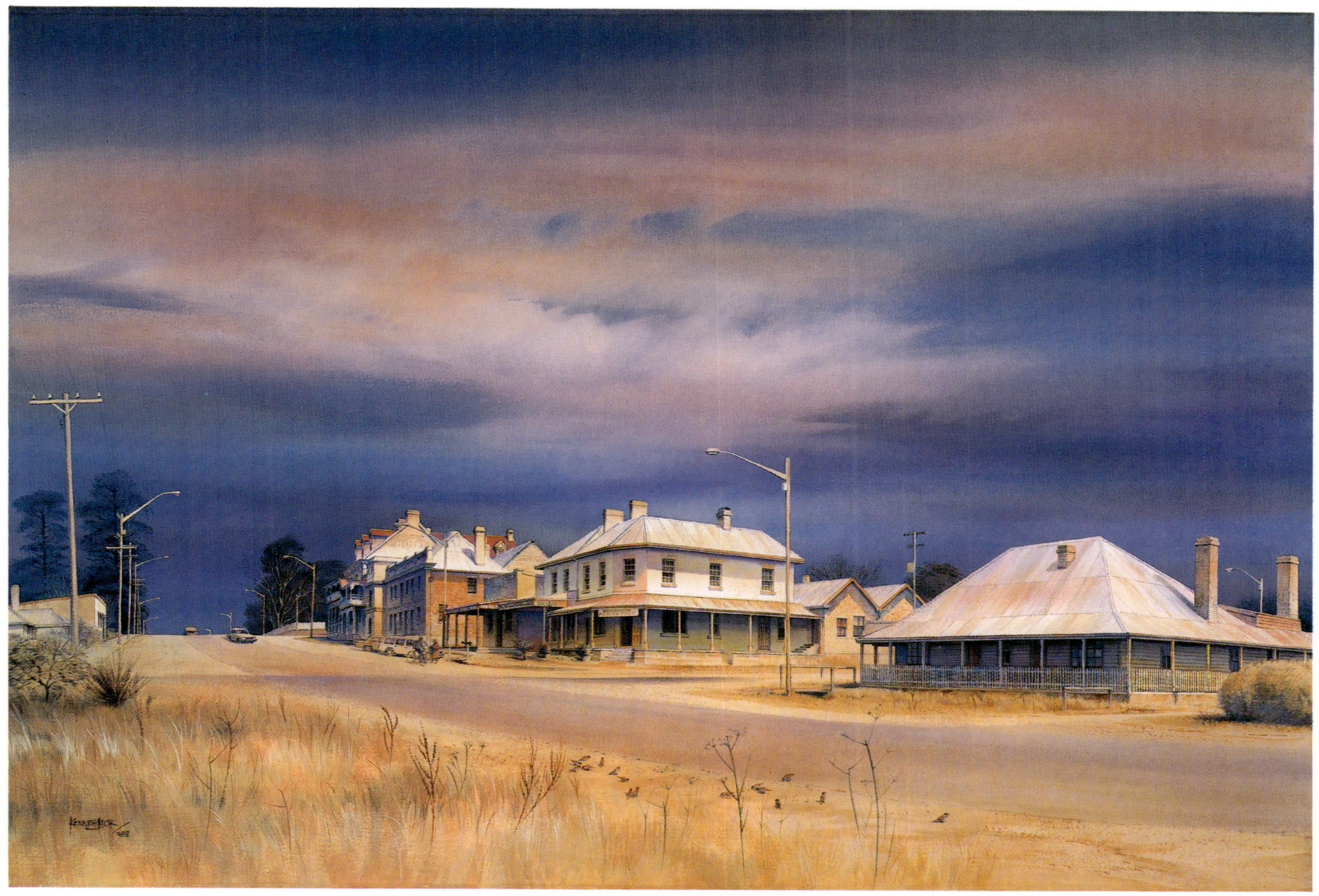

Plate 93 *Braidwood* 1988 (New South Wales) watercolour, 101 × 152 cm

This fine old town is situated mid-way between Canberra and Bateman's Bay. It has been declared an historic village by the National Trust because it has so many interesting old buildings.

On a recent visit I found that the central corner building had had its verandah rebuilt — years ago when I saw it, there was none. The large three-storey hotel on the hill is especially interesting, with cast iron verandah decorations and dormer windows in the roof. The orange colour of the stone wall is a key point in the composition.

FOOTNOTES

1 They were year nine students; Kenneth Jack was fourteen.

2 This and subsequent quotes from Kenneth Jack are from some notes prepared by the artist in 1971.

3 *Griffin*, 18 April 1947.

4 Ure Smith not only published *Art in Australia* but also diffused the work of modern Australian painters such as Dobell, Drysdale, Donald Friend and many others in such publications as *Present Day Art in Australia*, which were a revelation to the art students of Kenneth Jack's generation. It was in these books that he discovered the work of artists whose names he first heard from Donald Friend.

5 Douglas Dundas contributed the introduction to *Kenneth Jack*, published in 1972 by Collins—Australian Artist Editions.

6 Kenneth Jack: The Charm of Hobart, *The Art Bulletin of Tasmania*, The Tasmanian Museum and Art Gallery, Hobart 1986, p. 14.

7 Ibid. p. 14.

8 Ibid. p. 16.

9 Kenneth Jack had already done some etching, joining a Saturday morning class at Melbourne Technical College run by Ben Croskell, who had been taught by John Shirlow. In 1948 he also made some lithographs on zinc plates for the college magazine *Jargon*.

10 Artist's notes.

11 I am grateful to Barry Pearce for this information.

12 Artist's notes.

13 'There's never been a bus ride like this one with Matchbox Jack of the NEVER NEVER.' *Australasian Post*, 11 April 1968.

14 Artist's notes.

15 Artist's notes.

16 From transcript of opening address.

17 Letter from Lloyd Rees, 30 December, 1973.

18 Artist's notes.

19 The development broadened to take in city and urban subjects, and from coastal areas through to the lonely uninhabited areas of inland Australia, embracing country towns and straggling outback buildings.

20 Heinrich Wölfflin: *Principles of Art History* (first published in German in 1915), Dover 1950, reprint of the English translation 1932, p. 230.

21 Conversation with the artist.

22 Artist's notes.

23 W. Gilpin: *Observations on the River Wye and Several Parts of South Wales*, London 1782.

24 See Bernard Smith: *European Vision and the South Pacific 1768–1850*, Oxford University Press 1960, pp. 149–153.

25 The picturesque was satirised in the famous series of aquatint illustrations by Thomas Rowlandson to William Combe's *The Tour of Doctor Syntax, In Search of the Picturesque*, first published in book form in 1812.

26 W. Gilpin: ibid. p. 18.

27 Andrew Wyeth is often referred to as a phenomenon because he is the rare instance of a painter totally out of step with the general trend of American painting and yet is probably the most admired painter in the United States. Certainly his works bring astronomical prices and he is the only living painter to have been accorded the honour of a retrospective at the Metropolitan Museum of Art in New York. Kenneth Jack might well have wondered at the way that Wyeth was acclaimed in his country while his own work was dismissed here by those with a partisan viewpoint.

28 Werri Beach, 16 June 1971.

29 Artist's notes.

BIOGRAPHICAL NOTES

1924 Born in Caulfield, Melbourne, on October 5, the first child of Harold James Jack (1900–1977) and Ethel Gertrude Orr (1894–1950). A sister was born in 1926.

1930–42 Educated in State Primary and Secondary Schools

1939–42 Melbourne High School. Attended evening art classes at Melbourne Technical College, obtaining Drawing Teacher's Primary and Secondary certificates simultaneously with Leaving Certificate. Art editor of school magazine *The Unicorn*.

1942–45 Service in the RAAF as survey and cartographic draughtsman.
In 1944–45, in New Guinea, Morotai and North Borneo; met Donald Friend. Completed 500 drawings and paintings in spare time.

1945 September, discharged. resumed studies for Art Teacher's Certificate at Melbourne Technical College, now R.M.I.T. Awarded Churchill Art Prize, Bendigo, watercolour section.

1946 Full-time student at R.M.I.T. (C.R.T.S.), studying A.T.C. and A.T.D. Drawings reproduced in Ure Smith's *Australia, National Journal*, March and July.

1947 Full-time student at Melbourne Teachers College, gaining T.T.C. (Manual Arts); read Erle Loran's *Cézanne's Composition* (University of California, 1943), which had an important influence on his painting, as well as his teaching method, from 1947–57.

1948 Teaching art at Box Hill High School for one term, then at Upwey High School 1948–50.
Continued studies for A.T.C. and A.T.D. in the evenings.
Awarded three first prizes in C.R.T.S. exhibition.
The Melbourne Book, published by Ure Smith, containing 34 drawings by Jack.

1949 Makes drawings in Hobart for *The Charm of Hobart*, published by Ure Smith in 1950 using 52 drawings. First one-man exhibition at Grosvenor Gallery, Sydney. Works acquired by Art Gallery of N.S.W. and Mitchell Library.

1950 January, married Betty Dyer; daughter Judith born in December.
One-man exhibition at The Bookshelf Library, Hobart.
Begins thesis 'On the Drawing of Architecture'.

1951 Appointed art teacher at Prahran Technical College. Completed thesis; accepted and qualified for Art Teacher's Diploma.

1952 Assistant to Inspector of Art, Technical Schools, also part-time lecturer at Caulfield Institute of Technology, both positions until 1955.
One-man exhibition at Marodian Gallery, Brisbane.

Joined Victorian Artists Society; member until retired in 1964.
Attends evening classes in printmaking run by Harold Freedman at R.M.I.T.

1953 Perth Prize for painting. Dunlop Prize for painting.

1954 Son David born.
Bendigo Watercolour Prize (judged by Douglas Dundas).

1955 Part-time instructor in design at Melbourne School of Printing and Graphic Arts; designed and illustrated diary for MSPGA.
Dunlop Prize for Painting. Member of Australian Watercolour Institute from 1955.
Daughter Heather born.

1956 Senior lecturer in painting and printmaking at Caulfield Institute of Technology; held position till 1968.
Awarded Aubrey Gibson Prize (Victorian Artists Society). Exhibited, 4th Giles Bequest Exhibition of contemporary woodcuts and linocuts, Victoria and Albert Museum, London. Linocut *Macedonia House, Lancefield* purchased by the Museum.

1957 Silver medal, Royal Adelaide exhibition. Wagga Wagga Watercolour Prize (judged by Lloyd Rees).

1958 Exhibited, Cincinnati Colour Lithography Biennial, one lithograph purchased; exhibited, 5th Giles Bequest Exhibition of contemporary woodcuts and linocuts, Victoria and Albert Museum, London; linocut of *Town Hall, Talbot* purchased by the Museum.

1959 Bendigo Prize for oils (judged by Arnold Shore).

1960 Ballarat Watercolour (Minnie Crouch) Prize (judged by Lloyd Rees).

1961 Maude Vizard-Wholahan Watercolour Prize, Adelaide; Certificate of Merit — Fourth International Exhibition of Contemporary Art, New Delhi, for best exhibit from Australia. Darcy Morris Prize for Religious Painting.

1962 Begins making serigraphs. Does series of drawings of historic buildings of Brisbane for Johnstone Galleries. *Australian Gold and Ghost Towns*, a portfolio of linocuts, published by Porpoise Press, San Francisco.

1963 Won watercolour and print sections of Maude Vizard-Wholahan Prize, Adelaide.
E. J. Harvey Prize for Drawing, Brisbane Gallery (judged by Robert Campbell).
Included in Australian Print Survey exhibition to tour Australian galleries.

1964 Commissioned to draw aspects of present day and future Canberra for the book *The Future Canberra* published by Angus and Robertson for the Capital Territory Commission.

1965   One-man exhibition of prints, Johnstone Galleries, Brisbane. Awarded certificate of honour at Graphic Art of Five Continents exhibition, Leipzig.

1966   Included in Australian Prints Today exhibition, Smithsonian Institute, Washington D.C.
Painting presented by the Prime Minister to the Queen Mother during her visit to Australia.

1967   Invited to become official war artist in Vietnam, declines.
Awarded Trustees' Watercolour Prize, Art Gallery of N.S.W. for *The Diamantina*; work purchased by the Gallery.
Mural for Australian Pavilion, Expo '67 (8 × 24 feet), Montreal.
On 6 months' long-service leave, makes bus tour across N.S.W., Queensland to Darwin, to Broome, Port Hedland, Marble Bar, Tanami Desert and return via Alice Springs.
Camberwell Watercolour Prize.

1968   Deputy head of Caulfield (now Chisholm) Institute of Technology Art School (January to September). Retired from teaching to paint full time.
Caltex Award; Rural Bank Prize for oils.

1969   Member of Council of Caulfield Institute of Technology (1969–76).
Watercolour Prize, Royal Easter Show, Sydney. Rural Bank Prize for oils. Camberwell Oil Prize.

1970   Watercolour Prize, Royal Easter Show, Sydney.
Designed tapestry of Coat of Arms for the Australian Pavilion, Expo '70, Osaka.
Retrospective exhibition organised by David Dridan (John Martin's Gallery) for the Adelaide Festival.
Travels with Douglas Dundas from Adelaide to the Flinders Ranges and then to Broken Hill.
Rural Bank Prize for oils.

1971   Sketching holiday at Nimmitabel with John Eldershaw and John Brackenreg. Sketching holiday at Broken Hill, Milparinka, across to north Flinders Ranges between Lakes Frome and Callabonna.

1972   Trustees' Watercolour Prize, Art Gallery of N.S.W. for *Lake Hart*.
Kenneth Jack monograph published by Collins and Australian Artist Editions, with introduction by Douglas Dundas.

1973   First overseas tour, to England.

1974   One-man exhibition at Australian Galleries, Melbourne. Sketching trip to Western Australia and the south.

1975   One-man exhibition at Leicester Galleries, London. Sketching and gallery tour of Great Britain and Paris, Chartres and Rheims.

1977   Elected Associate of Royal Watercolour Society of London.

1978   Retrospective organised by David Dridan (John Martin's Gallery) for the Adelaide Festival (178 works).
Two long trips to Western Australia, travelling widely throughout the State.

1979   President of Australian branch of the Old Watercolour Society Club, London (1980 and 1981).
Sketching tour of U.S.A. (California, Texas and Washington) and Canada.

1980   Appointed foundation member of the Board of Artbank (1980–83).

1981   Patron, Australian branch of the O.W.S.C.

1982   Awarded M.B.E. for services to art.

1983   Elected full member of Royal Watercolour Society, London.
Sketching and gallery tour of England, France, Italy, Austria and Holland.

1984   Publication by Australian Artist Editions of *The Flinders Ranges of South Australia*, text and paintings by Kenneth Jack. Publication by The Beagle Press of portfolio of six original lithographs, *Old Mining Towns of Australia*.
Joint exhibition with Lloyd Rees, Artarmon Galleries, Sydney. Travels in Flinders Ranges to two remote areas, Nuccaleena and Mt. Patawarta.

1985   Two sketching trips to Western Australia, travelling widely throughout the State.

1986   April, sketching trip in the Flinders Ranges and Broken Hill.

1987   Awarded Member of the Order of Australia (AM) 'for services to art particularly watercolour painting'.
Sketching tour and gallery visits, Great Britain.
One-man exhibition, Australian Galleries.

1988   One-man exhibition, Adelaide Festival, Barry Newton Gallery.

Bibliography

Books

Walter Shaw Sparrow, *Advertising and British Art*. The Bodley Head, London, 1924.

Douglas Dundas, *Kenneth Jack*. Collins and Australian Artist Editions, 1972.

Franz Kempf, *Contemporary Australian Printmakers*. Lansdowne, Melbourne, 1976.

Oliver Millar, *The Queen's Pictures*. Weidenfeld and Nicholson, London, 1977.

Lou Klepac (ed.), *Contemporary Australian Drawing*. Catalogue, Art Gallery of Western Australia, 1978.

Max Germaine, *Artists and Galleries of Australia and New Zealand*. Lansdowne Editions, 1979.

Bianca McCullough, *Each Man's Wilderness* (Reflections by Australian Artists). Rigby, 1980.

Lillian Wood (ed.), *Directory of Australian Printmakers*, Print Council of Australia, 1982.

Alan McCulloch, *Encyclopedia of Australian Art*. Hutchinson, Australia, 1984.

William Kelly, *Heritage of Australian Art*. Macmillan Australia, Melbourne, 1984.

Graham Hopwood, *Handbook of Art*. Published by the author, North Balwyn, 1984.

Jennie Boddington, *Drysdale Photographer*. National Gallery of Victoria, 1987.

Newspapers and Periodicals

The Melbourne Book. *The Age*, 18 December 1948.

This is why Melbourne is what it is. *The Herald*, Melbourne, 22 December 1948.

Warwick Lawrence, A tale of two cities. *The Courier-Mail*, Brisbane, 29 January 1949.

Kenneth Jack's Art. *Contact*, Melbourne, March 1949.

James Gleeson, Fine work at two art exhibitions. *The Sun*, Sydney, 22 November 1949.

Old Houses. *The Bulletin*, 30 November 1949.

Arnold Shore, Old Masters and Current Scene. *Argus*, 17 December 1949.

Laurie Thomas, A series worth the money. *The Herald*, Melbourne, 31 December 1949.

Some Recent Australian Graphic Art. *Bulletin of the National Gallery of South Australia*, Vol. 22, No. 3, July 1960.

Alan McCulloch, Creative art is not too tidy. *The Herald*, 14 September 1960.

Daniel Thomas, This month's cover. *Hemisphere*, Sydney, April 1961.

Maude Vizard-Wholahan Competition 1961. *Bulletin of the National Gallery of South Australia*, Vol. 23, No. 1, July 1961.

Frank Sullivan, Wide-awake art from 'Down Under'. *The Straits Times*, Kuala Lumpur, 28 June 1963.

The Maude Vizard-Wholahan Competition. *Bulletin of the National Gallery of South Australia*, Vol. 25, No. 2, October 1963.

Elizabeth Young, exhibition review, *The Advertiser*, Adelaide, 15 April 1964.

Gertrude Langer, Print show by Kenneth Jack. *Courier-Mail*, 17 May 1965.

The Perth Prize. *The Western Australian Art Gallery Bulletin*, Vol. 1, No. 17, October 1965.

Betsy Gamble, Christmas Material. *Saturday Evening Mercury*, 10 December 1966.

Lou Klepac, S.A. assailed by displays. *The News*, Adelaide, 13 September 1967.

Robert Campbell, A unique artist. *The Advertiser*, Adelaide, 5 March 1970.

Rod McFarlane, Two strange views of the same land. *Daily Telegraph*, London, 15 April 1972.

James Gleeson, A new brand of realism. *The Sun-Herald*, 5 November 1972.

Nancy Borlase, Some tallish poppies in the mediocre corn. *The Bulletin*, 27 January 1973.

Terence Mullaly, Australia's image is established. *Daily Telegraph*, London, 23 June 1975.

Paul Heinrichs, The case for realism. *The Age*, 29 July 1978.

Linley Hartley, Kenneth Jack's adventure with Australia. *Diamond Valley News*, 29 June 1982.

Rosslyn Beiby, They recognised the talent but not the face of feted painter Jack. *The Age*, Melbourne, 6 October 1984.

Ronald Millar, Throwaways, in best taste. *The Herald*, Melbourne, 6 October 1984.

Lou Klepac, introduction to brochure for *Old Mining Towns of Australia*. Portfolio of six original lithographs, The Beagle Press, Sydney, 1984.

Articles by Kenneth Jack

The Gothic Cathedral, *Unicorn*, magazine of Melbourne High School, July 1942.

England, *Unicorn*, December 1942.

More About Art, letter to editor, *Griffin*, Melbourne Teachers' College, 18 April 1947.

Mozart, *Trainee*, Teachers College Magazine, Melbourne, 1947.

Interview with Hazel de Berg, National Library, Canberra. Tape 154, 1 December 1965 (transcript).

Each Man's Wilderness ed. Bianca McCullough, Rigby, 1980.

The Flinders Ranges of South Australia, Australian Artist Editions, Sydney, 1984.

The Charm of Hobart, *The Art Bulletin of Tasmania*, 1986. The Tasmanian Museum and Art Gallery, Hobart.

Books illustrated by Kenneth Jack

CLIVE TURNBULL, *The Melbourne Book,* Ure Smith, Sydney, 1948.

GEORGE BEIERS, *Houses of Australia*, Ure Smith, Sydney, 1948.

CLIVE TURNBULL, *The Charm of Hobart*, Ure Smith, Sydney, 1949.

Baraiyon, Australian essays, stories, verse, The Hawthorn Press, Melbourne, 1962.

Portfolio, *Australian Gold and Ghost Towns*, containing seven colour prints by Kenneth Jack, The Porpoise Bookshop, San Francisco, 1962.

The National Development Commission, *The Future Canberra*, Angus and Robertson, 1965.

ALLEN INCH, *Honour the Work*, A History of Melbourne High School, Lloyd O'Neill Pty Ltd, 1977.

M. BEILKE, *Shining Clarity — The Works of Robinson Jeffers*, Quintessence Publications, California, USA, 1977.

JEAN NUNN, *Soldier Settlers* War Service Land Settlement, Kangaroo Is., Investigator Press, 1981.

Portfolio, *Old Mining Towns of Australia*, containing six original lithographs by Kenneth Jack, The Beagle Press, Sydney, 1984.

OLGA HARDY, *Like a Bird on the Wing*, Lutheran Publishing House, Adelaide, 1984.

The Australian Landscape in Oils and Watercolour, Australian Artist Editions, 1984.

EXHIBITIONS

One-Man

1949	November/December Grosvenor Galleries, Sydney
1950	March Fullers Bookshop, Hobart
	August Johnstone Galleries, Brisbane
1952	Johnstone Galleries, Brisbane
1957	April Johnstone Galleries, Brisbane
	November Terry Clune Galleries, Sydney
1960	May Sixteen drawings of 'Como'. Australian Galleries, Melbourne
1961	October The Gallery, Carrick, Tasmania
1962	April Johnstone Galleries, Brisbane
1964	April Royal South Australian Society of Arts Gallery, Adelaide
	April The Gallery, Carrick, Tasmania
	October The Bistro Gallery, Hobart
1965	January Raffins Gallery, Orange
	May Johnstone Galleries, Brisbane
	June Townsville University
1966	February North Adelaide Galleries, Adelaide
	October Darlinghurst Galleries, Sydney
	November Heritage Fine Arts, Albury
	December Art Centre, Hobart
1967	September North Adelaide Galleries, Adelaide
1968	June/July Coombe Downs Galleries, Geelong
	July/August John Gild Galleries, Perth
	November National Gallery of Victoria (50 prints)
	November Johnstone Galleries, Brisbane
	November Prints, Sale Regional Arts Centre
	December Benalla Gallery, part of the prints exhibition from the National Gallery of Victoria
1969	March Art Centre, Hobart
1970	March Retrospective Exhibition, John Martin Gallery, Adelaide, Adelaide Festival
1972	October/November Artarmon Galleries
1974	October Australian Galleries, Melbourne (First Melbourne one-man)
1975	June Leicester Galleries, London
1976	March Lister Gallery, Perth
1978	February/March Retrospective (178 works), John Martin Gallery, Adelaide, Adelaide Festival

1980	September Greythorn Galleries, North Balwyn
1984	October Australian Galleries, Melbourne
1985	October Beehive Corner Gallery, Adelaide
1986	November Artarmon Galleries, Sydney (with Clifford Bayly)
1987	October Australian Galleries, Melbourne
1988	February Barry Newton Gallery, Adelaide, Adelaide Festival

Group

1943	January All Australian Exhibition of Art by Australians in the services, Athenaeum Gallery, Melbourne
1952–64	Exhibited as member of Victorian Artists Society
1955–	Exhibited with Australian Watercolour Institute
1956	September Prints by the Melbourne Graphic Artists, Peter Bray Gallery, Melbourne
	Opening Exhibition, Australian Galleries, Melbourne
1958	November/December The 5th Giles Bequest Exhibition, Victoria and Albert Museum, London
1958	November Prints by Melbourne Graphic artists, Australian Galleries, Melbourne
1963	October Australian Print Survey, Art Gallery of South Australia, then travelling to other State Galleries during 1964
1966	July Australian Prints Today, Smithsonian Institution, Washington D.C.
1970	March Ryecroft Invitation Exhibition, Ryecroft Cellars, Adelaide
1974	October Australian Printmakers, Brown Street Gallery, Hamilton, Victoria
1975	The Australian Image, Arts Victoria 75
1977	Focus 77, Six Prominent Australian Artists, Newton Gallery, Adelaide
1977	Royal Watercolour Society London, Autumn and Spring Exhibitions each year
1984	July Artarmon Galleries, Sydney — joint exhibition with Lloyd Rees
1985	June Ten watercolourists salute Victoria, State Bank, Melbourne, then Freeland Gallery, London (July)

PRIZES

1945	Bendigo Watercolour Prize
1948	Three prizes C.R.T.S. Exhibition
1953	Perth prize (oils)
1954	Bendigo Watercolour Prize
1956	Aubrey Gibson Prize (oils), Victorian Artists Society; Wagga Art Prize
1957	Watercolour section, Wagga Art Prize
1959	Bendigo Prize (oils)
1960	Minnie Crouch Prize for watercolour, Ballarat Gallery
1961	Darcy Morris Prize for Religious Painting
1961	Maude Vizard-Wholahan Watercolour Prize, Adelaide
1963	E. T. Cato Prize, watercolour, shared with Len Annois
1963	Maude Vizard-Wholahan Watercolour and Print Prizes, Adelaide
1963	E. J. Harvey Prize for drawing, Queensland Art Gallery
1967	Trustees Watercolour Prize, Art Gallery of N.S.W.
1967	Camberwell Rotary Club Watercolour Prize
1968	Rural Bank Art Prize (also 1969 and 1970) and Caltex Award
1969	Watercolour Prize, Royal Easter Show, Sydney; Camberwell Rotary Club (oils)
1970	Awarded Rural Bank and watercolour prizes at Royal Easter Show, Sydney
1972	Trustees Watercolour Prize, Wyne Competition, Art Gallery of N.S.W.

COLLECTIONS

Kenneth Jack is represented in the following public collections:

Adelaide City Council
Albury Regional Art Gallery
Artbank
Art Gallery of New South Wales
Art Gallery of South Australia
Art Gallery of Western Australia
Australian National Gallery, Canberra
Australian War Memorial
Ballarat Art Gallery
Bendigo Art Gallery
Brisbane City Council
Broken Hill Art Gallery
Castlemain Art Gallery
Caulfield City Council

Chisholm Institute of Technology
Cincinnati Art Museum, U.S.A.
Dandenong City Art Gallery
Dunedin Art Gallery, New Zealand
Geelong Art Gallery
H.M. Queen Elizabeth
H.M. The Queen Mother
Kuala Lumpur Art Gallery, Malaysia
Latrobe Library, Melbourne
Melbourne High School
Melbourne University and Teachers College
Mertz Collection, Austin, Texas
Mildura Art Gallery
Mitchell Library, Sydney
National Gallery, Kuala Lumpur
National Gallery of Victoria
Ormond College, Melbourne University
Otemon University, Osaka
Oxley Library, Brisbane
Queensland Art Gallery
Queensland University
Queen Victoria Museum and Art Gallery, Launceston
RMIT Collection
RWS Diploma Collection, London
Sale Regional Art Gallery
Shepparton Art Gallery
State Library, Hobart
Swan Hill Museum
Tasmanian Museum and Art Gallery
Townsville University
University of Adelaide
University of Western Australia
Victoria and Albert Museum, London
Warrnambool Art Gallery
Waverley City Art Collection

and in the following private collections:
Broken Hill Associated Smelters
Comalco
Conzinc Rio Tinto
Elders-IXL
Electrolitic Zinc
Finance Corp of Australia
Hayman Island
Myer Collection
National Trust of South Australia
New Norcia Monastery
North Broken Hill Pty Ltd
Rural and Industries Bank of Western Australia
State Bank of New South Wales
State Bank, Victoria
The Bank of Adelaide
and innumerable other private collections in Australia, USA and UK.

LIST OF PLATES AND FIGURES

Plate 40 *Evening Shadows, Mt. Egerton*
1980 (Victoria) pencil, oil pastel and
watercolour, 46 × 64 cm
Private collection

Plate 41 *Old Eucalypts, Buckaringa Gorge*
1980 (South Australia) pencil, oil pastel
and watercolour, 39 × 55 cm
Private collection

Plate 42 *Tarnagulla*
1980 (Victoria) watercolour, 34 × 56 cm
Private collection

Plate 43 *Chillagoe, North Queensland*
1981, watercolour, 33 × 55 cm
Private collection

Plate 44 *Tilba*
1980 (New South Wales) acrylic,
42 × 57 cm
Collection: Franklin Mint Pty Ltd ©

Plate 45 *Sydney from Kirribilli*
1980–81, acrylic, 81 × 122 cm
Private collection

Plate 46 *Balladonia Triptych*
1986 (Western Australia) 114 x 382 cm
Left panel: *The Woolshed* watercolour,
114 x 110 cm
Centre panel: *The Homestead*
watercolour, 114 x 162 cm
Right panel: *Old Telegraph
Station* watercolour, 114 x 110 cm
Collection: Hayman Island

Plate 47 *Evening Shadows, Skipton*
1981 (Victoria) pencil, oil pastel and
watercolour, 51 × 71 cm
Collection: Artbank

Plate 48 *Hotel at Cowell*
1981 (South Australia) pencil, oil pastel
and watercolour, 35 × 48 cm
Private collection

Plate 49 *Gwalia*
1981 (Western Australia) acrylic,
122 × 183 cm
Private collection

Plate 50 *Jamieson*
1981 (Victoria) pencil, oil pastel and
watercolour, 32 × 46 cm
Private collection

Plate 51 *Imperial Hotel, Ravenswood*
1981 (Queensland) watercolour,
47 × 72 cm
Collection: Sir James and Lady Foots

Plate 52 *Evening Shadows, Blinman*
1982 (South Australia) acrylic, 64 × 91 cm
Collection: Mr and Mrs Peter Jeffery

Plate 53 *Hot Afternoon, Cue*
1982 (Western Australia) pencil, oil pastel
and watercolour, 50 × 79 cm
Private collection

Plate 54 *Lower Gellibrand*
1982 (Victoria) carbon pencil, oil pastel
and watercolour, 50 × 79 cm
Private collection

Plate 55 *Moonrise, Dysart*
1982 (Tasmania) acrylic, 40 × 60 cm
Private collection

Plate 56 *Mt. Chambers*
1982 (South Australia) watercolour,
31 × 49 cm
Private collection

Plate 57 *Eastwards to Lake Frome (Salt)*
1987 (South Australia) watercolour,
101 × 151 cm
Private collection

Plate 58 *Chapel at Chewton*
1983 (Victoria) watercolour, 27 × 39 cm
Private collection

Plate 59 *Desolate Wasteland, Lake Eyre*
1983 (South Australia) watercolour,
36 × 53 cm
Private collection

Plate 60 *First Light, the Amphitheatre,
Palm Valley*
1983 (Northern Territory) watercolour and
oil pastel, 50 × 71 cm
Private collection

Plate 61 *Low Tide, Kangaroo Island*
1983 (South Australia) pencil, oil pastel
and watercolour, 33 × 48.3 cm
Private collection

Plate 62 *Moonrise over the Opal
Diggings, White Cliffs*
1983 (New South Wales) watercolour,
46 × 72 cm
Private collection

Plate 63 *Mt. Giles, Central Australia*
1983, watercolour, 35 × 55 cm
Private collection

Plate 64 *The Devil's Kitchen, Piggoreet*
1983 (Victoria) pencil, oil pastel and
watercolour, 31 × 46 cm
Private collection

Plate 65 *The Town Hall, South
Melbourne*
1983, pencil, aquarelle crayon and
watercolour, 21.6 × 30.5 cm
Private collection

Plate 66 *Zeehan*
1983 (Tasmania) watercolour, 41 × 59 cm
Private collection

Plate 67 *Between Showers; The Rock*
1984 (New South Wales) pencil, oil pastel
and watercolour, 37 × 54.5 cm
Private collection

Plate 68 *Ruined Farm, Mt. Blackwood*
1984 (Victoria) acrylic, 51 × 76 cm
Private collection

Plate 69 *Abandoned Port, Cossack*
1984 (Western Australia) acrylic,
42 × 57 cm
Private collection

Plate 70 *Abandoned Goldmine Office,
Day Dawn*
1988 (Western Australia) watercolour,
70 × 101 cm

Plate 71 *Across the Diggings, Hill End*
1984 (New South Wales) pencil, oil pastel
and watercolour, 50.2 × 78.2 cm
Collection: Art Gallery of New South
Wales

Plate 72 *Carcoar*
1984 (New South Wales) pencil, oil pastel
and watercolour, 44 × 73 cm
Private collection

Plate 73 *Hartley*
1984 (New South Wales) acrylic,
61 × 91 cm
Private collection

Plate 74 *Leonora*
1984 (Western Australia) watercolour,
69 × 102 cm
Private collection

Plate 75 *Middle River, Kangaroo Island*
1984 (South Australia) watercolour,
69 × 102 cm
Private collection

Plate 76 *National Trust Museum,
Wallaroo*
1984 (South Australia) pencil, oil pastel
and watercolour, 33 × 54 cm
Private collection

Plate 77 *Towards Lake Frome (Salt)*
1984 (South Australia) watercolour,
51 × 72 cm

Plate 78 *Main Street, Mt. Magnet*
1985 (Western Australia) gouache,
50 × 71 cm
Private collection

Plate 79 *Mine Building, Day Dawn*
1985 (Western Australia) pencil, oil pastel
and watercolour, 35.5 × 48 cm
Private collection

Plate 80 *Mine Building, Day Dawn II*
1985 (Western Australia) watercolour,
70 × 101 cm
Collection: Rural and Industries Bank of
Western Australia

Plate 81 *Sheep on a Salt Lake, Lake
Bumbunga*
1985 (South Australia) watercolour,
77 × 119.3 cm
Private collection

Plate 82 *Gal Gal Reach, Lower Murray*
1986, watercolour, 101 × 152 cm
Private collection

Figures

INDEX